West Academic Publish
Emeritus Advisory Bo

WILLS, TRUSTS, AND ESTATES

OBJECTIVE

Second Edition

PATRICIA A. CAIN
Professor of Law, Santa Clara University School of Law
Aliber Family Chair in Law, Emerita, University of Iowa College of Law

E. GARY SPITKO
Presidential Professor of Ethics and the Common Good and Professor of Law
Santa Clara University School of Law

DANAYA C. WRIGHT
T. Terrell Sessums & Gerald Sohn Professor of Constitutional Law
University of Florida, Levin College of Law

Exam Pro®

WEST ACADEMIC

860 Blue Gentian Road, Suite 350
Eagan, MN 55121
1-877-888-1330

Published in the United States of America

ISBN: 978-1-64708-437-0

"For Jean." PAC

"For Brian Michael Spitko, in loving memory." EGS

"For my family, who motivate all I do." DCW

About the Authors

Patricia A. Cain

Professor Cain is a professor of law at Santa Clara University and a prior holder of the Inez Mabie Distinguished Professorship. She has been in law teaching for over 40 years and has been teaching Trusts and Estates since 1977. She has taught as a tenured member of the law faculty at the University of Texas and at the University of Iowa. In addition, she has taught as a visiting professor at numerous law schools around the country, including the University of Wisconsin, the University of Southern California, Tulane University, the University of San Francisco, and Washington University in St. Louis. She is a member of the American Law Institute (ALI), an elected fellow of the American College of Trust and Estate Counsel (ACTEC) and a fellow of the American College of Tax Counsel. (ACTC). She was the inaugural recipient of the lifetime achievement award presented by the Tax Section of the Association of American Law schools in 2024.

E. Gary Spitko

Professor Spitko is the Presidential Professor of Ethics and the Common Good and Professor of Law at Santa Clara University. He has taught Trusts and Estates as a member of the law faculties at Santa Clara University and Indiana University, and also as a visiting professor at the Ohio State University College of Law and the University of California College of the Law, San Francisco. Previously, he served as Chair of the Association of American Law Schools Section on Donative Transfers, Fiduciaries and Estate Planning. In 2016, Professor Spitko was elected an Academic Fellow of the American College of Trust and Estate Counsel.

Danaya C. Wright

Professor Wright is the T. Terrell Sessums and Gerald Sohn Professor of Constitutional Law and Director of the Center for Governmental Responsibility at the University of Florida, Levin College of Law. She has taught Trusts and Estates for nearly 30 years and has written a casebook on the subject, a simulations book, and a specialty treatise/casebook on Future Interests. She has also written a Trusts and Estates book for non-lawyers and her scholarship on probate reform and heirs' property is leading efforts to solve intractable title problems and save family wealth.

About the Authors

Table of Topics

Table of Contents

WILLS, TRUSTS, AND ESTATES

OBJECTIVE

Second Edition

EXAM I

1. T's purported will was all on a single sheet of paper. The purported will contained three typewritten paragraphs identified as a will and making numerous bequests 1 through 9. This typewritten portion was undated, unsigned, and unwitnessed. After the three typed paragraphs was one paragraph in the handwriting of the deceased, dated and signed, which read "To my brother, James, I give $10 only. This will, which shall incorporate the typed matter above, shall be complete unless hereafter altered." May the court give effect to devises 1 through 9. Assume a jurisdiction that recognizes holographic wills.

   (a) Yes, under the doctrine of integration.

   (b) Yes, under the doctrine of incorporation by reference.

   (c) Yes, under the doctrine of republication by codicil.

   (d) No.

2. D dies domiciled in California. All of D's property will pass by intestacy. The bulk of D's estate consists of personal property located in Nevada. D also owns real property in Georgia. The law of which state will govern the passing of D's property?

   (a) California, Nevada, and Georgia.

   (b) California and Nevada.

   (c) California and Georgia

   (d) California.

3. Jurisdiction X has adopted an intestacy scheme that is grounded in large part upon the conduit theory and in large part upon empirical studies that show that most people have a strong preference that, if they die intestate, their estate should go to their surviving spouse to the exclusion of their surviving parents. In which of the following family situations would you expect the surviving spouse to take the largest share of the decedent's intestate property?

   (a) The decedent and the surviving spouse have "joint children" (that is, children of both the decedent and the surviving spouse), and the surviving spouse has children not of the decedent.

   (b) The decedent and the surviving spouse have "joint children," and the decedent has children not of the surviving spouse.

   (c) The decedent and the surviving spouse have "joint children" and neither the decedent nor the surviving spouse has any other children.

   (d) The decedent has children not of the surviving spouse, and the surviving spouse has no children.

4. Which of the following doctrines could be used to validate a pourover will at common law?

   (a) Republication by codicil and acts of independent significance.

   (b) Acts of independent significance and incorporation by reference.

   (c) Incorporation by reference and republication by codicil.

   (d) Republication by codicil, acts of independent significance, and incorporation by reference.

5. T executed Will #1 in Year 1. T executed Will #2, which expressly revoked Will #1, in Year 2. In Year 3, T revoked Will #2 by physical act believing that this revocation would revive Will #1. In Year 4, T died. The legatees under Will #2 argue in court that the court should nevertheless probate Will #2 under the doctrine of dependent relative revocation. The court agrees. What approach to revival does this jurisdiction employ?

   (a) Will #1 was never revoked because Will #2 is not effective until T's death. (#2 just covered up #1).

   (b) Will #1 cannot be revived unless re-executed with testamentary formalities.

   (c) Upon revocation of Will #2, Will #1 is revived if T so intends.

   (d) One cannot say from just the facts given.

6. T devises "My house to my sister Susan. The residue of my estate to my brother Jeff." At the time of the will's execution, T lives at 1307 W. James St. One year later, T sells that house and buys and moves into a new house at 11 Shawnee Lane. One year later, T dies. Who gets the house at 11 Shawnee Lane in a jurisdiction that adheres to the identity theory of ademption?

   (a) Susan.

   (b) Jeff.

   (c) T's heirs.

   (d) We cannot tell from the facts given.

7. In Year 1, T executes a will leaving her estate to Marc. In Year 2, T plans to execute a new will revoking the gift to Marc and leaving her estate to Fred. T's lawyer drafts the will in favor of Fred. T asks Jake to come to T's home to witness the will. But when Jake learns that the new will favors Fred, he fraudulently prevents T from revoking her first will and executing the second will. He does so by lying to T and telling her that Fred is a drug addict. He does this because he truly dislikes Fred. Thus, if the first will is probated and given effect as written, T's property will pass to Marc, who is wholly innocent of any fraud. At T's death, the court should

   (a) Probate the first will and allow the wholly innocent Marc to take T's property.

(b) Find that T died intestate and allow T's heirs to take T's property.

(c) Probate the first will but impose a constructive trust on the wholly innocent Marc for the benefit of Fred.

(d) Probate the second will and allow Fred to take T's property.

8. BW is unrelated to T and is one of two necessary witnesses to T's Will #1, and Will #2, which wholly revokes Will #1. Will #1 devises to BW $170,000 in Google stock. Will #2 devises to BW $70,000 in real property. What, if any, of T's property does BW take in a jurisdiction that has a modern purging statute, i.e., one that purges excess gain?

(a) BW takes nothing because T dies intestate as his wills lack the necessary two witnesses.

(b) BW takes nothing as the purging statute purges his excess gain.

(c) BW takes $70,000 in real property.

(d) BW takes $170,000 in Google stock and $70,000 in real property.

9. The State of Nirvana has adopted the harmless error principle (see UPC § 2–503). The Nirvana probate code does not recognize or even mention holographic wills. T handwrites a document that he intends to be his last will. T titles the document "My last will and testament," dates the document, and signs the document. The document remains unwitnessed at T's death. Should the Nirvana probate court probate the will?

(a) Yes, if it concludes that the material provisions of the will are in T's handwriting.

(b) No, because the Nirvana probate code does not recognize holographic wills.

(c) Yes, if it concludes that there is clear and convincing evidence that T substantially complied with the formalities for execution of a will.

(d) Yes, if it concludes that there is clear and convincing evidence that the testator intended the document to be his will.

10. O creates a trust giving A income for life, remainder to B. The corpus is principally comprised of several apartment buildings located within walking distance of one another, which the settlor in the trust instrument forbids the trustee from selling within 20 years of the time the trust was created. After a certain period of time, the apartment buildings start declining in value because of a general deterioration of the neighborhood. Upon petition of the trustee, should the court allow the trustee to sell the buildings if it finds that the purpose of the trust would be frustrated by retention of the buildings?

(a) No, so long as the buildings are producing a sufficient income for the life tenant.

(b) Yes, under the *Claflin* doctrine.

(c) No, as this would defeat the intent of the settlor.

(d) Yes, under the doctrine of administrative deviation.

11. T wishes to revoke her will. She directs Mark, who is in her presence, to mark an X on each page of a copy of her will and to make certain that each X touches the words of the will. Mark so marks the copy of T's will.

    (a) T's will is not revoked.

    (b) T's will is revoked.

    (c) T's will is revoked only if the jurisdiction allows partial revocation by physical act.

    (d) T's will is revoked only if Mark is an attorney.

Use the following fact pattern to answer questions 12–14:

Scott and Zelda were married to each other for 8 years. In Year 8 they both died from injuries suffered in an automobile accident. Scott predeceased Zelda in death by 72 hours. Zelda was survived by two children, Victor and William, from a previous marriage. They remain alive today. Scott had three children from a previous marriage—Anna, Bob, and Charlie. However, none of them survived Scott. They all died in a plane crash six years before Scott's death. Anna left two children—Ed and Fred. Bob left three children Gary, Harry and Ida. Charlie left two children—John and Kennedy. All of these grandchildren of Scott survived him. Assume the jurisdiction has adopted the Revised Uniform Simultaneous Death Act, which has also been followed by the UPC.

12. If Scott dies intestate, who takes his probate estate in a classic per stirpes (also known as a strict per stirpes) jurisdiction?

    (a) 1/5 to V, 1/5 to W, 1/10 to E, 1/10 to F, 1/15 to G, 1/15 to H, 1/15 to I, 1/10 to J and 1/10 to K.

    (b) 1/6 to E, 1/6 to F, 1/9 to G, 1/9 to H, 1/9 to I, 1/6 to J and 1/6 to K.

    (c) 1/7 to E, 1/7 to F, 1/7 to G, 1/7 to H, 1/7 to I, 1/7 to J and 1/7 to K.

    (d) 1/2 to Z, 1/12 to E, 1/12 to F, 1/18 to G, 1/18 to H, 1/18, to I, 1/12 to J and 1/12 to K.

13. If Scott dies intestate, who takes his probate estate in a modern per stirpes (also known as a per capita with representation) jurisdiction?

    (a) 1/5 to V, 1/5 to W, 1/10 to E, 1/10 to F, 1/15 to G, 1/15 to H, 1/15 to I, 1/10 to J and 1/10 to K.

    (b) 1/6 to E, 1/6 to F, 1/9 to G, 1/9 to H, 1/9 to I, 1/6 to J and 1/6 to K.

    (c) 1/7 to E, 1/7 to F, 1/7 to G, 1/7 to H, 1/7 to I, 1/7 to J and 1/7 to K.

    (d) 1/2 to Z, 1/12 to E, 1/12 to F, 1/18 to G, 1/18 to H, 1/18, to I, 1/12 to J and 1/12 to K.

14. Assume further that before Scott's death, his grandson Ed had died leaving three children. Mona, Nan, and Owen. In addition assume his grandson Gary had died, leaving one son, Patrick. If Scott were to die

intestate at this time, who would take his probate estate in a per capita at each generation jurisdiction?

(a) 1/5 to V, 1/5 to W, 1/10 to F, 1/10 to H, 1/10 to I, 1/10 to J, 1/10 to K, 1/10 to G, 1/30 to M, 1/30 to N and 1/30 to O.

(b) 1/18 to M, 1/18 to N, 1/18 to O, 1/6 to P, 1/6 to H, 1/6 to I, 1/6 to J and 1/6 to K.

(c) 1/14 to M, 1/14 to N, 1/14 to O, 1/14 to P, 1/7 to F, 1/7 to H, 1/7 to I, 1/7 to J and 1/7 to K.

(d) 1/2 to Z, 1/12 to E, 1/12 to F, 1/18 to G, 1/18 to H, 1/18, to I, 1/12 to J and 1/12 to K.

15. Doug executes a will devising "90% of my estate to my spouse Eric and 10% of my estate to my alma mater State U." Eric predeceases Doug. Doug dies survived by his two children Sophia and Elizabeth, who are also children of Eric. The relevant anti-lapse statute applies only to devises to a testator's predeceasing issue. The statute names as the substitute takers the issue of the predeceasing beneficiary. The jurisdiction has abolished the no-residue-of-a-residue rule. Who takes Doug's estate?

(a) Sophia and Elizabeth will split the estate 50/50.

(b) State U.

(c) 10% to State U and 90% to the estate of Eric.

(d) 10% to State U and 90% split between Sophia and Elizabeth.

16. Which of the following are reasons why a legatee or heir might disclaim her inheritance?

(a) To avoid adverse estate and gift tax consequences, and to avoid having the heir's or legatee's creditors seize the property.

(b) To avoid adverse estate and gift tax consequences, and to avoid ineligibility for public assistance.

(c) To avoid adverse estate and gift tax consequences, to avoid ineligibility for public assistance, and to avoid having the heir's or legatee's creditors seize the property.

(d) To avoid ineligibility for public assistance, and to avoid having the heir's or legatee's creditors seize the property.

17. Which of the following is not true of the Uniform Prudent Investor Act?

(a) Forbids the trustee from delegating the discretionary duty of investing.

(b) Evaluates the investment portfolio as a whole rather than evaluating each investment in isolation.

(c) Abandons the view that the trustee must avoid "speculative" investments.

(d) Has been widely adopted in the United States.

18. T's will provides: I leave the rest and residue of my estate to my good friend, Frank, for him to manage for the benefit of those I have secretly identified to him. Who should take the residue of T's estate?

    (a) Frank, as constructive trustee in favor of the intended beneficiaries.

    (b) Frank, as a resulting trustee in favor of the testator's heirs.

    (c) Frank, who will not be legally bound to distribute to any beneficiaries of a trust, but will be viewed as holding the assets in a precatory trust.

    (d) Frank, as trustee of an honorary trust in favor of the beneficiaries who are otherwise unable to enforce the trust.

19. Which of the following future interests may be created in the transferor?

    (a) Reversion.

    (b) Vested remainder.

    (c) Contingent remainder.

    (d) Executory interest.

20. Ollie transferred Blackacre by deed in Year 1 to Andy for life, then to Ben and his heirs, but if Ben dies without issue surviving him, then to Carol and her heirs. In Year 15, Ben died survived by his oldest son, Seth. Andy is still alive. At Ben's death, who has what interests in Blackacre? Apply general principles of common law.

    (a) Andy has a life estate and Ben's estate has a vested remainder.

    (b) Andy has a life estate and Seth has a vested remainder.

    (c) Andy has a life estate, Ben's estate has a vested remainder subject to divestment, and Carol has a shifting executory interest.

    (d) Andy has a life estate, Carol has a contingent remainder, and Ollie has a reversion.

21. Assume basically the same facts as in the prior question, except that Ollie transfers the interests in Blackacre by will. The will provision says: "I leave Blackacre to Andy for life, then to Ben, but if Ben dies without issue surviving him, then to Carol." Ollie's will also contains a residuary clause that provides: "I leave the rest of my property to Carol." Ben dies in Year 15 survived by his oldest son Seth. Then Andy dies. Under the UPC:

    (a) Ben's estate is entitled to Blackacre because there was no express condition of survivorship.

    (b) Seth is entitled to Blackacre as a substitute taker for Ben.

    (c) Seth is entitled to Blackacre because there is an implied condition of survivorship.

    (d) Carol is entitled to Blackacre under the residuary clause.

22. Linda and Brent have been best friends since childhood. They are now in their late 50s. Brent has been diagnosed with a terminal illness. His

primary physician predicts that he will die within 9 months. Brent, terrified of the pain he will likely endure, begs Linda to help him end his life. She agrees and saves up a large dose of her sleeping medication which she gives to him. Brent's will, executed after she agreed to help him, but without her knowledge, leaves his entire estate to Linda and names her executor. Brent dies after he takes a lethal dose of the sleeping medication. After Brent's death, his brother, Ben, learns of Linda's participation in Brent's suicide and moves to have himself substituted for Linda as executor of his brother's estate. He claims that the gift to Linda in the will must be voided and that he, as the next of kin, will be entitled to the entire estate. His best argument for this position is:

(a) Brent and Linda colluded to prevent Ben from inheriting what was rightfully his.

(b) Brent, due to his terminal illness, did not know the natural objects of his bounty and thus did not have the mental capacity required to execute a valid will.

(c) Linda committed a wrongdoing in providing Brent with the lethal dose and she should not be allowed to benefit from the wrong.

(d) Under the UPC, Linda will not be able to take because her actions are sufficient to constitute an intentional killing.

23. Arthur's will leaves his entire estate to his second wife, Mary, and names Lucas, his grandson, as the Executor. At Arthur's death, the fair market value of property in his probate estate is approximately $1.0 million. Mary also takes as beneficiary of his life insurance ($1.5 million) and as the surviving joint tenant on realty ($1.0 million) and joint bank and stock accounts ($1.0 million). Mary is thinking of not probating the will, in which case, Arthur's estate would pass via intestacy half to Mary and half to his grandson, Lucas, son of a deceased daughter from his first marriage. If Mary fails to probate the will:

(a) She cannot be penalized because even one entrusted with the custody of a will is not under an affirmative obligation to offer the will for probate.

(b) She will be treated as having made a taxable gift of $500,000 to Lucas.

(c) The executor must probate the will because the estate is too large to administer informally.

(d) Arthur's creditors are "interested parties" and so can force a probate of the will in order to force an administration of the estate.

24. Harold and Elizabeth have been married for 20 years. They have two children, Kate (age 16) and Kim (age 12). Harold also has a son, Ronald, from a prior marriage. Ronald's mother (Harold's first wife) died when Ronald was 2 and he was raised by Harold and Elizabeth. In a UPC jurisdiction, if Harold dies intestate, what will be Elizabeth's share of his estate, unadjusted for inflation?

(a) She will receive the entire estate provided its value is under $300,000.

(b) She will receive the entire estate provided its value is under $225,000.

(c) She will receive the entire estate provided its value is under $150,000.

(d) She will receive the entire estate.

25. Thomas wants to be sure that his brother, Ned, gets no part of his estate. Thomas has two sisters, Sally and Serena. Both of his parents are dead and he has no spouse or issue. Under the intestacy law, if Thomas dies intestate, his estate will be split equally among his three siblings. Thomas lives in a UPC state. Which of the following methods is certain to disinherit Ned?

(a) Thomas executes a valid will that leaves everything he owns to his sisters, Sally and Sarah.

(b) Thomas executes a document with wills formalities and testamentary intent that says "If my brother Ned survives me, I want him to take nothing from my estate."

(c) Thomas executed a valid revocable inter vivos trust leaves everything he owns to his sisters, Sally and Sarah.

(d) To put all of his property into joint tenancy with right of survivorship with his sisters.

EXAM II

1. Settlor creates an irrevocable trust of which he is a beneficiary. Settlor's creditor seeks to attach settlor's interest in the trust. Under the Uniform Trust Code and traditional doctrine, still in effect in most American jurisdictions

   (a) The settlor's beneficial interest is immune from the creditor's claim because the trust is irrevocable.

   (b) The settlor's beneficial interest is immune from the creditor's claim but only if the trust contains a spendthrift provision.

   (c) The creditor may attach the settlor's beneficial interest provided that the trust is not a discretionary trust.

   (d) The creditor may attach as much of the trust as the trustee could distribute to or for the settlor's benefit.

2. T devises "My personal residence at 1307 W. James St. to my sister Susan. The residue of my estate to my brother Jeff." At the time of the will's execution, T lives at 1307 W. James St. One year later, T sells that house and buys and moves into a new house at 11 Shawnee Lane, which he uses as his personal residence. One year later, T dies. At T's death, to what is Susan entitled under UPC § 2–606 (the intent theory of ademption)?

   (a) The difference in value between the two houses.

   (b) Presumptively nothing.

   (c) The value of the house at 1307 W. James St. at the time it was sold.

   (d) Presumptively the house at 11 Shawnee Lane.

3. T devises "$100,000 to A, to be paid from the sale of my home, or from other sources if the sale is insufficient." After T's death, T's executor sells T's home for $500,000. If A's gift is subject to abatement, A's gift will abate with

   (a) the residuary gifts.

   (b) the general gifts.

   (c) the specific gifts.

   (d) the class gifts.

4. Which of the following is not part of the augmented estate under the UPC's elective share provisions?

   (a) Property passing from the decedent to one other than the surviving spouse by a payable-on-death account.

   (b) Property passing at the decedent's death from the decedent to the surviving spouse by means of an inter vivos revocable trust.

(c) Certain inter vivos transfers from the surviving spouse within two years of the decedent's death.

(d) An irrevocable trust created prior to the marriage.

5. In year 1, T executes his will, leaving everything to his wife, Wanda, in a testamentary trust, and, if she fails to survive him, to his mother, Maude. The will does not mention or otherwise provide for any child born after execution of the will. In year 2, T's child C is born. In year 3, T executes a codicil to his will which changes the trustee of his testamentary trust. In year 4, Wanda dies and six months later T dies. In a jurisdiction in which the pretermitted heir statute applies only to children born after execution of the will, should the probate court apply the doctrine of republication by codicil?

(a) Yes, if T has no other children.

(b) No, if, but only if, Maude agrees.

(c) Yes, if T would have wanted to disinherit C.

(d) No, if T would have wanted to disinherit C.

6. Is the following a valid attempt at creation of a trust? "I give $100,000 to me as trustee to be held in trust for my benefit."

(a) Yes, this trust has a settlor, property, a beneficiary, and a trustee.

(b) No, one person may not be a settlor, trustee and beneficiary.

(c) No, there has been no delivery.

(d) No, a trust must have at least one beneficiary who is not the sole trustee.

7. T executes a will the first lines of which state "I am going on a long trip into the jungle. If I do not return from the jungle, my estate should be distributed as follows:" T journeys to the jungle, returns home, and two months later dies of a rare illness. Should the court probate T's will?

(a) No, because the condition—"If I do not return from the jungle," was not satisfied.

(b) No, unless it can be shown that T contracted the rare illness while in the jungle.

(c) Yes, because there is no evidence that T wanted to die intestate.

(d) Yes, because there is no evidence that T wanted the will to be effective only if he did not return from the jungle.

8. Testator's will gives to Daniel the power to appoint Testator's property "to such person or persons as Daniel shall appoint." Daniel holds a

(a) Inter vivos general power of appointment.

(b) Testamentary non-general (special) power of appointment.

(c) Testamentary general power of appointment.

(d) Inter vivos non-general (special) power of appointment.

9. D had two children, Alex & Barbara. Alex predeceased D leaving three children Elaine, Francesca, and Greg. D then died intestate, survived by Barbara, Barbara's son Carlos, and Alex's three children. Barbara disclaims her inheritance. Who takes D's intestate estate under the Uniform Probate Code, which has a per capita at each generation scheme?

   (a) Carlos, Elaine, Francesca, and Greg each take 1/4.

   (b) 1/2 to Alex, 1/2 to Carlos.

   (c) 1/2 to Carlos, 1/2 split between Elaine, Francesca, and Greg.

   (d) We cannot tell from the facts given.

10. Mike executes a will leaving his estate to his wife Carol, if she survives him, and if not to his children (from a prior marriage) Greg, Peter, and Bobby. Carol executes a will leaving her estate to her husband Mike, if he survives her, and if not to her children (from a prior marriage) Marcia, Jan, and Cindy. Mike and Carol are involved in a car accident that ends up taking both of their lives. Mike dies on Tuesday, and Carol dies on Friday. Who takes Mike's estate in a jurisdiction that has adopted the Revised Uniform Simultaneous Death Act, which has been adopted by the UPC?

   (a) Carol's estate.

   (b) Greg, Peter and Bobby will take as Mike's intestate heirs.

   (c) Greg, Peter and Bobby will take as Mike's devisees.

   (d) Marcia, Jan and Cindy will take as Carol's devisees.

11. Under the Uniform Trust Code and in most American jurisdictions, a spendthrift provision in a trust is valid

   (a) If it restrains voluntary alienation of a beneficiary's interest, even if it does not restrain involuntary alienation.

   (b) If it restrains involuntary alienation of a beneficiary's interest, even if it does not restrain voluntary alienation.

   (c) Only if it restrains both voluntary and involuntary alienation of a beneficiary's interest.

   (d) Only if it restrains neither voluntary nor involuntary alienation of a beneficiary's interest.

12. Which of the following is not a trustee's defense to a claim of self-dealing?

   (a) The settlor authorized the self-dealing, and the transaction was fair and reasonable with respect to the beneficiaries.

   (b) The beneficiaries consented to the self-dealing after full disclosure, and the transaction was fair and reasonable with respect to the beneficiaries.

   (c) The transaction was fair and reasonable with respect to the beneficiaries.

   (d) The court approved of the transaction before-hand.

13. Helen executed a will in Year 1 that provided in part that "Certain of my real and personal property shall be distributed to such person or persons as I will designate in a memorandum that I will title 'Distribution of My Real and Personal Property.' " Helen later drafted a memorandum so titled and from time to time revised it. In Year 5, Helen included in the revised memorandum an entry "To Ginny, my house on Di Lido Island." Helen never signed any version of the memorandum. In Year 9, Helen executed a codicil to her will changing the designation of the trustee of a testamentary trust set up by the will. In Year 10, Helen died. Will Ginny take the home on Di Lido Island under Helen's will?

    (a) Yes, pursuant to the doctrines of incorporation by reference and republication by codicil.

    (b) No, because the doctrine of incorporation by reference does not apply to devises of real property.

    (c) No, because the testator did not sign the memorandum.

    (d) No, because the memorandum designating Ginny as the taker of the home on Di Lido Island was not in existence at the execution of the will.

14. Anna told her family that she intended to leave all her property to the local animal shelter. Her cousins, who were her closest relatives, were shocked, but agreed to help her with her estate plan. In fact, several of them actively shielded her from any outside contact and although they told her they had asked an attorney to draft the will she requested, they had not actually done so. Six months later, never having executed a valid will in favor of her intended beneficiary, Anna slipped and fell in her home and died shortly thereafter. The animal shelter has been informed of Anna's intent by one of the cousins. If the animal shelters wants to make a successful claim to Anna's estate, its best argument is:

    (a) A precatory trust.

    (b) An honorary trust.

    (c) A resulting trust.

    (d) A constructive trust.

15. Testator died leaving a will devising the residue of her estate in trust to pay the income to her three children Kevin, Brian, and Danny for their respective lives. The will further provided that at the death of the last surviving beneficiary, the trust was to terminate and the residue was to be distributed to the testator's "then surviving issue." What future interests are created by this will?

    (a) Reversion and vested remainder.

    (b) Vested remainder and executory interest.

    (c) Executory interest and contingent remainder.

    (d) Contingent remainder and reversion.

16. Klare loaned Bob $10,000 on an unsecured note two years ago and Bob used the funds to pay off an old gambling debt. At Bob's death, Klare wants to file a claim against Bob's estate for the unpaid balance of $8,000. Bob's primary asset was a ten-acre tract of land valued at $150,000, held for investment and owned by Bob and his spouse, Ellen, as joint tenants with right of survivorship. Bob created the joint tenancy five years ago. The few assets he owned individually at his death were all exempt from creditors (e.g., clothing, a funeral plot, a small life insurance policy). Bob and Ellen were domiciled in a UPC common law property state. What is the best way for Klare to proceed?

    (a) File a claim against Bob's estate in order to force a sale of the land.

    (b) File a claim directly against Ellen since she is the current owner of the land.

    (c) Write his claim off as a bad debt because joint tenancy real assets of a decedent cannot be reached by creditors after the decedent's death.

    (d) Make a fraudulent transfer claim against half the joint tenancy asset now held by Ellen.

17. Larry Lawyer represented Ted Testator and helped him with his estate plan. Ted left his entire estate to his paramour, Pam, cutting out his wife of 40 years, Flo. After Ted died, Flo sued to have the will set aside, claiming lack of testamentary capacity and undue influence. In addition, Flo asserted her statutory elective share as an alternative claim against the estate. Larry Lawyer acted as attorney for the estate and successfully defended the validity of the will. However, the court ruled in favor of Flo on her elective share claim. Pam, upset that her inheritance has been virtually cut in half, sues Larry Lawyer for malpractice.

    Lawyer's best defense to this claim is:

    (a) A spouse cannot waive her right to an elective share.

    (b) Lawyer did not know that Ted was married for 40 years because Ted did not reveal that he had a wife on the questionnaire Lawyer asked Ted to fill in summarizing his family relationships and his property holdings.

    (c) Lack of privity.

    (d) It is unreasonable for Pam to recover since it is against public policy for a testator to leave his estate to a paramour.

18. Harold and Elizabeth have been married for 20 years. They have two children, Kate (age 16) and Kim (age 12). Harold also has a son, Ronald, from a prior marriage. Ronald's mother (Harold's first wife) died when Ronald was 2 and he was raised by Harold and Elizabeth. Elizabeth adopted Ronald when he was four. In a UPC state, if Harold dies intestate, what will be Elizabeth's share of his estate?

    (a) She will receive the entire estate.

    (b) She will receive the first $300,000 and 75% of the rest.

(c) She will receive the first $225,000 and 50% of the rest.

(d) She will receive the first $150,000 and 50% of the rest.

19. Evelyn is the sole child of Testator and is named as the sole beneficiary in Testator's will. Testator's estate is worth approximately $15.0 million. At the time of Testator's death, Evelyn is 75 years old and is in a nursing home, recovering from a stroke. It is unlikely that she will ever fully recover, and she may need to stay in the nursing home for the rest of her life. The costs of the nursing home are currently being paid by her private insurance, but it has a $300,000 cap, which is expected to cover her costs only for the next several years. Her son, Evan, has a valid power of attorney and has consulted you about the possibility of exercising the power in order to disclaim the $15.0 million testamentary gift from Testator. What do you tell him?

(a) He cannot exercise the power of attorney to disclaim because disclaimers generally cannot be exercised by agents, but instead must be exercised by the principal.

(b) He can exercise the power of attorney to disclaim but it will not avoid any estate tax due by Testator's estate.

(c) He can exercise the power of attorney to disclaim and it will avoid both Testator's estate taxes due and creditors' claims.

(d) He can exercise the power of attorney to disclaim, and it will not affect his mother's right to continued care at the nursing home, even if she runs out of insurance.

20. George's will provides that his executor shall destroy his home after his death. The rest and residue of his property, including the land on which the home sits, is left to his son, Bill. The house is in perfectly fine condition and Bill thinks the only reason his father included the provision regarding its destruction in his will is because his father had become very antisocial in his later years and never wanted to let anyone come into the house. Bill asks the executor not to follow the direction to destroy the home. Which of the following is the most likely outcome of this request?

(a) Even if the executor wants to agree to Bill's request, litigation of the issue is still possible as the executor has no right to agree to such a request.

(b) If the executor and Bill litigate over this issue, a court will likely rule that the destruction shall not occur because it violates public policy.

(c) If the executor and Bill litigate over this issue, a court will likely uphold the provision in the will because of the strong policy supporting freedom of testation.

(d) If the executor and Bill litigate over this issue, a court will likely uphold the provision in the will because George could have destroyed the house while he was alive.

21. Frank wants his family to understand clearly why his estate plan leaves some of them out. He makes a video of himself using a webcam that will explain it all. He dies two years later. After his death, the video was found on his computer but no will was found. In the video, Frank appears to be reading from a set of note cards. He announces that he is of sound mind and intends for the video to serve as a recording of his testamentary intent. He then says: "To my oldest daughter, Fran, I give nothing, because she has had the bad sense to hang out with people who will take advantage of her. To my next daughter, Claire, I give the sum of $2.0 million, but she must use it to do good in the world as I know she will. To my son, Victor, I leave enough money to fly home for my funeral. Finally, to my wife, who I doubt has ever been faithful to me, I leave one year's allowance of $250,000, which should give her enough time to find another sucker. If I have anything left over, I give it to the American Red Cross." The Red Cross wants to know whether it can collect the legacy.

    (a) The Red Cross may be able to collect if Frank died in a state that recognizes holographic wills.

    (b) The Red Cross may be able to collect if Frank died in a state that recognizes nuncupative wills.

    (c) The Red Cross may be able to collect if Frank died in a state that had adopted a harmless error statute.

    (d) The Red Cross is not likely to be able to collect.

22. Mildred's will leaves everything to her husband, Lon, and if he fails to survive her, then to Lon's nephew, Ted. Five years later, Mildred divorces Lon. However, they remain good friends and she dies six months later, never having changed her will. Mildred died in a non-UPC state in which the applicable state statute provides: "Any gift in a will in favor of a spouse is revoked upon divorce. The property will be distributed as if the beneficiary had predeceased the testator." Mildred is survived by her mother, Mona, and by Lon and Ted. The most likely distribution of Mildred's estate is:

    (a) Everything to Lon because that was her intent.

    (b) Everything to Ted because the gift to Lon is revoked by statute.

    (c) Everything to Mona because the gift to Ted should be revoked along with the gift to Lon.

    (d) Everything to Mona because Lon did not in fact predecease Mildred and so the condition precedent to Ted's taking has not occurred.

23. Van cares about what will happen to his body after his death. He has asked his good friend Rip to see that his body is cremated and his ashes are buried next to his dog's ashes in the field behind the farmhouse where Van currently lives. Rip told Van he would try to carry out his wishes but advised Van to see a lawyer. In the absence of any applicable statutory provision, which of the following is the best advice to Van:

(a) Van should devise his body to Rip so that Rip will have the authority to request a cremation.

(b) Van should give Rip a durable power of attorney and specifically authorize Rip to arrange for a cremation.

(c) Van should execute a living will that makes it clear that he wishes his body to be cremated.

(d) Historically, a person had no power to control the disposition of his own body after death. Thus, Van can only hope that a court will allow Rip to carry out Van's wishes.

24. Prince married Zoe and they had one daughter, Clarissa. Five years later, Prince died intestate. When the administration of his estate was opened, a woman named Minnie came forward and proved that she had been legally married to Prince 10 years earlier, that they had two children, and that she and Prince had never been divorced. State law provides that nonmarital children can inherit from their fathers only if their parents marry after the birth of the child. Otherwise, the state follows the intestacy scheme of the UPC. Which of the following is not true with respect to the distribution of Prince's estate?

(a) Minnie is the only legal spouse of Prince and is thus entitled to an intestate share.

(b) Clarissa will be considered an illegitimate or nonmarital child of Prince.

(c) Clarissa will inherit from Prince.

(d) Zoe has no basis for claiming part of the estate.

25. The State of K has a statute that protects omitted spouses by giving them an intestate share. An omitted spouse is described as someone who married the testator after the testator had executed a will. In the absence of children from another marriage, the omitted spouse would be entitled to 100% of the testator's estate as her intestate share. The State of K has another statute that allows spouses to elect against the will. This statute limits the amount that the spouse can claim to one-third of the testator's estate. What is the best explanation for the difference in these two remedies?

(a) The elective share is derived from the law of dower which limited recovery to a life estate in one-third of the estate.

(b) The omitted spouse provision is based on a presumption of testamentary intent and the elective share is based on a policy of protecting disinherited spouses.

(c) The omitted spouse provision is rarely triggered whereas the elective share is often used by disinherited spouses.

(d) The difference in distribution amounts really does not matter because the surviving spouse can decide which remedy is preferable.

EXAM III

1. To compute the spouse's elective share under UPC 2–202 (as modified in 2008), the spouse must consult the table contained in UPC 2–203 that indicates the percentage of the augmented estate that is deemed to be marital property, depending on the length of the marriage. For a marriage of five years duration, the percentage in the table is 30%. This means that, a survivor can claim as an elective share:
   (a) 30% of the augmented estate.
   (b) 30% of the decedent's net probate estate.
   (c) 15% of the augmented estate.
   (d) 60% of the augmented estate.

2. Is the following a valid attempt at creation of a testamentary trust in an otherwise validly executed will? "I devise my cattle ranch in Texas to my sister Susan, and I desire that she use the profits from the ranch to benefit my brother Jeff."
   (a) No, because the devise lacks words of direction.
   (b) No, because we cannot be sure that the ranch will produce any profits.
   (c) Yes, because Susan is the trustee.
   (d) Yes, because a testamentary trust will not fail for want of a trustee.

3. Jurisdiction X has reduced the formalities for execution of a will. However, if the formalities are not met, the document will be probated so long as there is clear and convincing evidence that T intended the document to be his will. Jurisdiction X is a
   (a) Harmless error jurisdiction, such as the UPC.
   (b) Strict compliance jurisdiction, such as a majority of American jurisdictions.
   (c) Substantial compliance jurisdiction.
   (d) Holographic will jurisdiction.

4. Assume you are in a jurisdiction that follows the *Claflin* doctrine. Assume further that the settlor is dead and all trust beneficiaries agree to early termination of the trust. Which of the following trusts cannot be terminated?
   1. "Such income to A for life as is needed for A's support, remainder in principal at A's death to B."
   2. "Income to H for life, and upon H's death, income to Son until he reaches the age of 35, at which time Son is to receive the principal in fee."

3. "Income to A for life, remainder in principal at A's death to B."

4. "Income to A for life to be used for A's support, remainder in principal at A's death to B."

5. "Income to A for life, remainder in principal at A's death to B. A's interest may not be assigned or attached."

(a) 1, 2, 4, and 5.

(b) 1, 2, and 5

(c) Only trust 2 cannot be terminated.

(d) None of these trusts can be terminated.

5. Steven possesses an inter vivos general power of appointment. He contracts with Harriet to appoint the property to Harriet's two children, who are the default takers under the power. Is the contract likely to be enforceable?

   (a) No, because the donee of a power of appointment that is not presently exercisable may not contract to make an appointment.

   (b) No, unless the court construes the contract as one to release the power and allow the property to pass in default of appointment.

   (c) Yes, because Steven holds a power that is tantamount to ownership of the appointive property in that he has the power to vest himself in ownership at any time.

   (d) No, if the exercise benefits Steven. Such a contract would be a "fraud on the power."

Use the following fact pattern to answer questions 6–8:

T executes a typed will which contains a $50,000 devise to Benny but no residuary clause. Later, T crosses out the "$50,000" and writes "$60,000," signs and dates the change.

6. After T dies, to what is Benny entitled to in a non-UPC state that allows partial revocation by physical act, recognizes holographic wills, and does not have the doctrine of dependent relative revocation?

   (a) $110,000.

   (b) $60,000.

   (c) $50,000.

   (d) $0.

7. After T dies, to what is Benny entitled to in a state that has adopted UPC § 2–503 (the harmless error rule), and does allow partial revocation by physical act, recognize holographic wills, and has the doctrine of dependent relative revocation?

   (a) $110,000.

   (b) $60,000.

(c) $50,000.

(d) $0.

8. After T dies, to what is Benny entitled to in a non-UPC state that allows partial revocation by physical act, recognizes holographic wills, and has the doctrine of dependent relative revocation?

   (a) $110,000.

   (b) $60,000.

   (c) $50,000.

   (d) $0.

9. D died intestate survived by five children and no spouse. D left a net probate estate of $800,000. While D was alive, he gave Child A a $150,000 home. While D was alive, he gave Child B a $100,000 boat. While D was alive, he gave Child C a $25,000 car. D gave no large gifts to his two remaining children, E and F. Assume that the gifts to A, B and C were advancements. Who takes what portion of D's intestate estate?

   (a) Each child takes $160,000.

   (b) E and F take the entire intestate estate.

   (c) A takes $65,000, B takes $115,000, C takes $190,000, E and F each take $215,000.

   (d) Each child takes $105,000.

10. Frank, the testator's son, intentionally misrepresented to his father, the testator, that Daughter Dora was back on drugs. Frank knew that his father had threatened to disinherit Dora if she ever went back on drugs. Taking Frank at his word, the testator amended his will by codicil, removing all gifts to Dora. Under these facts, Frank has committed

    (a) Fraud in the execution.

    (b) Fraud in the inducement.

    (c) Constructive fraud.

    (d) Resulting fraud.

11. The law of the marital domicile at the time personal property is acquired generally controls

    (a) Title, but only if the property is held in the state of the domicile.

    (b) Characterization (separate or community) of the property.

    (c) The survivor's marital rights (such as an elective share).

    (d) Who will inherit the property if one of the spouses dies intestate.

12. Testator devises the residuary of her estate to the Reverend Wells in trust to be administered "in such manner as in his discretion shall appear best calculated to carry out wishes which I have expressed to him or may express to him." This donative transfer is

(a) An honorary trust.

(b) A secret trust.

(c) A semi-secret trust.

(d) A precatory trust.

13. Testator devises property in trust "to my only child, Elizabeth, for her life and at her death to my heirs." In most states, at what date is a court likely to determine the testator's heirs for the purposes of this devise?

(a) At Elizabeth's death.

(b) At the testator's death.

(c) At Elizabeth's death, but only if Elizabeth has issue.

(d) At the testator's death, because Elizabeth is the only heir of the testator.

14. At Jerry's death, he owned the following property: a personal residence held in joint tenancy with his wife Samantha; two joint bank accounts also held with Samantha; a POD savings account naming his daughter, Jocelyn, as the beneficiary; a life insurance policy and retirement account, both acquired through his employer and naming his wife as beneficiary, various personal items, including clothing, a model train collection, and jewelry, and $30,000 worth of Rockwell stock that he inherited from his father, held in his name alone. He had no debts. Samantha can find no will and comes to you for advice on whether she needs to begin a formal estate administration.

(a) She will need to institute a formal estate administration in order to clear up title to all the property owned by Jerry at death.

(b) She can collect the personal property by providing an affidavit that she is Jerry's only heir, but only if the daughter is not a minor.

(c) She does not need to institute any administration because all of Jerry's property passes outside of probate.

(d) She will need to institute some form of estate administration in order to clear up title to the Rockwell stock.

15. Jane and Larry have been married for 5 years. Larry has a $100,000 face amount life insurance policy that names Jane as the beneficiary and his mother, Esther, as the contingent beneficiary. Jane and Larry have no children. Both of their fathers are dead, but Larry's mother, Esther, and Jane's mother, Mildred, are both in good health. While vacationing in Florida, Jane and Larry are both killed in a freak boating accident which appears to have killed everyone on board instantaneously. Both of them died intestate. The applicable state simultaneous death act provides that "when there is no sufficient evidence that two individuals died otherwise than simultaneously, each individual's property is distributed as if he or she survived the other." The insurance company should pay the $100,000 as follows:

(a) Under the State's Simultaneous Death Act, to Esther.

(b) Under the State's Simultaneous Death Act to Jane's estate.

(c) Under the State's Simultaneous Death Act to Mildred and Esther equally.

(d) Under the State's Simultaneous Death Act to Larry's estate.

16. Lawrence died many years ago, leaving a will that left his entire estate in trust, with the following instruction to the trustee: "distribute all income to my wife, Maureen, for her life, and then to my stepdaughter, Dorothy, for her life, and then to Dorothy's then living issue if any, and if none, then distribute to my heirs." At Lawrence's death, he was survived by a brother, Benjamin and Benjamin's son, Luke, and by his stepdaughter, Dorothy. His wife (Dorothy's mother, Maureen) had predeceased him.

    Income was paid to Dorothy for 15 years until her death last year. Dorothy had no surviving issue at her death. Benjamin died 10 years ago, with a will that left everything to his wife, Millie, if she survived, and if not, to his son Luke. Millie did survive. She is still alive and so is their son, Luke, and Luke's two children, born after Lawrence's death.

    Assume there is no statutory provision covering this gift and there is no modern case law changing the traditional common law rules. To whom should the trustee distribute the trust corpus?

    (a) Millie

    (b) Benjamin's estate, to be distributed to his intestate heirs.

    (c) Dorothy's estate

    (d) Luke

17. Assume the same facts as in the previous question but now assume that the UPC provision that covers this fact situation is part of the probate code of the state in which Lawrence died. In this event, the trust corpus will go to.

    (a) Maureen's estate

    (b) Benjamin's estate

    (c) Millie

    (d) Luke

18. Harry's will leaves "everything I own to my wife, Willa, if she survives me by 30 days. If she fails to survive me by 30 days, then I leave my entire estate to Willa's sister, Stella." Harry also has an insurance policy naming Willa as beneficiary. Harry and Willa are divorced. Two years later Harry dies, never having changed his will. He has no living relatives at the time of his death. He is survived by Willa and Stella and their mother, Maude. Under the UPC:

    (a) Stella is entitled to Harry's probate estate and Willa is entitled to the insurance proceeds.

(b) The state is entitled to the insurance proceeds and Stella is entitled to Harry's probate estate.

(c) The state is entitled to Harry's probate estate and Willa is entitled to the insurance proceeds.

(d) The state is entitled to Harry's probate estate and to the insurance proceeds.

19. Truman's will provided: "I leave the contents of the drawers in my desk to Annie." At Truman's death, Annie and others go through his desk drawers. Included in the top drawer was an original gelatin silver photograph by Ansel Adams, signed by Adams, and valued at $35,000. The residuary takers under the will argue that Annie should not be entitled to the photograph. It is not clear when Truman purchased the Ansel Adams photograph. Which of the following arguments would you make on behalf of the residuary takers?

(a) Putting a valuable photograph in a desk drawer is not an act of independent significance.

(b) There are insufficient testamentary formalities attached to the inclusion of this photograph in the gift to Annie.

(c) People are always putting things in desk drawers and taking them out. A desk drawer is different from a safety deposit box.

(d) All of the above.

20. Which of the following does not have standing to contest a will that has been submitted for probate?

(a) An adopted child of the testator who was left out of the will.

(b) A contingent beneficiary in an earlier will that was revoked by the will submitted to probate.

(c) A trustee named in the will.

(d) A divorced spouse, cut out of the will completely, who claims that the testator promised to leave half of his estate to her disabled sister.

21. Betsy's will leaves all her property to her best friend, Will. Will predeceases Betsy, but she fails to change her will. He is survived by a son, Darwin. At Betsy's death, she is survived by Darwin and a distant cousin, Colin, who is the grandchild of her mother's great aunt, Sarah. Betsy lives in State M, which has adopted the UPC. At Betsy's death, the probate estate will go to:

(a) Will's estate

(b) Darwin

(c) Colin

(d) The State of M

22. Harvey and Ellen are about to get married. Harvey is asking Ellen to waive her rights in his estate in exchange for a current payment of $2.0

million. He proposes to pay the $2.0 million by transferring $2.0 million worth of real estate to the two of them as joint tenants with right of survivorship. She consults you to ask whether this arrangement sufficiently protects her right to the $2.0 million. She realizes that if she dies first, she would get nothing and isn't worried about that. But she wants to be certain that she receives at least $2.0 million in value at his death in the event he dies first. Which of the following best protects her right?

(a) The joint tenancy with right of survivorship.

(b) A tenancy in common backed up by a will leaving all the property to Ellen.

(c) A tenancy by the entirety.

(d) A deed granting the property to Harvey and Ellen for their joint lives with alternative contingent remainders to the survivor of them.

23. State G adopted the intestacy provisions of the Uniform Probate Code in 1999. Then the State Probate Code was amended in 2005 to provide as follows:

> **§ 53-2-1. Determining heirs of decedent who died without will**
>
> (a) For purposes of this Code section:
>
> (1) Children of the decedent who are born after the decedent's death are considered children in being at the decedent's death, provided they were conceived prior to the decedent's death, were born within ten months of the decedent's death, and survived 120 hours or more after birth.

Decedent died intestate in 2006, survived by his mother and two brothers. Six months later his fiancé became pregnant using decedent's frozen sperm. If she gives birth to a healthy baby who lives for at least 120 hours, what is the most likely distribution of Decedent's estate by a State of G Probate Court?

(a) Everything to his mother.

(b) Half to his brothers and half to his mother.

(c) Everything to his child.

(d) Everything to his fiancé as the guardian of his child.

24. Gene and Frank were brothers. Before going on an extended cruise around the world, Gene transferred $100,000 from his savings account to Frank and asked Frank to purchase a ten acre tract of land close to Gene's farm that was to be auctioned off at a tax sale the next month. Frank bought the land and took title in his own name and recorded the deed, intending to transfer the property to Gene when Gene returned from the cruise. Shortly after Gene returned but before Frank transferred the property, Frank died. His will leaves everything to his daughter, Rose. Rose, as

executor, has included the ten acre tract in Frank's probate estate. Gene challenges that characterization. What is the most likely outcome of this conflict?

(a) The court will honor record title and Rose will win.

(b) The court will impose a constructive trust and Gene will win.

(c) The court will give the property to Gene under a resulting trust theory.

(d) The court will presume a gift from Gene to Frank and Rose will win.

25. Testator visited his lawyer to ask to change his will. The change affected only Article V, which included a list of charitable beneficiaries to whom the testator was giving various amounts of stock. The change added a number of charities and altered the amounts given to each previously listed charity. The lawyer's secretary retyped Article V and inserted it in the will in place of the existing Article V. She then told the Testator that the will had been changed and there was nothing more he needed to do. At Testator's death, if someone wants to challenge the gifts to charitable beneficiaries, which of the following requirements in the law of wills is likely to be most useful?

(a) Each page of the will must be signed by the testator.

(b) An amendment to a will is not valid unless there is evidence of testamentary intent.

(c) The doctrine of integration.

(d) Stock is not tangible personal property.

EXAM IV

1. Gary left the residue of his estate to Harold for life and then as Harold appoints by will to any or all of Oscar, Oprah, and Andrew. Gary failed to specify any takers in default. Harold died intestate, survived by Oscar, Oprah, and Andrew. The property is likely to pass to:

   (a) Harold's heirs.

   (b) Oscar, Oprah, and Andrew in equal shares.

   (c) The class of appointees in equal shares.

   (d) Gary's estate.

2. T devises "$100,000 to A, to be paid from the sale of my home, or from other sources if the sale is insufficient." After T's death, T's executor sells T's home for $200,000. If A's gift is subject to abatement, A's gift will abate with:

   (a) the residuary gifts.

   (b) the general gifts.

   (c) the specific gifts.

   (d) Both (b) and (c).

3. What result in the above question if the home had sold for only $80,000? Assuming that the gift to A is subject to abatement, which class of gifts will it abate with?

   (a) the residuary gifts.

   (b) the general gifts.

   (c) the specific gifts.

   (d) Both (b) and (c).

4. In the State of Nirvana, persons who are equally related to the intestate decedent and who take a share of the intestate estate, take the same proportion of the estate. The Nirvanans believe that this approach best carries out the likely intent of the typical intestate decedent. Which intestacy scheme has the State of Nirvana adopted?

   (a) Classic or strict per stirpes

   (b) Modern per stirpes

   (c) Either (a) or (b), depending on the facts

   (d) Per capita at each generation

5. Under the Uniform Trust Code and in many American jurisdictions, certain "exception creditors" might be able to attach a beneficiary's interest in a trust notwithstanding an otherwise valid spendthrift

provision. "Exception creditors" under the Uniform Trust Code and in many jurisdictions include

(a) One who has obtained a tort judgment against the beneficiary.

(b) A former spouse of the beneficiary who has a judgment or court order against the beneficiary for spousal support.

(c) A child of the beneficiary who has a judgment or court order against the beneficiary for child support.

(d) Both (b) and (c).

6. Settlor creates a revocable trust of which he is not a beneficiary. Under the Uniform Trust Code and in most American jurisdictions

(a) The settlor's creditors generally cannot reach the trust assets as "the power to revoke is not property."

(b) The settlor's creditors can reach the trust assets only if the creation of the trust involved a fraudulent conveyance.

(c) The settlor's creditors can reach the trust assets only if the trust does not contain a spendthrift provision.

(d) The settlor's creditors can reach the trust assets.

7. Jane and Larry have been married for 5 years. Larry has a \$100,000 face amount life insurance policy that names Jane as the beneficiary and his mother, Esther, as the contingent beneficiary. Jane and Larry have no children. Both of their fathers are dead, but Larry's mother, Esther, and Jane's mother, Mildred, are both in good health. While vacationing in Florida, Jane and Larry are both killed in a freak boating accident. Larry died instantly, but Jane was rushed to a nearby hospital, where she died two days later. Under the UPC, the insurance company should pay the \$100,000 as follows:

(a) To Jane's estate since she survived, but is now dead.

(b) To Esther as the contingent beneficiary under the life insurance policy.

(c) To Mildred as Jane's only living heir.

(d) None of the above.

8. Nick and Nora, who are cousins, opened a joint bank account with right of survivorship at Bank One. There is no evidence to suggest that their intent was anything other than establishing a true joint account. Nick made the initial deposit to the account and most of the subsequent deposits, but Nora contributed by making small deposits now and then. Nick's will, executed three years later, states as follows: I give the sums on deposit in the joint bank account at Bank One to my friend, Frank. At Nick's death, there was \$50,000 on deposit in the joint bank account. Under the UPC, what is the most likely result?

(a) Nora will take the full \$50,000 because of her survivorship rights in the bank account.

(b) Frank will take the full $50,000 because the provision in the will effectively revoked the joint account.

(c) Frank and Nora will split the $50,000 equally.

(d) Frank and Nora will split the $50,000, but from these facts, we can't tell what the split will be.

9. Carson's will provides as follows: "I leave the sum of $100,000 to whoever turns out to be the beneficiary in the last will of my sister, Stella. The rest and residue of my property shall be distributed equally among my issue." Two years later Stella executes a will that leaves all her property to her daughter, Donna. Stella died six months ago. Carson died last month. Under general principles of common law, what is the most likely distribution of Carson's $100,000 specific bequest?

   (a) The $100,000 gift fails because Stella's will was not in existence when Carson executed his own will.

   (b) The $100,000 gift fails under the doctrine of integration.

   (c) The $100,000 gift is valid but only if Donna can show that Carson intended Donna to be the beneficiary.

   (d) The $100,000 gift to Donna is valid.

10. At common law, which of the following types of gifts would not fall into the residue if the gift lapsed.

   (a) A residuary gift.

   (b) A general gift.

   (c) A specific gift.

   (d) A demonstrative gift.

11. Gary died intestate survived only by the following lineal descendants: three grandchildren, all children of a deceased daughter Joan, and three great-grandchildren, Kim, Karl, and Kathy. Kim and Karl were the children of a deceased son of Joan named William. Kathy was the granddaughter of Gary's only son, Harry, who died many years ago in a boating accident that also took the lives of Kathy's parents.

   Gary lives in a UPC state. The most likely distribution of Gary's estate will be:

   (a) One-sixth to each of the surviving lineal descendants.

   (b) One-half to be split among the three children of Joan and the other one-half to be split between Kim, Karl, and Kathy.

   (c) One-fifth each to the three grandchildren and to Kathy, and one-tenth each to Kim and Karl.

   (d) One fifth each to the three grandchildren and 2/15 to each of the three great grandchildren.

12. Maureen's will leaves "my house at 214 Dover Street to my good friend Annie." It turns out that Maureen doesn't own 214 Dover Street, but she

does own 215 Dover Street. There are three people who claim to be her good friend Annie. In most United States jurisdictions:

(a) The gift fails because there is no remedy for correcting a scrivener's mistake in a will.

(b) The court will allow parol evidence to prove which of the three people named Annie was the "Annie" that Maureen intended to give her property to.

(c) The court will probably give the house equally to all three Annies if they can all prove that they are good friends of Maureen's.

(d) The court will change 214 to 215 since this is a patent ambiguity.

13. Marc has been adjudicated incompetent to manage his property. From that fact, we can conclude

(a) Marc lacks the capacity to execute a will.

(b) Marc might have the capacity to execute a will.

(c) Marc necessarily lacks the capacity to execute a will unless he has a "lucid interval" during which he executes his will.

(d) Marc lacks the capacity to execute a will but might have the capacity to revoke a will.

14. Susan created a testamentary trust in the residuary clause of her will that provided as follows: "All income shall be paid to my son, Thomas, for his life and then to his then living issue, if any. And if none, then to my then living heirs."

Susan died survived by Thomas and an estranged son, Samuel. Samuel dies several years later, survived by a daughter, Rachel. Thomas dies some years later with no living issue. Rachel seeks a distribution of the trust assets to herself as the only living heir of Susan.

Assuming there is no statutory provision that applies to this situation. At the death of Thomas, the trust corpus should be distributed to:

(a) The estate of Thomas.

(b) The estate of Samuel.

(c) Equally between the estates of Samuel and Thomas.

(d) Rachel.

15. Clara was in the hospital. She called her lawyer to give directions about certain changes she wanted made in the disposition of her estate under her current will. In particular, she wanted to add two sizeable legacies to her two friends, Bert and Jane. In addition, she wanted to change her residuary clause so that a larger portion would go to charity. The lawyer decided to draft a codicil to the will that would effectuate these changes. He brought the typed codicil to the hospital for Clara to review. It included a gift of $100,000 each to Bert and to Jane. And it changed the residuary

from a 10% gift to charity to a 50% gift to charity, thereby cutting back the size of the residuary gift to her daughter Hallie.

Clara read the codicil and said she approved it. The lawyer went to find some hospital employees who might agree to be witnesses to her execution of the document. When he returned with two nurses, Hallie had already signed the codicil. She and the lawyer began to discuss the effect of that and whether or not the nurses could now witness the execution of the will. She said it was her signature and she would be willing to sign it again if that was necessary. She opened her bedside drawer to pull the pen back out to sign again and was suddenly overtaken by a massive coronary. She was immediately rushed out of the room and the lawyer stuffed the codicil into his briefcase. Clara survived the attack, went home from the hospital, regained her health for a while, but died six months later. The lawyer wants to probate the will, but realizes that the witnesses never signed the codicil. He signs it himself at that time and goes to the hospital to find one of the nurses who was in the room that day and gets her to sign as well.

In a state that has a UPC-style will execution statute, but no harmless error statute, a probate court will most likely:

(a) Disallow probate of the codicil because no one ever witnessed Clara's signature.

(b) Disallow probate of the codicil because the witnesses signed six months after the codicil was signed by Clara.

(c) Disallow probate of the codicil because it was signed by the lawyer rather than one of the intended witnesses.

(d) Allow probate of the codicil because the witnesses did witness Clara's acknowledgement of her own signature and ultimately signed the codicil themselves.

16. Hank and Wilma have been married for over 40 years. They have two children and three grandchildren. Before Hank goes into the hospital for surgery, they agree to sign a will. They write it together, with Hank dictating out loud to Wilma who does the writing. They state that they intend for this document to serve as the will of both of them. The will provides: "Our property shall go to whichever one of us survives the other and then it shall go to our two children." They both sign at the end and when Hank goes to the hospital the next day they take it with them, show it to the receptionist, and ask her and her co-worker to sign the will as witnesses. They do. Hank dies, survived by Wilma and the two children. They probate the will and Wilma takes title to all the couple's assets.

    Five years later Wilma marries Henry. At her death 2 years later, the children try to re-probate the will that she and Hank had executed years before. Henry claims that he should be entitled to Wilma's estate as her surviving husband. Under the UPC, Henry's most successful claim is:

    (a) A joint and mutual will is insufficient to raise a presumption of a contract between Wilma and Hank.

(b) The will was not properly witnessed because the witnesses did not see Wilma sign the will.

(c) He is a pretermitted spouse and is entitled to an intestate share.

(d) He has the right to an elective share.

17. Henry and Mary were married for 30 years. Henry started dating his secretary and tried to keep it from Mary. When Mary discovered the affair, she had a huge fight with Henry that became physical. During the fight, she picked up a heavy object in the kitchen and hit him on the head with it. Henry died two days later in the local hospital. Mary is convicted of homicide and sentenced to prison. Her children are supportive of her and are worried about her financial stability. Henry's will leaves everything to Mary, but if she predeceases him then to the children. He also has an insurance policy that names Mary as the primary beneficiary. The oldest child, Shirley, is executor of the estate and she wants to know whether she can distribute any of the assets to her mother.

(a) If the state has no slayer statute, then Shirley can distribute the assets to her mother.

(b) If the life insurance is part of an ERISA controlled pension plan, then Shirley can distribute the assets to her mother.

(c) If Henry and Mary lived in a community property state, then Shirley can distribute all the assets to her mother.

(d) The safest way to ensure that Mary receives the assets in Henry's estate is for the children to distribute the assets to themselves and then gift them to Mary.

18. Which of the following is *not* true about real estate held as joint tenants with right of survivorship?

(a) The survivor cannot disclaim any of the property at the death of the first joint tenant.

(b) The real estate will not be included in the probate estate at the death of the first joint tenant.

(c) The joint tenancy can only be severed by agreement of all joint tenants.

(d) Both (a) and (c).

19. Constance wants to be buried in her wedding gown next to her husband who died 20 years ago. In addition, she wants all of her jewelry buried with her. The jewelry is valued at $20,000. The best way to ensure that this happens is:

(a) For Constance to instruct her Executor to make these arrangements in her will.

(b) For Constance to direct an attorney in fact to make these arrangements on her behalf after her death.

(c) For Constance to create a trust fund that provides the necessary funds for burial and includes a substantial additional sum to be paid to the named beneficiary provided her burial wishes are carried out, and if not, the gift will revert to a charity.

(d) For Constance to make the payment of funeral expenses under the will conditional on burial in accord with her wishes.

20. Father died without a spouse. Father's first will devised his entire estate to his daughter Mary, and expressly disinherited his sons Peter and Paul. Father's second will expressly revoked his first will and left one half of his estate to Mary and one half of his estate to Peter. Peter, Paul, and Mary are his only children. Who might have standing to challenge the second will?

(a) Peter, Paul, and Mary.

(b) Peter and Paul, but not Mary.

(c) Paul, but not Peter or Mary.

(d) Paul and Mary, but not Peter.

21. Tom Testator executed a will on June 1, 2012 and provided for a specific bequest of $250,000 to be paid to the John Jones trust and distributed under the terms of that trust. The John Jones irrevocable trust was created on July 15, 2012 by Tom's brother, John, who transferred $1.0 million to the trust. The trust provided for all trust funds to be accumulated until July 15, 2023 and then distributed to the then living descendants of Tom and John. Tom died in 2020 and his will was probated. The residuary takers under his will are attacking the specific bequest of $250,000 and argue that it should be distributed to them. The trustee of the John Jones trust argues that the $250,000 is a valid gift to the trust. The most likely outcome of this dispute, in a UPC state, is:

(a) The gift will fail because the creation of a trust is not an act of independent significance.

(b) The gift is valid.

(c) The gift will fail because this trust was not created by the testator.

(d) The gift will fail because the trust was created after the will was executed.

22. State O has a probate statute providing that children born outside of wedlock can inherit from their fathers provided "paternity has been determined by a court of competent jurisdiction during the life of the father." M and F were engaged to be married. They were expecting a child to be born in six months and had set the wedding date to occur one month before the birth. Two days before the wedding F died unexpectedly from a congenital heart defect that had been unknown until his death. One month later, child S was born. S claims to be F's intestate heir. Which of the following is S's strongest claim:

(a) His parents should be considered constructively married at the time of F's death.

(b) It is unfair to penalize him solely because his father died before the marriage.

(c) S has a fundamental right to inherit.

(d) State O's statute regarding inheritance by nonmarital children violates the equal protection clause of the U.S. constitution.

23. John created a trust in his will for his family, naming First Bank as trustee. The trust document provided "The trustee shall distribute all income to my wife, if she survives me, and then at her death, the trustee shall distribute among my then living issue as my trustee in its sole discretion determines is in their best interests. Twenty-one years after the death of my wife, the trust shall terminate and the assets shall be distributed to my then living issue per stirpes." At John's death, his wife disclaims her interest in the trust in order to make the income available for younger generations. John's oldest son, Tim, asks for a distribution to help him start a new business. The Trustee declines. Tim wants to sue the Trustee for abuse of discretion. What advice do you give him?

(a) There is no chance of success in such a suit because the trustee has absolute discretion.

(b) If Tim can prove a breach of trust, he will be able to obtain the funds needed for the new business.

(c) While suits like this are not generally successful, Tim might win if he can prove that the trustee bank declined to distribute the income because another bank client wanted to start a similar business.

(d) Both (b) and (c).

24. Tim Testator executed three wills in succession, one each year. Will #1, executed in year one, provided a bequest to his friend, Anna, of 100,000 and the rest and residue to my brother, Bill. He also provided that he intended to leave nothing to his sister, Sally. In year two, having patched up things with his sister, he executed Will #2, leaving her $100,000 and everything else to brother Bill and to friend Anna, equally. But the next year, after a quarrel with Sally, he executed Will #3. This will did not provide for any bequests. All it said was: "I hereby revoke Will #2." All three wills were validly executed. In a non-UPC state, the most likely distribution of Testator's $1.0 million estate is:

(a) Testator died intestate and therefore his heirs, Bill and Sally take.

(b) If the state recognizes dependent and relative revocation, Will #2 may be probated.

(c) If the state recognizes dependent and relative revocation, Will #1 may be probated.

(d) Will #2 will be probated because Will #3 is a "negative will" and is not recognized at common law.

25. Frank directs his lawyer to draft a will for him leaving his estate to Frank's girlfriend Mary. The lawyer drafts the purported will. Franks executes it complying with the formalities for the execution of a will required by the state at the time. But at the execution ceremony, Frank tells the two witnesses that he does not wish or intend to leave his estate to Mary. Rather, he is executing the will to induce Mary to sleep with him. Several years later Frank dies leaving the purported will intact. Does Mary take Frank's estate under the purported will?

    (a) No, because Frank committed fraud in the inducement.

    (b) Yes, because Frank complied with the formalities required for the execution of a will.

    (c) Yes, if Frank changed his mind about leaving his estate to Mary in the time between the purported will execution and Frank's death.

    (d) No, because Frank lacked testamentary intent.

EXAM V

Use the following fact pattern to answer questions 1 and 2:

The decedent died intestate survived only by (1) her first cousin twice removed Sonny (the grandchild of the decedent's great-great grandparents, who are the first common ancestors between Sonny and the intestate decedent) (2) her second cousin once removed Buddy (the great-great grandchild of the decedent's great grandparents, who are the first common ancestors between Buddy and the intestate decedent), and (3) her first cousin thrice removed Happy (the great-great-great grandchild of the decedent's grandparents, who are the first common ancestors between Happy and the intestate decedent).

1. Who takes the decedent's intestate estate in a jurisdiction that applies a degree of kinship (aka degree of relationship) system to this fact pattern?
   (a) Sonny takes all.
   (b) Buddy takes all.
   (c) Happy takes all.
   (d) Sonny and Buddy split the property 50-50.

2. Who takes the decedent's intestate estate in a jurisdiction that applies a parentelic system to this fact pattern?
   (a) Sonny takes all.
   (b) Buddy takes all.
   (c) Happy takes all.
   (d) Sonny and Buddy split the property 50-50.

3. Testator devises his home to Anthony, $150,000 to Brittany, and all the rest of his estate to Carlos. At the testator's death, the testator's obligations to creditors are such that these gifts cannot be paid in full. One or more of the gifts must abate. What is the most likely order of abatement?
   (a) The gifts will abate equally pro rata.
   (b) Anthony's gift will abate first, Brittany's gift will abate second, and Carlos's gift will abate third.
   (c) Brittany's gift will abate first, Carlos's gift will abate second, and Anthony's gift will abate third.
   (d) Carlos's gift will abate first, Brittany's gift will abate second, and Anthony's gift will abate third.

4. Which of the following is not true of will substitutes?
   (a) They avoid probate.

(b) They are inter vivos transfers.

(c) They are testamentary gifts.

(d) They have the effect of passing property at the donor's death.

5. Testator devises "$10,000 each to Amanda, Lisa, and Tyler." The devises to Amanda, Lisa, and Tyler are

(a) Residuary gifts.

(b) General gifts.

(c) Specific gifts.

(d) Demonstrative gifts.

6. When a person intentionally misrepresents the contents or the character of a document, thereby causing the testator to execute the document as her purported will, that person has committed

(a) Fraud in the execution.

(b) Fraud in the inducement.

(c) Constructive fraud.

(d) Technical fraud.

7. Michael conveys property in trust "to Anna for life, remainder to Jackie." Jackie dies during Anna's lifetime having devised his estate to Edward. Under general principles of common law, who takes the remainder?

(a) Edward as the devisee of Jackie.

(b) Michael (or Michael's estate) by way of a reversion.

(c) Anna's estate by way of a contingent remainder.

(d) Jackie's issue by way of the anti-lapse statute.

8. Harold and Wanda were married 20 years ago in Texas, a community property state. They have lived in Texas throughout their married lives. During the marriage, they acquired a 100-acre tract of land from their own wages at a cost of $100,000 and Harold inherited some stock from his mother. At Harold's death, the land was worth $2.0 million and the stock was worth $1.0 million. Assuming no other assets, which of the following is true?

(a) Harold's gross estate for federal estate tax purposes is $3.0 million.

(b) Harold's gross estate for federal estate tax purposes is $1.0 million.

(c) Harold's gross estate for federal estate tax purposes is $2.0 million.

(d) If Harold leaves all his property to Wanda, his estate will pay estate taxes only on his separate property.

9. In most states, the signing of a self-proving affidavit will create which of the following:

(a) An irrebuttable presumption that the will was duly executed.

(b) A rebuttable presumption that the will was duly executed.

(c) An irrebuttable presumption that the will is valid.

(d) An irrebuttable presumption that the testator was of sound mind.

10. Susan asked her brother Tom to serve as trustee of a small family trust. Tom was concerned about liability arising from serving as trustee given that he is not a professional trustee. To calm Tom's fears, Susan inserted a clause into the trust providing that Tom shall be exonerated from liability for his actions as trustee "including but not limited to liability arising from intentional and willful neglect, bad faith, and reckless indifference." Which of the following is generally true of this exculpatory clause?

    (a) The clause is enforceable to excuse intentional and willful neglect, bad faith, and reckless indifference given that Tom is not a professional trustee.

    (b) The clause is not enforceable to excuse intentional and willful neglect, bad faith, and reckless indifference.

    (c) The clause is enforceable to excuse intentional and willful neglect, bad faith, and reckless indifference if Susan consulted independent counsel about the clause prior to inserting the clause into the trust instrument.

    (d) The clause is not enforceable to excuse intentional and willful neglect, bad faith, and reckless indifference unless the trust also grants Tom absolute discretion as trustee.

11. Ursula's will provides as follows: "I leave the rest of my property in trust for the benefit of my grandson Amir for life, then to Amir's first child to graduate from college." Ursula is survived by Amir aged 25 and Amir's son, Sam, aged 2. How does the common law rule against perpetuities affect this gift?

    (a) The rule does not void any gifts because all of the potential beneficiaries are "lives in being" at Ursula's death.

    (b) The gift to Amir is valid, but the contingent remainder to his first child is void.

    (c) The gift to Amir is valid, but the gift to Sam will only take effect if he is in fact the first child to graduate from college.

    (d) The entire gift violates the rule.

12. Assume the same facts as the previous question, except that Amir predeceases Ursula. Under common law rules, who will benefit from the trust fund?

    (a) Amir's estate will collect the income from the gift until Sam graduates from college and then Sam will get the trust corpus.

    (b) Sam will get the trust corpus because his interest does not violate the rule against perpetuities.

(c) Sam will not benefit because his interest violates the rule against perpetuities.

(d) Sam will collect the trust corpus if he graduates from college.

13. Fred's will created a trust in which he gave his son, Mick, the income from the trust for life and "then as Mick shall appoint by last will and testament." The same will gave the "rest and residue of my property to Yale University." Mick was Fred's only child. At Mick's death, his will was probated. It was a simple will that appointed his wife, Molly, as executrix and then provided "I give all of my property, of every kind and wherever situated, to my wife Molly." Molly survived Mick. Under the UPC, the trust assets will go to:

    (a) Molly, because she was named as the residuary taker in Mick's will.

    (b) Mick's estate because he held a general power of appointment, but he did not exercise it.

    (c) Fred's residuary taker, Yale, because his reversionary interest would pass under his residuary clause.

    (d) The state in which Fred was domiciled because he has no living heirs to take his interest.

14. Assume the same facts as in the prior question except that Fred's will provided that the income would be paid to Mick and then the assets of the trust would be distributed "as Mick appoints by will to anyone other than himself, his estate, or his creditors." At Mick's death, under the UPC, the trust property will go to:

    (a) Molly, because she was named as the residuary taker in Mick's will.

    (b) Mick's estate because he held a general power of appointment, but he did not exercise it.

    (c) Fred's residuary taker, Yale, because his reversionary interest would pass under his residuary clause.

    (d) The state in which Fred was domiciled because he has no living heirs to take his interest.

15. The evidence at trial demonstrates that Testator told her lawyer to destroy her will and codicil. The lawyer suggested, however, that Testator keep the will and codicil as models in case she decided to draft a new will. The lawyer wrote 'null and void' on the back of the will and the back of the codicil and Testator signed underneath these notations. Testator died shortly thereafter leaving a large estate. In a harmless error jurisdiction, are the will and codicil revoked?

    (a) No. The attempts at revocation by physical act fail because the acts of cancellation do not touch the words of the will.

    (b) No. The attempts to revoke by subsequent writing fail because not all of the material portions of the purported revoking instruments are in the hand of the testator.

(c) Yes. The will and codicil are revoked by physical act.

(d) Yes. The will and codicil are revoked by subsequent instrument.

16. A court finds that Francis has equitably adopted Carlos. Which of the following statements generally is not true in most American jurisdictions that recognize the doctrine of equitable adoption?

(a) If Francis dies intestate, Carlos will inherit from Francis as would a biological and legal child of Francis.

(b) If Carlos dies intestate, Francis will inherit from Carlos as would a biological and legal parent of Carlos.

(c) If Francis predeceases Carlos, Carlos will inherit through Francis as would a biological and legal child of Francis.

(d) Both (b) and (c).

17. When Tom executed his will he had three living siblings—Peter, Paul, and Mary, and a niece Louise, who was Mary's daughter. Tom's will made certain specific bequests to Louise and devised the residuary of his estate to Peter and Paul. The will further provided that "I do not want any of my property to pass to Mary either under this will or by intestacy." At Tom's death, he is survived only by Mary and Mary's daughter Louise. Peter and Paul died without issue before Tom. Who takes Tom's residuary estate at common law?

(a) Peter's estate will take 1/2 and Paul's estate will take 1/2.

(b) Louise.

(c) Mary.

(d) Mary will take 1/3, Peter's estate will take 1/3, and Paul's estate will take 1/3.

18. June and Bill purportedly were married in Year 1 in a community property state. Bill, however, was already married to May at the time of his marriage ceremony to June. June, therefore, was never legally married to Bill. Bill died intestate in Year 10 survived only by May and June. He had no children. The court finds that May and Bill were never divorced and that June had no knowledge of Bill's earlier marriage to May. If the jurisdiction accepts the putative spouse doctrine, the court most likely will:

(a) Award Bill's entire intestate estate to June.

(b) Award Bill's entire intestate estate to May.

(c) Award at least some of Bill's intestate estate to June.

(d) Award all of the property acquired during years 1 through 10 to June.

19. Evan created a POD account at Second State Bank, naming his niece Nancy as the POD beneficiary. Shortly before his death, Evan wrote a codicil to his will that stated: I have $100,000 on deposit in a POD account at Second State Bank. I will that money to be split equally between my

niece Nancy and my nephew Norman. Assuming that Evan died in a UPC state:

(a) Nancy and Norman will split the $100,000.

(b) Nancy will take the entire $100,000 because codicils can only pass tangible personal property.

(c) Nancy will take the entire $100,000 because you cannot revoke or amend a POD account by will.

(d) The $100,000 will pass outside of probate, thereby avoiding federal estate taxes.

20. Tony's will left his entire estate to his friends, Sam and John. John failed to survive Tony but left a daughter, Debra. Tony's closest living relative at his death was his sister Sara. How should Tony's estate be distributed under the UPC?

(a) Sam should take the entire estate because he is the only surviving residuary taker.

(b) Sam should take half the estate and Debra should take the other half of the estate as a substitute taker for John.

(c) Sam should take half the estate and John's estate should take the other half.

(d) Sam should take half the estate and Sara should take the other half.

21. Joan's will made the following gifts: "I leave my home to Sally. I leave $100,000 to Josh. I leave my 100 shares of Rockwell stock, currently valued at $100 per share, to Pat. I leave the rest of my property to Gwen."

At Joan's death, she owned a home worth $500,000, but subject to a mortgage of $300,000, $350,000 in cash, and the 100 shares of Rockwell stock, which was trading at $50 a share. She had no debts, other than the mortgage. Under the UPC, how should Joan's estate be distributed?

(a) Sally should get the home free and clear since it was a specific devise and Josh should get the rest of the cash. Pat should get the Rockwell stock.

(b) Sally should get the home subject to the mortgage. Josh should get $100,000 in cash. Pat should get 100 shares of Rockwell stock, and Gwen should get the rest.

(c) Sally should get the home free and clear under the doctrine of exoneration. Josh and Pat should split the rest since they both got specific bequests.

(d) Sally should get the home subject to the mortgage. The executor should purchase another 100 shares of Rockwell stock so that 200 shares at $50 can be distributed to Pat. Josh should get $100,000 and Gwen should get the rest.

22. Gino declared himself trustee of $1.0 million in perpetuity for the purpose of granting college scholarships out of the income of the fund to any then

living issue of his top three managers. At the time of his death, he had awarded two college scholarships to qualifying children. The trust's ability to continue awarding scholarships in the future is threatened by:

(a) The rule against perpetuities.

(b) The identifiable beneficiary rule.

(c) The failure to name a successor trustee.

(d) A cy pres statute.

23. Blanche's will left everything to her brother Bob. She kept the original will in a drawer in her bedroom. One day, Blanche was rushed to the hospital after a severe stroke. She was in the hospital for weeks, but Bob never came to see her. One day when her neighbor Nellie was visiting, Blanche complained about Bob's absence. She then gave Nellie the key to her house and told her to go find the will and tear it up. Nellie did so and immediately called Blanche to tell her the will had been taken care of. Blanche died survived by her brother Bob and three sisters. When Bob learned about the will's destruction, he was very upset. He called his sisters and explained that he had called the hospital regularly to check on Blanche but had not visited her because he had a bad cold at the time and the nurses told him he should wait until he was over it because Blanche was very susceptible to germs.

Under the UPC:

(a) The will in favor of Bob can be probated under the Doctrine of Dependent Relative Revocation.

(b) The will in favor of Bob can be probated because it was never revoked.

(c) The will in favor of Bob can be probated under the revival statute.

(d) Bob will take one-fourth of Blanche's estate by intestacy.

24. 70 percent of the ABC Trust portfolio consists of First National Bank stock. 30 percent of the ABC Trust portfolio consists of Bank of the East stock. The Trustee of the ABC Trust is likely to be judged imprudent because of which of the following?

(a) The portfolio has excessive firm risk, excessive industry risk, and excessive market risk.

(b) The portfolio has excessive firm risk and excessive industry risk.

(c) The portfolio has excessive firm risk, and excessive market risk.

(d) The portfolio has excessive industry risk and excessive market risk.

25. Uncle Marvin, age 80, has a favorite niece, Samantha. He has decided to leave his entire estate to her, but he is worried that his other nieces and nephews will challenge the will. His estate is valued at over $5.0 million, so his fears seem well founded. He has asked for your advice on how best to protect Samantha after his death from claims by his other relatives. His current will names Samantha as his sole beneficiary. You advise him to:

(a) Put everything he owns into joint tenancy with right of survivorship.

(b) Adopt Samantha.

(c) Add a codicil to the will that reconfirms Samantha as sole beneficiary and provides that anyone who challenges the will shall lose his intestate share.

(d) Include a provision in his will explaining why he is disinheriting all his other heirs.

EXAM VI

1. Feeling he was about to die, Tony called his nephew Johnny and asked him to come around to his house. When Johnny arrived, Tony handed him the claim check for a necklace he had sent to a jeweler to be repaired and told Johnny that his mother, Carmen, was to have the necklace. That night Tony died and the next day Johnny remembered about the claim check and gave it to his mother Carmen. Tony's wife, Isabella, is the personal administrator of his estate and is seeking return of the necklace from Carmen. Will Isabella be successful?

   (a) Yes because the necklace was an attempted testamentary gift and it fails because it was not executed with the will formalities.

   (b) Yes because the necklace was an attempted gift causa mortis and it fails because Carmen did not take possession of the necklace until after Tony had died.

   (c) No because the necklace was a gift causa mortis and Tony had relinquished possession through the claim check he gave to Johnny and delivery was therefore complete.

   (d) No because the necklace was an inter vivos gift and the claim check was constructive delivery.

2. Laura decided to execute a will, so she went to a lawyer and had a lovely will drafted that represented her exact wishes. However, she wanted to think over the devises so she asked to take it home and promised that she would have her friends execute the will in front of a notary. The lawyer carefully explained how the execution ceremony should be done and she took detailed notes. After sleeping on it, she decided she was happy with the will so she asked her neighbor to come over to witness the will. The neighbor wasn't home, however, but her 16-year-old daughter was and she agreed to come witness the will. Her other neighbor wasn't home at all, so she asked her son to serve as a witness. Her son was 45 years old and his wife was a notary and she was there too and agreed to notarize the self-proving affidavit. Laura called them all into the dining room where she told them they were witnessing her sign her will. Each of them signed the will as required, in the presence of Laura and in the presence of each other, and the self-proving affidavit was notarized by her daughter-in-law. After Cynthia's death, her granddaughter challenges the will for failure to conform to the will formalities. What is the likely outcome of the will challenge in a state that follows the UPC?

   (a) It will succeed because the neighbor's daughter was a minor and a minor may not serve as a witness.

   (b) It will succeed because Laura's son is an interested witness and may not serve as a witness.

(c) It will succeed because Laura's daughter-in-law is legally prohibited from notarizing any document for a family member.

(d) It will fail because the will was properly executed.

3. Peter left all his property, valued at $300,000, in trust with the following instructions:

> I give my wonderful spouse Beth all the income for the duration of her life. At her death, I wish my two children, Carmen and Felix, to split the income for the duration of their lives. When the first child dies, that child's income share shall pass to their issue, if any. If they have no issue, then the income passes to the other child. At the death of my last child, I give all the rest and residue of my trust property to my grandchildren, the issue of any deceased grandchild to take that grandchild's share. At any time, my trustee may invade principal for the benefit of any grandchild's college education, even during the lifetime of my spouse and children.

At Peter's death, his spouse Beth, his two children Carmen and Felix, and 2 grandchildren were alive. Those grandchildren, Ashley and Bree, were 4 and 2 respectively and were the daughters of Carmen. During Beth's life estate, one more grandchild was born, Devoe, the daughter of Felix. During the life estates of Carmen and Felix, two more grandchildren were born, Constance the daughter of Carmen, and Edgar, the son of Felix. Ashley reached age 18 and went to college during Beth's lifetime, after the birth of Devoe, but before the birth of Constance and Edgar. At the death of the last child, who is in the class of grandchildren entitled to a distribution of principal?

(a) Ashley and Bree because they were the only grandchildren alive at the death of Peter.

(b) Ashley, Bree, and Devoe because they were the only grandchildren alive at the death of Beth.

(c) Ashley, Bree, Devoe, Constance, and Edgar because they were the only grandchildren alive at the death of the last child to die.

(d) Ashley, Bree, and Devoe because they were the only grandchildren alive when the first distribution of principal was made for a grandchild's college education.

4. Darren died with a valid will that gave his home to his daughter, Jennine, his car to his nephew Antonio, and the residue to his son. At his death he owned the following property and the following debts.

- A house valued at $500,000
- Personal property valued at $50,000
- A car valued at $35,000
- Cash in the bank to the amount of $75,000

- Individual Retirement Account valued at $700,000 with a beneficiary designation
- Securities account valued at $300,000 with a beneficiary designation

His debts include:

- $300,000 mortgage on his house
- $10,000 car loan
- $50,000 in credit card debts
- $40,000 in funeral and end of life medical expenses

How are Darren's debts paid?

(a) All $400,000 in debts are paid from the largest asset, the IRA.

(b) The mortgage on the house and the car loan go unpaid and pass with those assets, while the $90,000 in credit card and medical debts are paid first out of the bank account and then out of the securities account.

(c) The mortgage on the house and the car loan go unpaid and pass with those assets, while the $90,000 in credit card and medical debts are paid out of the bank account and personal property, proportionally.

(d) The mortgage on the house and the car loan go unpaid and pass with those assets, while the $90,000 in credit card and medical debts are paid first from the bank account, and the remaining $15,000 is paid out of the personal property.

5. Kendal was in a terrible car accident and suffered massive brain damage. However, she was placed on life support (artificial respiration and hydration) in order to allow her family to visit and say their final goodbyes. When her entire family was assembled in the hospital, her brother Jay instructed the doctors to remove the life support mechanisms, but her sister Gay disagreed and insisted that she remain on life support. Fortunately, Kendal had gone to a lawyer and had drafted a complete estate plan, including end-of-life instructions. In fact, she had a large notebook with every instrument prepared by her lawyers that Jay brought with him to the hospital. Which document should the parties consult to assist them in making this decision?

   (a) Health care proxy.

   (b) Durable Power of Attorney.

   (c) Living Will.

   (d) Last Will and Testament.

6. Calliope executed a will giving most of her vast fortune to charities and not to her children. However, she left bequests of $1 million to each of her three children. She also included a no-contest clause in her will stating that any beneficiary who challenged her will would be entirely

disinherited from her estate. Her children have come to you for advice as they would like to challenge the will but are concerned about that no-contest clause. Which challenge would you advise them will be the most likely to trigger enforcement of the no-contest clause?

(a) A challenge to the will on the grounds of incapacity.

(b) A challenge to the will on the grounds that the will formalities were not followed.

(c) A challenge to the will on the grounds of undue influence.

(d) A challenge to the will on the grounds of lack of testamentary intent to disinherit them.

7. Holly executed a will and included a section that stated: "I hereby give the tangible personal property to the persons listed in the appendix." At her death, Holly's will included a piece of paper titled "appendix" that listed dozens of names of friends and family members with items of property listed beside each name. Sometimes the names were marked out with other names written above them and sometimes the items of property were marked out with different items written in. These were all in Holly's handwriting. Holly executed her will in January, 2020, but she had signed the appendix page at the bottom and dated it January 15, 2025. She died on February 1, 2025 after a brief hospital stay following a car accident. Which doctrine is likely to validate the handwritten appendix with the marked-in names and property?

(a) Separate Writing Doctrine.

(b) Incorporation by Reference.

(c) Integration.

(d) Acts of Independent Significance.

8. Clarence executed a will in which he gave all the rest and residue of his property to his best friend Eric, in trust, to distribute \$5.00 to each first grade and second grade student at the local elementary school on the last day before the winter holiday and the last day of school before the summer holiday. Clarence's daughter Rachel is upset that Clarence did not leave any property to her, or to her three children, other than the \$5.00 they would get as school children. If Rachel challenges this provision of Clarence's will, what is the likely outcome?

(a) The trust will be upheld as a charitable trust and Eric will take the property and execute the trust.

(b) The trust will be voided as not meeting the definition of a charitable trust and a resulting trust will be created to return the property from Eric to Clarence's estate to pass by intestacy.

(c) The trust will be voided as not meeting the definition of a charitable trust and a constructive trust will be created to pass the property to the local school district.

(d) The trust will be upheld as an honorary trust and Eric will take the property and execute the trust.

9. Tom was convinced that the estate tax was unconstitutional and therefore chose to leave all his estate to a local law firm run by his best friend Peter, in trust, to use the proceeds to sue the government to have the estate tax declared void. Tom's children are upset that their father won't listen to reason, especially since his estate is not large enough to even generate any estate tax. What type of mistake will the children argue has influenced Tom's will?

   (a) mistake of law in the inducement.

   (b) mistake of fact in the inducement.

   (c) mistake of law in the expression.

   (d) mistake of fact in the expression.

10. Wilbur executed a valid will leaving "all my artwork to my daughter, Sabine," "my house at 1506 West 98th Street and all furniture and furnishings in my house to my son, Griffin," and "the residue of my estate to my wife, Doris." At his death, Wilbur's estate contained the following assets:

    - 1 sketch by Picasso worth $200,000 and $500,000 in cash that can be traced to Wilbur's sale of artwork that occurred after he executed the will.
    - badly worn furniture worth $50 and $500 from the guardian's sale of the contents of his home.
    - $100,000 cash in the bank from the state Department of Transportation that condemned his home to build a highway.

    How is Wilbur's estate distributed?

    (a) Sabine gets the Picasso, Griffin gets the $50 worth of furniture, and Doris gets the $650,000 in cash.

    (b) Sabine gets the Picasso, Griffin gets the $50 worth of furniture plus the $500 from the guardian's sale of the contents of the home plus the $100,000 cash from the condemnation of the home, and Doris gets the $500,000 from Wilbur's sale of the artwork.

    (c) Sabine gets the Picasso plus the $500,000 from sale of the artwork, Griffin gets the $50 worth of furniture, and Doris gets the $100,000 cash from the condemnation plus the $500 from the sale of the furniture.

    (d) Sabine gets the Picasso plus the $500,000 from sale of the artwork, Griffin gets the $50 worth of furniture, the $500 from the sale of the furniture, and the $100,000 from the condemnation of the house, and Doris gets nothing.

11. Roland died intestate with an estate worth $500,000. He was survived by his three children Abel, Bonnie, and Chelsea and the three children of his fourth child Donald who predeceased him (Evelyn, Frank, and Ginny). During life Roland had given Abel $50,000 for a world cruise, he had given Bonnie $100,000 for a downpayment on a house, he had given Chelsea $30,000 to buy a new car and he had given Donald $60,000 to start a business. Assuming all four gifts to his children are treated as advancements under the UPC, how is Roland's estate distributed?

    (a) Abel gets $85,000; Bonnie gets $35,000; Chelsea gets $105,000; and Donalds 3 children share $75,000.

    (b) Abel gets $135,000; Bonnie gets $85,000; Chelsea gets $155,000; and Donald's 3 children share $125,000.

    (c) Abel gets $120,000; Bonnie gets $70,000; Chelsea gets $140,000; and Donald's 3 children share $170,000.

    (d) Abel gets $120,000; Bonnie gets $70,000; Chelsea gets $140,000; and Donald's 3 children share $110,000.

12. Jocelyn left a properly executed will that devised "all the personal property located in my personal residence" to my daughter Sherry and "all the rest and residue of my property and estate, of every kind and character, to my son Kevin." At her death, Jocelyn had $50,000 stashed inside her mattress, along with stock certificates in Coca Cola, and a checkbook for her checking account at the local bank which contained $100,000. The only other property she owned was her personal residence. Who gets what property and under what rationale?

    (a) Sherry gets the tangible personal property and the cash, but Kevin gets the realty and the stock and the checking account because the term "personal property" is patently ambiguous.

    (b) Sherry gets the tangible personal property and the cash, but Kevin gets the realty and the stock and the checking account because the term "personal property" is latently ambiguous.

    (c) Sherry gets only the tangible personal property, and Kevin gets the cash, the stock, and the checking account, as well as the realty, because the term "personal property" does not include intangible property since it is latently ambiguous.

    (d) Sherry gets the tangible personal property plus the cash, the stock, and the money in the checking account because they are all personal property and there is no ambiguity. Kevin gets only the realty.

13. Jimmy filed suit to have his nonmarital son, Roman, legitimated and to change his name to Jimmy's last name when Roman was 7 years old. Although Roman never lived with Jimmy, he visited his father and Jimmy paid child support and sent birthday and holiday cards to Roman. When Roman was 10, however, Jimmy met Rosa and they married. They then had four children. When Jimmy wrote his will, he stated in the will that he had "four living children and no deceased children." He named his four

children with Rosa his beneficiaries and made no provision for Roman. After Jimmy died, Roman challenged Jimmy's will. If Roman alleges that Jimmy made a mistake, will he likely be successful?

(a) No because a mistake of fact must induce an erroneous bequest.

(b) No because a mistake of fact must be expressed in the will and affect the will.

(c) Yes because there is a mistake of fact in the expression.

(d) Yes because there is a mistake of fact in the inducement.

14. Bettina had no spouse or children, so she devised all her property in her will as follows:

> I give half my estate to my brother, Sven, or if he predeceases me then to Sven's wife, Olga. I give the other half of my estate to my sister Eva, but if she predeceases me then to Eva's husband, Klaus.

At Bettina's death, Sven, Olga, and Eva had died. Sven predeceased Olga and left children by his first marriage. Olga left children by her first marriage. And Eva left children by a prior marriage. Sven and Olga did not have children together. And Klaus had no children. How should Bettina's estate be distributed under the UPC?

(a) All to Klaus as the only surviving devisee.

(b) Half to Klaus and half to Sven's children under anti-lapse statute.

(c) Half to Klaus and half to Olga's children under anti-lapse statute.

(d) Half to Eva's issue and half to Sven's issue as the only relatives of Bettina.

15. Hamlet was unmarried and had no children. Hamlet's will bequeaths the entirety of his estate to Ophelia, his longtime girlfriend. Hamlet and Ophelia were in a car crash caused by a truck driver who fell asleep while driving, which killed Hamlet instantly. Ophelia was rushed to a hospital and died six days later, having never awoken from a continuous coma. Hamlet's only living relative is his mother, Gertrude. Hamlet's personal representative opened probate proceedings one month after Hamlet's death. Who will inherit Hamlet's estate in a UPC state?

(a) Ophelia, because she survived the crash.

(b) Ophelia, because she survived Hamlet by more than 120 hours.

(c) Gertrude, because Hamlet and Ophelia died from the same cause.

(d) Gertrude, because Ophelia is deceased at the time that Hamlet's estate is probated.

16. Prior to their marriage, Harriet and Tom entered into a pre-nuptial agreement. Assuming the agreement is validly executed in a UPC state, which of the following provisions would be upheld by a probate court?

I. A provision waiving Tom's right to statutory family allowance, homestead, and exempt property

II. A provision waiving Tom's right to an elective share

III. A provision waiving Tom's right to serve as personal representative

IV. A provision waiving disclosure of Harriet's property

(a) I and II only.

(b) I, II, and III.

(c) II, III, and IV.

(d) I, II, III, and IV.

17. Rupert died with a modest estate and a lot of debts. Which claim is not a valid debt of Rupert's estate?

(a) Claim for delinquent child support.

(b) Claim for future child support.

(c) Claim for a tort judgment against Rupert.

(d) Claim for estate taxes.

18. Back in 2001, Irving, childless and unmarried, executed a will giving all his property to his best friend, Eric. A few years later Irving met Charlene and they cohabited together. Eventually they had three children and lived together, although they never expressed any interest in being married and they never represented themselves as husband and wife. However, they had resided together for so long that everyone in the community assumed they were married. After their children were grown, Irving adopted a beautiful German Shepherd, Kali. Irving had completely forgotten about his 2001 will and assumed that since he had had children the will would be invalid anyway and he was happy with the default intestacy rule as to his property. Under intestacy, all of his property would pass to his children. But he wanted Kali to go to Charlene. So, one day he typed up an instrument stating that he wanted Charlene to get Kali at his death. He signed and dated the instrument, and it was signed by two witnesses. The next day Irving died. How will Irving's estate be distributed under the UPC and why?

(a) Charlene will take Kali plus an elective share because they will be considered married under common law marriage rules and the rest will pass to the children by intestacy.

(b) Charlene will take Kali and the children will take the rest of his estate because they are pretermitted.

(c) Charlene will take Kali and Eric will take the rest of the estate because the 2001 will is republished by codicil.

(d) Kali and his estate will pass to the children because Irving was mistaken as to the legal effect of his 2001 will so he will die intestate.

19. Vicki executed her will in year #1. Two years later, she executed a second will (will #2), specifically revoking will #1, but she never destroyed will #1. A year before her death, Vicki was adjudicated incompetent and her daughter was appointed as guardian under state law. Shortly before her death, she asked her daughter to bring her both wills. The daughter did and Vicki tore them both up. Vicki's estate should be distributed:

    (a) To the beneficiaries named in will #2 because she had no capacity to revoke.

    (b) To the beneficiaries in will #2 because tearing up both wills at the same time is not the way to revoke will #2.

    (c) To her intestate heirs because both wills were validly revoked by physical act.

    (d) To her intestate heirs provided they can prove that she was in a lucid moment at the time she tore up the wills.

20. Hilary and Bill had been married for thirty years when they decided they needed to do some estate planning to provide for their five children, two of whom were still minors. They went to an estate planning attorney who drafted reciprocal wills giving all their property to the other spouse if alive, but if deceased the property was to pass to the oldest child (Chelsea) in trust for the benefit of all five children. Shortly after they executed their wills, Hilary had an affair and Bill filed divorce proceedings. Ultimately, the property was split, custody of the minor children was granted to Bill and Hilary equally, and the final divorce and property settlements were signed. A week later, at a party for Chelsea's college graduation, Chelsea drank too much but insisted on driving her mother home. Chelsea had a blood alcohol level over the legal limit and, while arguing with her mother over her ability to drive, ran a red light and crashed into a telephone pole. The airbag deployed to save Chelsea's life, but Hilary was not wearing her seat belt and was thrown through the windshield. Chelsea, annoyed with her mother, refused to give aid and Hilary died before another car could come along and call 911. How is Hilary's estate distributed under the UPC?

    (a) Her entire estate passes to Bill according to the will.

    (b) Her entire estate passes by intestacy because Bill's gift was revoked by the divorce and Chelsea's gift was revoked under the slayer statute.

    (c) Her entire estate passes in trust to Chelsea to benefit the five children.

    (d) Her entire estate passes in trust to a different trustee to benefit her four children (omitting Chelsea).

21. David had a pre-marital child (Gregory) while he was in college. After he graduated, he married Alison, but they had no children. Shortly after his marriage, David executed a will, leaving all his property to Alison, but if Alison predeceased him then his property was to pass to his "heirs at law."

When Gregory was 9 (and after David had executed his will), David learned that he was Gregory's father and instituted proceedings to recognize his paternity and to change Gregory's last name to his. The court granted both motions but Gregory never lived with David. He did pay child support, however, and sent holiday and birthday cards to Gregory and they visited frequently. When Gregory was 13, David separated from Alison, but they never divorced. David moved in with Matilda, and they had a daughter, Ginny. Shortly after Ginny's birth, David died from choking on a fried pork rind. What rights do Gregory and Ginny have in David's estate?

(a) Gregory and Ginny are entitled to shares as pretermitted children.

(b) Gregory is not entitled to a share as a pretermitted child, but Ginny is.

(c) Gregory is entitled to a share as a pretermitted child, but Ginny is not.

(d) Neither child is entitled to a share as a pretermitted child and Alison will take everything under the will.

22. Ben suffered severe brain damage from a fight in a bar when he was 25 years old. At the time, Ben had a son, Newman, who was aged 3. After Ben was released from the hospital he had to live in an assisted living facility and shortly thereafter his wife, Katie, divorced him and took Newman to live in Arizona. Ben's mother became his legal guardian and was a trustee over the $5 million award Ben received from the bar's insurance company and she regularly paid the nursing home care until she died. At her death, Ben was moved to Tennessee to be closer to his brother and his wife, Caleb and Jenny. Caleb then took over as trustee of Ben's trust and he and Jenny regularly visited Ben in the nursing home. As Newman grew up, he naturally grew apart from his father Ben and never visited him once he had moved to Tennessee. Shortly before he died, Ben decided he wanted to write a will and he asked Caleb to make an appointment with an attorney. Caleb did so, drove him to the attorney, and also accompanied him in the meeting because Ben was unable to talk clearly and Caleb helped translate. Ben's will left his estate in equal thirds to Caleb, Jenny, and Newman. At Ben's death, Newman decides to challenge Ben's will. What is the most likely outcome?

(a) Ben's will will be void for lack of mental capacity because of his brain injury.

(b) Ben's will will be upheld because it provides for the natural objects of his bounty and shows that he had adequate capacity.

(c) Ben's will will be upheld because he intended to benefit Caleb, Jenny, and Newman.

(d) Ben's will will be void because Caleb procured it.

23. Janice executed a will that provided, in relevant part, that "my 20 shares of XYZ stock I give to my nephew, Jason." At her death, Janice had 60

shares of ABC stock. Under which of the fact situations below would Jason take all 60 shares of the ABC stock?

(a) Janice sold her shares of XYZ stock and used the proceeds to purchase the ABC stock.

(b) ABC corp bought out XYZ corp and issued 3 shares of ABC stock for each share of XYZ stock.

(c) XYZ corp bought back all of its stock and Janice used the money to purchase the ABC stock.

(d) Janice's guardian sold her XYZ stock and shortly before her death she inherited the 60 shares of ABC stock.

24. Giana was the trustee of a revocable living trust, created by her best friend Barbara. The trust consisted solely of money in a bank account that was to benefit Barbara's three children. The income was to be paid to them until they reached age 50, at which time each would be entitled to their share. During Barbara's lifetime, Giana had no role in the trust management, but upon Barbara's death she withdrew the funds and put them in a bank account in the bank she had her other accounts with, but she did not co-mingle the funds with hers. Once established, Giana began to take monthly payments of a small amount to compensate her for time as trustee. If Barbara's children come to you claiming that Giana's actions are highly suspicious and wondering if they are violations of her duty of loyalty, how should you instruct them?

(a) That Giana's transfer of the money to her bank and the withdrawal of compensation to herself are likely violations of her duty of loyalty.

(b) That only the deposit of the money in her bank is likely a violation of her duty of loyalty.

(c) That only her withdrawal of compensation is likely a violation of her duty of loyalty.

(d) That none of her actions are likely a violation of her duty of loyalty.

25. Abel was a childless widower when he made a will leaving all of his property to the Humane Society of New York. He also named his good friend Jeremy as his personal representative. At his death, Abel owed $50,000 to Citibank on his credit cards, his closest relatives were his two brothers, Don and Jon, and Jon's daughter Elsie. There was no such organization as the Humane Society of New York, but there was the New York Humane Society where Abel had volunteered in his spare time up until a few weeks before his death. At his death, who does not have standing to participate in the probate of Abel's will?

(a) Citibank.

(b) Don and Jon.

(c) Elsie.

(d) The New York Humane Society.

EXAM VII

1. Aidan executed a will that provided as follows:

> I give the rest and residue of my property to Salvador, my brother, as trustee, to pay income for life to my spouse, Louisa. Then, whatever property remains in the trust is to be given outright to my nieces and nephews.

At Aidan's death, he had six nieces and nephews who were all the children of his sister Aileen. By the time Louisa died, he had a total of nine nieces and nephews (all Aileen's children). In addition, one daughter of Aileen had predeceased Louisa, leaving issue. Aileen's children are asking Salvador to distribute the trust principal. However, Salvador had just married and was planning to have children. And so Salvador has refused, claiming that he cannot distribute funds until he knows how much each niece and nephew is entitled to, and he won't know that until he and Aileen die. He and Aileen are Aidan's only siblings. What should Salvador do as trustee?

(a) He should divide the trust assets into six shares, one for each niece and nephew who was alive at Aidan's death.

(b) He should divide the trust assets into nine shares, one for each living niece and nephew who was alive at Louisa's death.

(c) He should divide the trust assets into ten shares, one for each living niece and nephew and one for the issue of the deceased niece.

(d) He should refuse to distribute trust assets until he and his wife are done having children.

2. Robbie left a properly executed will that provided as follows:

> At my death I would like my body to be placed in a mushroom bag and buried under the chicken coop. I would also like my tattoos to be removed from my body, dried, and framed for display. Everyone who attends my funeral is to be given a pound of weed so every time they smoke they think of me. Please hold my funeral in Colorado where recreational marijuana use is permissible.

Robbie then buried his will in a mason jar under the chicken coop to keep it safe, but he left a note to his family and friends that said: "Being a vegetarian, I have left my will in a place it will be carefully guarded." Everyone was stumped by this instruction and were unable to find the will, so Robbie's mother, who was also named executor under the will, went ahead and had her son cremated, tattoos and all. Robbie's best friend Shaggy was convinced that Robbie's mom did not try very hard to find his funeral instructions or his will, so he set out to find it. After days of searching, he found the will and realizes that Robbie's wishes were not followed. Shaggy has come to you seeking advice about what remedy exists. Under general principles of common law, which piece of advice is NOT accurate.

(a) Robbie should not have put his instructions for the disposition of his remains in his will, but should have used a separate statement which could be easily found.

(b) Robbie was legally entitled to have his funeral wishes followed and Shaggy can sue his mom for damages.

(c) Robbie could have had his tattoos removed.

(d) Robbie could have been buried in a mushroom suit.

3. Roland died intestate. He was survived by his three children Abel, Bonnie, and Chelsea and the three children of his fourth child Donald who predeceased him (Evelyn, Frank, and Ginny). During life Roland had given Abel $50,000 for a world cruise, he had given Bonnie $100,000 for a down payment on a house, he had given Chelsea $30,000 to buy a new car and he had given Donald $60,000 to start a business. Bonnie is appointed personal representative for Roland's estate and has come to you for guidance on whether to treat the lifetime gifts as advancements or not. Under which fact scenario would the gifts NOT be treated as advancements?

(a) Roland gave each child their money in a birthday card in which he had written "the enclosed is an advancement on your inheritance."

(b) Roland gave each child their money in a birthday card and stated orally to them, in front of witnesses, that the money enclosed was an advancement on their inheritance.

(c) Roland handed each child their money and orally stated to them that the gifts were advancements and each child wrote a thank you note to Roland three weeks after their respective birthdays thanking him and acknowledging that the money was an advancement.

(d) Roland handed each child their money and each wrote to him a thank you note that said "I know how this is going to depreciate our inheritances, but I really want to thank you for your generosity."

4. Caroline bequeathed in her will $100,000 to ABC University to establish a scholarship for deserving football players. Shortly thereafter, she designated the scholarship fund at ABC University as the beneficiary on an Individual Retirement Account worth $100,000. When she changed the beneficiary on her IRA, she also executed a gift letter stating that the $100,000 in the account was to be used for the scholarship she was establishing. At her death, ABC University quickly collected the $100,000 from her IRA, and then it demanded an additional $100,000 from her estate. What is the likely outcome?

(a) ABC University will be successful because there is no ambiguity and the gift letter is not incorporated by reference into Caroline's will.

(b) ABC University will be successful because any ambiguity is latent and the extrinsic evidence of the gift letter is inadmissible to resolve any ambiguity.

(c) ABC University will not be successful because the gift letter drafted after the will can be admitted to show Caroline's intent when she drafted the will.

(d) ABC University will not be successful because the IRA designation can satisfy the contemporaneous writing requirement for ademption by satisfaction.

5. Kevin and Lesley were unmarried intimate partners who jointly ran a restaurant. Although they both did all the work and shared the profits, all the restaurant's accounts were in Kevin's name only. One day Kevin started to feel really sick, and so he dragged himself to the restaurant where he wrote checks to Lesley on each of the restaurant's two accounts, one for $200,000 and the other for $150,000. He handed both checks to Lesley when she drove him to their home that evening. She stayed with him all night, and he passed away early in the morning. The next day, after contacting the funeral home, Lesley went to the bank and deposited the two checks in her own checking account with the same bank. Herbert, the personal representative of Kevin's estate, contacted the bank and instructed them to put a hold on the checks and not allow the funds to be taken out of the restaurant's accounts. Will Lesley be successful in getting the money from the bank?

(a) Yes because the checks were gifts causa mortis and Kevin had died of the causes that motivated the gifts.

(b) Yes because the checks were inter vivos gifts and Kevin had delivered them to Lesley.

(c) No because checks were testamentary gifts and were not executed with the will formalities.

(d) No because the checks were gifts causa mortis but Kevin had not turned over full possession of the money represented by the checks because Lesley had not cashed them before Kevin's death.

6. Cynthia died intestate in a state that follows classic per stirpes for intestate distribution. She was survived by 1 living child, Anabelle, and six grandchildren. Two of the grandchildren (Britney and Cleo) are the daughters of her deceased son Michael. The other four grandchildren (Darren, Ernestine, Flaco, and Gabby) are the children of her deceased daughter Nadine. Michael also had a deceased son Herman who predeceased Cynthia and left two children (Imogene and Kristina). How is Cynthia's estate distributed?

(a) Anabelle takes 1/3; Britney and Cleo take 1/4 each; Darren, Ernestine, Flaco, and Gabby each take 1/10 each; and Herman takes 1/4.

(b) Anabelle takes 1/3; Britney and Cleo take 1/6 each; Darren, Ernestine, Flaco, and Gabby take 1/12 each; and Imogene and Kristina take 1/6 each

(c) Anabelle takes 1/3; Britney and Cleo take 1/9 each; Darren, Ernestine, Flaco, and Gabby take 1/12 each; and Imogene and Kristina take 1/18 each

(d) Anabelle takes 1/3; Britney, Cleo, Darren, Ernestine, Flaco, and Gabby each take 2/21; Imogene and Kristine take 1/21 each.

7. Jackson looked on the internet for a sample will, where he found one that was really simple. It stated "I hereby pour all my property into my revocable living trust." He properly executed it even though he wasn't really sure what it meant, but he thought it sounded good to have a trust and assumed that all trusts were just pre-established legal arrangements that everyone would understand. Five years later, however, Jackson met an old friend Eric in a bar who was an estates attorney and when he told Eric about his will, Eric told him he needed to execute a trust agreement. Eric explained how it worked and that night Jackson went home and wrote on a piece of notebook paper the following: "I, Jackson Pollock, hereby establish this as my revocable trust. I appoint my friend Eric as trustee after I die, and I am the trustee now. I also want all my property to be used for the benefit of my parents and my sister Marie, with any left over going to the Museum of Modern Art." Jackson then signed and dated the paper. The next day Jackson was killed in a car accident. Jackson's parents have come to your office for advice on whether the pour over will and revocable trust are valid or whether Jackson died intestate.

(a) Jackson's pour over will is invalid because it references a trust that was not in existence at the time the will was created, so Jackson died intestate.

(b) Jackson's revocable trust is invalid because it was not executed with the will formalities, which is necessary for an unfunded trust so the will has nothing to pour into and fails, thus causing Jackson to die intestate.

(c) Jackson's pour over will is valid but the trust is not because the trust was not executed with the will formalities, so the court will impose a constructive trust to use the property for the benefit of Jackson's parents and sister, with a portion of the estate passing to the Museum of Modern Art.

(d) Jackson's pour over will and revocable trust are valid because the Uniform Testamentary Additions to Trusts Act allows an unfunded trust to be created after the will and it does not require the will formalities for execution.

8. Helen executed a will that gave "all the rest and residue of my estate, both real and personal, to my heirs at law, living at the time of my decease." When she wrote her will, she believed that her 16 cousins were her heirs at law and she intended that they would receive her property. In fact, her

elderly aunt Carol was her actual heir at law. What mistake did Helen make?

(a) Mistake of fact in the expression.

(b) Mistake of law in the expression.

(c) Mistake of fact in the inducement.

(d) Mistake of law in the inducement.

9. Romeo and Juliet entered in a pre-marital agreement because the Capulet and the Montague families were both very wealthy and did not want any of their property to pass to the other side of the family. Which provision is not enforceable?

(a) A provision stating that each has no share in the estate of the other in case of death.

(b) A provision eliminating spousal maintenance in case the parties divorce.

(c) A provision eliminating child support in case the parties have children and divorce.

(d) A provision disposing of marital property in case the parties divorce.

10. Annie established a trust for the benefit of her three children, Mark, Karen, and Fred. Each child was entitled to a life income in the trust, plus the right to request up to 5% of the principal each year. Annie had also included the following provision in her trust: "No interest of any beneficiary in the income or principal of this trust shall be assignable in anticipation of payment or be liable in any way for the beneficiary's debts or obligations and shall not be subject to attachment." Mark has a number of debts against him but he is refusing to exercise his right to take the 5% from his mother's trust. Which of his creditors **cannot** pierce the trust and demand payment up to the 5% per year under the Uniform Trust Code?

(a) Mark's ex-wife Penelope for back payment of spousal maintenance

(b) Mark's ex-wife Penelope for back payment of child support for their two minor children for whom Penelope has primary custody.

(c) The IRS to whom Mark owes back income taxes and penalties.

(d) Mark's lawyer who represented him in his divorce from Penelope and to whom he still owes for legal services.

11. Rupert was a wealthy news and media company owner with billions of dollars in assets. He has six children from his first 3 marriages and is currently married to his 5th wife, Elena. He is 93 years old and suffers from congestive heart failure that can reduce the amount of oxygen reaching his brain. Otherwise, he is fit and is still active in his businesses. Rupert has been a client of a prestigious law firm for decades and they have prepared a series of trusts and wills over the years for him. Those documents all treated his children to a significant portion of his estate.

Shortly after his marriage to Elena, however, she began to control the news that reached him and she was convinced that immigrants were eating pets, the democrats were going to cancel Christmas, and that abortion was legal even after the child was born. In fact, she made sure that the only news Rupert saw was from his very own National Questioner, which can hardly be called a news magazine, and which peddled the same conspiracy theories. Whenever Rupert read the National Questioner his blood pressure would spike and he would start to rave. Shortly before his death, Elena called her own lawyer and made an appointment for Rupert to revisit his estate planning documents. She accompanied him to the appointment and helped to remind him that his six children had neglected him since he married her. Rupert then executed a new will drafted by Elena's lawyer that revoked all of his trusts and gave his entire estate to Elena. After Rupert died from a heart attack after reading the fake news, the children seek your advice about challenging the will that Elena has submitted to probate. Which theory is LEAST likely to be successful?

(a) That Elena exercised undue influence over Rupert.

(b) That Rupert lacked mental capacity to execute his will.

(c) That Rupert suffered from an insane delusion that the fake news was real.

(d) That Elena killed Rupert.

12. Jason died intestate leaving Rebecca, his surviving spouse, and three adult children—Alex, Brandi, and Cynthia. At his death, Jason owned the following property:

    - Tangible personal property
    - Their family home titled as tenants by the entirety with Rebecca
    - Cash in a bank account titled as joint tenants with rights of survivorship with Rebecca
    - A securities account naming the three children as beneficiaries
    - A cabin titled in his own name that he inherited from his parents

    How will Jason's estate be distributed if Rebecca is the mother of the three children and they live in a state that follows the Uniform Probate Code?

    (a) Rebecca will take the family home and the cash in the bank account directly as her inheritance, and the three children will divide among themselves the tangible personal property, the securities account, and the cabin.

    (b) Rebecca will take the family home and one-fourth of the tangible personal property, the cash in the bank account, and the cabin. The children will each take one-fourth of the tangible personal property, the cash, the cabin, and they will divide the assets in the securities account.

(c) Rebecca will take the family home and the cash in the bank account plus one-half of the tangible personal property and the cabin. The children will split the other half of the tangible personal property and the cabin and the assets in the securities account.

(d) Rebecca will take everything except the assets in the securities account, which will pass to the children.

13. Herbert and Julia dated in college but broke up before Julia realized she was pregnant with Herbert's child. Julia never told Herbert about the child (Abigail) and she gave birth and raised Abigail without Herbert's knowledge or financial contribution. A few years later, Julia met Greg and married him and they had two children, Bonnie and Carson. Greg treated Abigail as his own child, she called him father, and although he never adopted Abigail he included her in his will along with Bonnie and Carson. After all three children were grown, Greg died tragically in a car accident, and Julia ran into Herbert at Greg's funeral. They resumed their relationship and married shortly thereafter. After many years of wedded bliss, Herbert died intestate from old age. On his deathbed, Julia told Herbert that Abigail was his natural child. Is Abigail entitled to a share of Herbert's estate?

(a) Yes because she is a biological child of Herbert.

(b) Yes because Herbert married Julia.

(c) No because Herbert did not know Abigail was his child and never contributed to her support.

(d) No because Abigail did not seek a judicial adjudication of parentage before Herbert died.

14. Tony Stark was a wealthy industrialist who died testate at a relatively early age after living many years convinced he was a superhero. He was survived by his spouse and two young children. At his death, his wife found a document titled "Last Will and Testament of Tony Stark" which left half his property to Jarvis, his computer avatar named after his former butler who had died. The rest of his property he devised to "any man named Bruce Banner living in Philadelphia." The document was handwritten and signed by Tony. There were also two other signatures on the page, but Tony's wife could not read their signatures well enough to decipher who they were. The document was dated two months before Tony's death and nominated his good friend, Happy Hogan, to be the personal representative of his estate. Happy has filed the will for probate in the county of Tony's domicile, but his wife and children wish to contest it as being invalid. What is the best argument for its invalidity?

(a) The will is invalid because the witness signatures are indecipherable.

(b) Tony made a mistake because Bruce Banner lives in Boston.

(c) Tony lacked capacity because he left his property to a computer.

(d) Tony lacked capacity because he did not acknowledge his wife and children.

15. Albert executed a valid will in which he left his house to his sister, Bonnie; he left all cash and securities to his brother, Clyde; he left his artwork to his niece, Dania (who is one of Bonnie's three children); he left his car to his nephew Edward (who is one of Clyde's two children); and he left the residue of his estate to his intimate unmarried partner, Isabel. Bonnie and Clyde both predeceased Albert. How is his estate distributed in a UPC state?

    (a) Bonnie's estate takes the house, Clyde's estate takes the cash and securities, Dania takes the artwork, Edward takes the car, and Isabel takes the residue.

    (b) Dania takes the house and the artwork, Edward takes the cash and securities and the car, and Isabel takes the residue.

    (c) Dania and her two siblings share the house and Dania takes the artwork. Edward and his sibling share the cash and securities and Edward takes the car. Isabel takes the residue.

    (d) Dania takes the artwork, Edward takes the car, and Isabel takes the house, the cash and securities, and all the rest and residue.

16. Wilma executed a will in which she poured all of her estate into her unfunded but fully executed revocable living trust. Her trust then provided that the income would be payable to her spouse, Linda, for life, and then to their three children, Alexi, Barbie, and Connie for the duration of their lives. At the death of each of their children, that child's share of the trust principal was to pass to each child's lineal descendants. At the time of Wilma's death, Alexi had two children, Barbie had two children, and Connie had one child. What present estates and future interests do the parties have in Wilma's trust under the UPC?

    (a) Linda has a life estate; Alexi, Barbie, and Connie each have remainders in life estates; and the five grandchildren have contingent remainders in fee simple absolute contingent on surviving to distribution and subject to open to take in new members.

    (b) Linda has a fee simple subject to an executory limitation; Alexi, Barbie, and Connie have shifting executory interests in life estates; and the five grandchildren have vested remainders in fee simple absolute.

    (c) Linda has a life estate; Alexi, Barbie, and Connie have absolutely vested remainders in a life estate; and the five grandchildren have vested remainders subject to open in fee simple absolute.

    (d) Linda has a fee simple absolute because the pour over into an unfunded trust is invalid so the estate passes by intestacy entirely to Linda.

17. More than fifty years ago, in 1972, Juan executed a will (will 1) when he was eighteen years old and about to go into the military, leaving all of his

meager possessions to his parents and his siblings. But in 2022, after a long and successful life as a real estate developer after leaving the Marines, he decided it was time to finally get his financial house in order and he drafted and executed a will (will 2) leaving all his property in trust for the benefit of his wife Maria, and his four children and twelve grandchildren. He did not create a trust during his lifetime, but instead provided that his estate would be put into trust upon his death. A year later in 2023, however, he got angry at Maria and his children for acting like they were entitled to his wealth, so he executed another will (will 3) leaving all his property in trust for charitable purposes. The 1972 and 2023 wills were validly executed according to the wills act formalities (wills 1 and 3), but during execution of the 2022 will, one of the witnesses had to leave the room to take a phone call and did not see the other witness sign. The absent witness returned and signed the will after the first witness had left the room. After making it up with Maria and his kids, Juan tore up his 2023 will with the intention that his 2022 will would be revived. He died suddenly the next day. What is the effect in a UPC state and why?

(a) The first will is valid because the second was not validly executed and the third was revoked.

(b) The second will is valid because it expresses the clear intentions of the testator at his death and was validly executed.

(c) The third will is valid because it was the last valid will he wrote.

(d) The first will is valid because it was revived when the third will was revoked and the second will was never validly executed.

18. Raleigh properly executed a form will that he got off the internet in which he left all his property to his parents. Two weeks later he remembered that he had promised to give his miniature poodle to his best friend, Elise. Not wanting to mess around with re-executing the will, he took out a piece of notebook paper and handwrote the following: "If my miniature poodle muffin is still alive at my death, I give her to my best friend Erica." He then signed the page and stapled it to the back of his will. In a UPC state, what is the best argument for validating the gift of the poodle?

(a) Republication by Codicil.

(b) Incorporation by Reference.

(c) Valid holographic will.

(d) Separate Writing Doctrine.

19. Valerie was an elderly resident of an assisted living facility who suffered from mild Alzheimer's disease. Her caregiver, a nurse named Kurt, frequently asked Valerie about her past and her finances and whether she would be able to stay in the facility. This worried Valerie, which made her more anxious and more forgetful. Kurt also befriended Valerie and often told Valerie that her family didn't care about her, but that he did, and that he would always watch out for her. This made Valerie think of Kurt

as loyal and special, more than just a caregiver. Several times she told Kurt that she needed to redo her estate plan since her family never came to visit her. Kurt guessed that she might favor him in a new estate plan. To help nudge her in that direction, one day he told her that he was going to have leave the facility and stop caring for her as his mom was ill and needed Kurt's care. He said he did not make enough as a caregiver to help his mother out and so he really had no choice. All of this was a lie. In fact, Kurt's mom was no longer alive. This news made Valerie decide she really needed to change her estate plan immediately. She told Kurt she wanted to name him as a primary beneficiary and asked him to find her a lawyer and take her to see him. Kurt gave her the name of one of the lawyers recommended by the facility and, at Valerie's request, he drove her to the appointment with the lawyer. Valerie told the lawyer that she wanted half of her estate to go to Kurt and the other half to her nieces and nephews. In a suit by Valerie's heirs contesting the will, which cause of action is the strongest?

(a) Valerie was under duress.

(b) Valerie was subjected to undue influence.

(c) Valerie was subjected to fraud in the inducement.

(d) Valerie was subjected to fraud in the execution.

20. Esperanza was a wealthy business owner who worked hard and played hard. She had had numerous intimate relationships but she was deeply in love with Pablo, a talented artist. Although their relationship ebbed and flowed, they did not marry until Esperanza was diagnosed with terminal cancer. On the day she learned of her diagnosis, she called and asked Pablo to marry her. Three weeks later, they participated in a civil marriage ceremony at the courthouse. Two weeks later Esperanza died. After her death, Pablo found Esperanza's will, which left all her property to the American Cancer Society and naming her friend Valeria as personal representative. Her will had been drafted in the three weeks after she learned of the cancer diagnosis but before her marriage to Pablo. Hurt that Esperanza had never thought of making him a bequest, Pablo intervenes and challenges the will. What is Pablo's most likely grounds for intervention in a non-community property state?

(a) Esperanza lacked mental capacity.

(b) Pablo is entitled to a share as a pretermitted spouse.

(c) Pablo is entitled to an elective share.

(d) Pablo should be appointed personal representative as her surviving spouse.

21. Janice executed a will that provided, in relevant part, that "my 20 shares of XYZ stock I give to my nephew, Jason." At her death, Janice had 60 shares of XYZ stock. Which of the fact situations below would **NOT** be the result under the UPC ademption rules?

(a) Jason is entitled only to 20 shares because that is all Janice mentioned in the will.

(b) Jason is entitled only to 20 shares, because Janice purchased the additional 40 shares which will pass through her residuary clause.

(c) Jason is entitled only to 40 shares because those were the result of a stock split, and the additional 20 shares Janice inherited from her father pass through her residuary clause.

(d) Jason is entitled to all 60 shares because 40 were the result of reinvested dividends, and the additional 20 shares were the result of a stock split.

22. Penelope executed a will that established a testamentary trust to dispose of the residue of her estate. She named her best friend Molly to be her trustee and instructed Molly to distribute the trust proceeds to the "10 nicest people who come to my funeral in Molly's sole discretion." Molly dutifully took possession of the trust property and took note of every person who attended Penelope's funeral. She then looked up each person's charitable giving record and decided to give the property to those who had donated to animal rescue organizations, medical research organizations, or climate mitigation organizations. Before she could distribute the trust principal, however, Penelope's brother Jackson, who was her closest living heir, filed for an injunction to prevent Molly's distribution and to declare that the trust was invalid. What should happen to the money in the trust?

(a) It should be distributed to the 10 beneficiaries Molly had identified.

(b) It should escheat to the state.

(c) It should be kept by Molly because the trust was invalid and Molly was given the property.

(d) It should pass to Jackson because the trust fails and the residue lapses and passes by intestacy.

23. Alex had a securities account with Morgan Stanley that contained $100,000 worth of mutual funds and securities. He decided one day that he wanted his daughter, Elizabeth, to get the fund at his death, so he went into the Morgan Stanley office and added Elizabeth's name as a joint tenant with right of survivorship. Alex continued to receive all notices and he managed the account entirely. In fact, Elizabeth had no knowledge of the account at all. Shortly before his death, however, Alex felt bad that he had not also provided for his son, Sebastian, and so he went to the Morgan Stanley office and withdrew all the funds from the account he held jointly with Elizabeth and transferred them into an account he owned individually in his own name. At his death, Sebastian claims the funds in the account as the residuary beneficiary of Alex's will. Alex had stated in his will, which he had executed a few days after adding Elizabeth to his account, "I am leaving nothing to my daughter Elizabeth because she is already provided for." Who takes the funds in the account and why?

(a) Elizabeth as joint tenant because Alex could not revoke the joint tenancy when he withdrew the funds.

(b) Elizabeth by intestacy because the will reflects a mistake of fact in the inducement since Alex had not provided for her.

(c) Sebastian because Alex owned the funds at his death and without a beneficiary designation they pass to his estate and are disposed of pursuant to the will.

(d) Sebastian and Elizabeth equally because the funds were not named in the will and therefore pass by intestacy equally to his children.

24. Hazel bequeathed her wedding ring to her granddaughter, Isabel. However, several years after executing her will, Hazel gave her wedding ring to her grandson Ethan, who used it to propose to his wife Carol. Ethan and Carol were married for roughly ten years before they divorced, but Carol kept the wedding ring in the divorce. When Hazel died, Isabel asserts that she should be entitled to the ring and the court should order Carol to return it to her. What is the most likely outcome?

(a) The court will order Carol to give Isabel the ring.

(b) The court will give Isabel the monetary value of the ring out of Hazel's estate.

(c) The court will give Isabel the monetary value of the ring out of Ethan's share of the estate.

(d) The court will not make any order regarding the ring and Isabel will be out of luck.

25. Kamala believed strongly in the power of higher education to lift people up from poverty. In keeping with this belief, she left $1.0 million of her estate in trust to pay out education expenses as needed, in the discretion of the trustee, for any of the lineal descendants of her parents. Kamala's closest heir at her death challenges this gift in trust. In most states, a court is likely to rule as follows:

(a) Uphold the trust since it is committed to charitable/educational purposes.

(b) Strike it down because there are no vested interests.

(c) Wait at least 90 years to see if the trust fund has been depleted.

(d) Uphold the trust since the beneficiaries are identifiable.

EXAM VIII

California Questions

Answer all of the questions in this exam according to California law.

1. Husband Harry and Wife Wanda have been married for 10 years. Before their marriage, Harry had purchased a home in Palo Alto and a vacation home in Monterrey. He purchased both for cash, using funds he had inherited from his parents. Harry and Wanda have two minor children, Caleb and Cindy. Since their marriage, the couple has purchased various stocks and bonds. Both have retirement accounts through their employers. Harry is consulting you about drafting a will for him. He asks you who would inherit all his property if he were to die without a will. You tell him:

   (a) Wanda will take everything.

   (b) Wanda and his two minor children will take everything equally, as co-tenants.

   (c) Wanda will take all of the stocks and bonds, but will share ownership of the real estate equally with the minor children.

   (d) Wanda will take half of Harry's share of the stocks and bonds, and will share ownership of the real estate equally with the minor children.

2. Trustor created a revocable inter vivos trust that provided as follows: "Income to Trustor during Trustor's life, together with any principal that the Trustor needs, and at Trustor's death to Son, Steve." Steve predeceased Trustor, leaving a daughter, Diane. At Trustor's death, the successor trustee of the trust should distribute the trust assets to:

   (a) Steve's estate because Steve had a vested remainder.

   (b) Trustor's estate because the remainder to Steve fails.

   (c) Diane, because she has a future interest in a trust.

   (d) Diane, because her father Steve was the beneficiary of an "at-death transfer."

3. Jane opened a joint account at Bank One and named Jules as the joint account holder. Jane deposited $10,000 in the account. No other deposits or withdrawals were made to this account. At Jane's death her revocable trust contained her dispositive plan. The trust provided that at her death, all of her assets, including the bank account at Bank One should go to her sister, Jean. The bank should distribute the funds in the bank account to:

   (a) Jules because he was named on the bank documents as the person who would be entitled to the funds in the account at Jane's death.

(b) To Jean, but only if Jean can prove that the account was opened by Jane as a "convenience account."

(c) To Jane's estate because she has effectively cancelled the survivorship right in the bank account, but the trust cannot effectively provide where the funds in the account are to go.

(d) To Jean because Jane has clearly established that she had a different intent than the one she had when she opened the account.

4. Which of the following statements is *not* true about the California intestacy scheme?

   (a) A stepchild can never inherit.

   (b) Distribution "by right of representation" means strict per stirpes distribution.

   (c) An heir must survive by 120 hours.

   (d) Both (a) and (b).

5. Testator's will provides that he leaves Blackacre to his son, Samuel, if he survives me. The rest and residue of the estate goes to T's daughter, Deb. Samuel fails to survive T, but he leaves a son, Sam. Deb does survive. Blackacre should be distributed to:

   (a) Samuel's son, Sam, under the anti-lapse statute.

   (b) Daughter Deb.

   (c) T's estate, because he didn't provide otherwise.

   (d) Deb and Sam, equally.

6. Alice created a revocable inter vivos trust. Article III of the trust provided: "This trust may be revoked by a statement in writing delivered to the trustee during the trustor's life." Alice was the trustee and beneficiary of the trust. The trust provided that at her death, all of her property was to go to Ben. Five years after executing the trust, Alice executed a will that provided that all of her property, including any property in trust, was to go to Carl. At Alice's death, all of her property should be distributed to:

   (a) Carl, because the will revoked the gift in the trust.

   (b) Ben, because the will could not revoke the trust.

   (c) Alice's intestate heirs.

   (d) Alice's estate.

7. Mark was married to Mary. His will and his revocable inter vivos trust left everything to Mary. Mark also had a $100,000 life insurance policy naming Mary as the beneficiary. One year before his death Mark and Mary divorced, but Mark never changed any of his estate planning documents. At Mark's death, Mary is entitled to:

   (a) All of Mark's property and the life insurance proceeds because Mark never revoked any of these documents.

(b) Any of the assets in the trust and the life insurance proceeds because divorce revoked the gift in the will.

(c) Nothing because divorce revokes all deathtime transfers.

(d) Only the life insurance proceeds.

8. Herman died with a will that left everything to his wife, Wilma. She failed to survive him. He made no provision for alternative takers.

Herman was survived by his adopted son, Sam, who was the natural child of Wilma. He was also survived by another son, Quince. Quince was a nonmarital child, born when Herman was living with his then girlfriend, Hannah. Herman had admitted paternity and paid child support to Quince's mom until Quince was 18, Quince was adopted by his mother's new husband when he was just over one year old and had no memory of Herman.

Quince died two years before Herman. Quince was survived by 3 children, Abby, Beth, and Chance.

What is the most likely distribution of Herman's estate and why? Apply California law.

(a) Herman's estate will pass to Sam under the anti-lapse statute since Sam was an "issue" of Wilma.

(b) Herman died intestate. Son Sam will take as his only intestate heir.

(c) Herman died intestate. Son Sam will take half and Abby, Beth, and Chance will share the other half equally.

(d) Herman died intestate, Son Sam will take half and the estate of son Quince will take the other half.

9. Tom downloaded a will form from a legal documents web site. He chose the correct form for California. It contained an attestation clause for two witnesses to sign. In the middle of the page where there was a blank to fill in the names of beneficiaries, he wrote: "Everything to Betty." He then signed and dated it and crossed out the attestation clause and the blank lines for witnesses to sign. In a contest between Betty and Tom's intestate heirs, what is the most likely outcome under California law?

(a) The heirs will win because the will is not wholly in the handwriting of Tom.

(b) The heirs will win because Tom did not handwrite any words indicating testamentary intent.

(c) Betty will win only if she can prove by clear and convincing evidence that Tom intended this will form to be a valid will.

(d) Betty will win because Tom executed a valid holographic will.

10. Dick's will provided as follows: "My executor may find a memorandum signed by me and left in my desk drawer that designates certain beneficiaries to take my personal property." After Dick's death, the duly appointed executor did find such a memorandum. It provided that $4,000

should go to Jane and the painting of "Spot," worth $4,000 should go to Dick's nephew, Ned. The effect of this memo under California probate law is as follows:

(a) Jane and Ned should take because the gifts are small enough to qualify under California statutes dealing with the passing of property under a memorandum executed after the will.

(b) Only Ned should take.

(c) Only Jane should take.

(d) Neither Ned nor Jane should take because the memorandum was not in existence prior to will execution.

11. Ursula's will provides as follows: "I leave the rest of my property in trust for the benefit of my grandson Amir for life, then to Amir's first child to graduate from college." Ursula is survived by Amir aged 25 and Amir's son, Sam, aged 2. Under California law, what is the effect of the rule against perpetuities?

(a) All gifts are valid because all of the potential beneficiaries are "lives in being" at Ursula's death.

(b) The gift to Amir is valid, but the contingent remainder to his first child is absolutely void.

(c) The gift to Amir is valid, and Sam will take the remainder if it turns out that he is in fact the first child of Amir to graduate from college.

(d) The gift to the first child to graduate from college is void because it is not certain that it will take effect within 90 years.

12. Stella died at home in early 2021. Her husband had predeceased her. She was survived by her husband's two children (her stepchildren) and her own four children (from a prior marriage). An envelope containing her will was found in her safety deposit box at First Bank. The will was signed and witnessed and dated September 15, 2015. It left everything to her husband and if he failed to survive her to her two stepchildren and her four children in equal shares. Her husband died in 2016. Inside the will was another piece of paper folded carefully. It said: "This is an amendment to my will. My husband died recently and I want my estate to pass to my four children. Signed and dated: February 2, 2017." All of this was in Stella's handwriting. But there was no actual signature on the document. All six children survive Stella. Under California law, Stella's estate should be distributed:

(a) Only to her four children provided there is clear and convincing evidence that she intended the amendment to be a testamentary document.

(b) To her four children, under the doctrine of integration.

(c) To her four children, under the doctrine of incorporation by reference.

(d) To all six children, including the two stepchildren.

13. Helen and William have lived their entire lives in California. They have been married since 1968 and have accumulated a community estate in the range of $800,000 total value. Helen's will, executed two years ago, leaves all her property, including her interest in the community estate, to her alma mater, Santa Clara University. At her death in December of 2008, William was stunned to learn that he had been disinherited in favor of Santa Clara. He consults you for advice about what he can do to make a claim against Helen's estate. You advise him:

    (a) He can make no viable claim against the estate.

    (b) He can make a claim to a spousal elective share.

    (c) He can make a claim to his intestate share of the community estate as a pretermitted spouse.

    (d) He can claim that the bequest is in fraud of his rights as a spouse.

14. Decedent died intestate and was survived by no spouse, no issue, and no parents. His brother, Buck, predeceased him leaving two children, Niece Nan and Nephew Ned. His sister Sue predeceased him, leaving one child, Nephew Nick. His other sister, Sara, also predeceased, as did her daughter Deb. But Deb was survived by two children, grandnieces Greta and Glenda. Under California law, how should Decedent's estate be distributed?

    (a) 1/6 to each of Buck's two children, 1/3 to Sue's child and 1/6 each to the grandchildren of Sara.

    (b) 1/4 to each of Buck's two children, 1/4 to Sue's child, and 1/8 each to the grandchildren of Sara.

    (c) Per capita to each of the collateral heirs, i.e., 1/5 each.

    (d) 1/3 to each of Buck's two children and 1/3 to Sue's child, because they are related through the closest ancestor to Decedent.

15. Jack and Jill owned Blackacre as joint tenants. One day, driving home from the airport together, they were in a horrible car accident. Jill was pronounced dead at the scene and Jack died one day later in the hospital. Jack is survived by his son Sam, but he has a will that leaves everything to the Red Cross. Jill died intestate survived by her son, Saul. Who becomes the owner of Blackacre as a result of these deaths?

    (a) Sam and Saul will own Blackacre as tenants in common.

    (b) Sam will own Blackacre.

    (c) The Red Cross will own Blackacre.

    (d) The Red Cross and Saul will own Blackacre as tenants in common.

16. Ted died intestate. He had three sons, Carl, Cam, and Chet. They were all the children of Ted and his ex-spouse, Nora. Carl died one day before Ted. Cam died the day after Ted and Chet died one week later. All three sons died intestate, but only Chet died with surviving issue, his son, Graham.

None of the sons was survived by a spouse. Who ends up with Ted's property?

(a) The three sons each take one-third, equally.

(b) Only Cam and Chet can take. The facts don't say who will inherit from Cam, but Chet's son, Graham will take one-third.

(c) Chet's son, Graham, will inherit everything through Chet.

(d) Graham will inherit directly from Ted.

17. Tom consulted his estate planning lawyer about the possibility of changing the provisions of his revocable trust to give a larger share to his new wife. Tom also told his wife, Wanda, that he planned to increase her share in his separate property trust to half, from the current one-third. Six months later, Tom died without having made any changes to his separate property trust. Wanda sued the estate planning lawyer for negligence in not carrying out Tom's wishes in a timely manner. The lawyer demurs. What should the court rule?

(a) It should sustain the demurrer because failing to complete estate planning documents in a timely manner is not negligence.

(b) It should sustain the demurrer because there is no privity between Wanda and the lawyer.

(c) It should overrule the demurrer because Wanda can show that she was an intended beneficiary of the contract between Tom and the lawyer.

(d) It should overrule the demurrer to give Wanda the opportunity to prove negligence.

18. The State of California recognizes registered relationships other than marriage. A couple can file with the Secretary of State and become a registered domestic partnership. Under state law, such RDPs have exactly the same rights as married couples, including being subject to the community property regime. Which of the following statements is not true about the status of RDPs?

(a) They must file income tax returns as married for state purposes, but not for federal purposes.

(b) At the death of the first partner, only half of the property acquired during the marriage is likely to be included in the taxable estate for federal estate tax purposes.

(c) If one partner earns $1,000,000 in salary during a year and the other earns nothing, the earning partner will be viewed as making a $500,00 gift to the non-earning partner.

(d) A surviving partner is entitled to social security survivor benefits, based on the working credits of the deceased partner.

19. Frank, who never knew who his biological father was, was removed from the care of his mother and her rights were terminated when he was 3

years old. He was placed as a foster child with Howard and Wendy Dean, who had a daughter, Mary. Frank lived with the Deans until he married and moved away at age 20. He always called Howard and Wendy Dad and Mom. He clearly had a sibling-like relationship with Mary. When Wendy died, he and Mary met and made decisions about her funeral and disposition of remains. Then Mary died, and everyone looked to Frank to make the decisions. Finally, Howard died. He died intestate, never having officially adopted Frank. Frank claims to be the intestate heir. A distant third cousin of Howard's named Randy claims he is the sole heir. At trial, the court should rule:

(a) In favor of Frank because he was functionally the child of Howard.

(b) In favor of Frank because he was equitably adopted by Howard.

(c) In favor of Frank under California Probate Code § 6454, statutory adoption of a foster child.

(d) In favor of Randy.

20. T's will left Blackacre in trust: for the benefit of my surviving children for life and at the death of the last survivor, to my grandchildren per capita. T was survived by two children, Ben and Cindy and by a grandchild named Ginny who was the daughter of a predeceased son, Sam. However, Ginny failed to survive her aunt and uncle, Cindy and Ben. She left a daughter, Gretchen. Under California law, what is Ginny's interest in Blackacre?

(a) Ginny takes a lifetime income interest as a representative of Sam

(b) Ginny can take nothing because her parent failed to survive T.

(c) Ginny takes a vested remainder in Blackacre which will go to her estate at the death of both Ben and Cindy.

(d) Ginny's daughter Gretchen will take as a substitute taker for Ginny since Ginny failed to survive the life tenants, Ben and Cindy.

21. Hal and Wang were married in 2017. It was Hal's first marriage, but Wang's second. Wang had a daughter, Deb, who became a stepchild of Hal. Hal and Deb were very close and so when Hal and Wang divorced in 2022, Deb (aged ten) continued to live with Hal. In 2023 Hal died intestate survived by Wang and Deb, and also by his great aunt, Mary. Who should take Hal's estate?

(a) Mary.

(b) Deb.

(c) The state.

(d) Wang.

22. Under California law, which of the following is a valid reason for contesting a will?

(a) The will was not notarized.

(b) The testator lacked the mental capacity to understand the nature of the act and its consequences.

(c) The testator did not sign the will in front of any witnesses.

(d) The will was executed in another state.

23. In California, when is a living trust typically used instead of a will?

(a) To avoid probate.

(b) To distribute property only after the testator's death.

(c) To reduce estate taxes.

(d) To make gifts to heirs who are minors.

24. Susie and Willie were in love with each other in high school. But then they went their separate ways. Willie married Beth and Susie married Steve. In their 70s, after the deaths of both spouses, they found each other again. Willie asked Susie to marry him, but she said no. So Willie promised if she would just quit her job and move in with him he would leave her everything he owned. He also pronounced that everything he did own would be owned jointly with her with right of survivorship. And, at other times, he promised he would support her for life. Susie did quit her job and moved in with Willie. He did add her to several joint bank accounts, but not enough to fulfill his promise of lifetime support if she outlived him for long. Willie died intestate. Susie's best claim to share in his estate is:

(a) As a cohabitant, she is entitled to an intestate share.

(b) That the Statute of Frauds does not apply to Willie's promise of support.

(c) Under the *Marvin* case, she is either entitled to lifetime support or to Willie's full estate.

(d) She has a *quantum meruit* claim to the value of her services.

25. Steve died testate with a will that left Blackacre to "my sons who survive me," The rest of his estate was left to his "daughter Debby for life, then to my heirs." Steve had two sons but neither survived him. Each son was survived by a wife and one child. These wives and children (Steve's grandchildren, Gus and Garth) also survived Steve. Steve's daughter Debby died 25 years after Steve. Debby was survived by a husband, but no children or other issue. One of Steve's grandchildren, Gus, predeceased Debby, but the other one, Garth, survived. Gus was survived by a child, Cathy. At Debby's death, her life estate ended. Who should now own the property that Steve owned at his death?

(a) Gus and Garth (or their estates) now own Blackacre under the anti-lapse statute, and Garth and Cathy own everything else as the remainder owners of the estate.

(b) Debby, Gus, and Garth (or their estates) now own everything because they were Steve's actual heirs.

(c) Garth and Cathy own everything.

(d) Gus's estate and Garth and Cathy own everything.

EXAM I
ANSWER KEY AND EXPLANATIONS

1. **The best answer is (b).** Under the doctrine of incorporation by reference as it existed at common law, a document that has not been executed with the formalities for the execution of a will can be given testamentary effect under a will provided that (1) the document was in existence at the execution of the will, (2) the will manifests the testator's intention to incorporate the document into the will, and (3) the will sufficiently identifies the document to be incorporated. Technically, the document that is being incorporated by reference does not become a part of the will. In the hypothetical, if we treat the handwritten portion of the single sheet of paper as a separate document from the typed portion, the handwritten portion would seem to be a valid holographic will. Since T referred to "this will" as incorporating the typed material, there is a good argument that T thought of the typed material as separate from the will and it should be treated as separate from the holographic will. A holographic will may incorporate by reference a document that is typed. The holographic will sufficiently expresses an intention to incorporate the typed matter, and sufficiently identifies the document to be incorporated ("the typed matter above"). Finally, the typed matter seems to have been in existence at execution of the holographic will. Therefore, a strong argument exists that the doctrine of incorporation by reference may be used to give effect to devises 1 through 9.

   Answer (a) is not correct. The doctrine of integration provides that a document that is present at the execution of the will and that T intends to be a part of the will is a part of the will. The doctrine of integration cannot be used to validate devises 1 through 9, however, because if those devises are considered a part of the purported executed will, the entire will fails (and devises 1 through 9 necessarily fail as well). If the typed matter is a part of the will, then will is not a valid holographic will because the will contains material provisions that are not in T's handwriting. Moreover, the will cannot be a valid non-holographic will because it has not been witnessed.

   Answer (c) is not correct. When applied, the doctrine of republication by codicil re-executes an earlier will and brings the date of execution of the earlier will up to the date of execution of the codicil. The doctrine of republication by codicil is properly applied only to a validly executed prior will and only if doing so will carry out the intent of the testator. A court may not properly apply the doctrine on the facts of this hypothetical, therefore, because the typed matter is not a validly executed prior will. (It is unsigned and unwitnessed.)

2. **The best answer is (c).** In general, the law of a decedent's domicile at his death provides the law governing the intestate passing of his personal property. In general, the law of the situs of real property provides the law governing the intestate passing of that real property at the death of the owner. California law, therefore, will govern the passing of D's intestate personal property, even though most of that personal property is physically located in Nevada. Georgia law will govern the intestate passing of D's real property because that real property is located in Georgia. A court may respect a testator's or settlor's direction that the law of a given state shall govern, respectively, a will or a trust. A court may refuse to give effect to such a designation if such application of law would defeat a public policy (such as the policy supporting provision of an elective share to a surviving spouse) of the forum state or, in some cases, the state with the most significant relationship to the matter. In this hypothetical, however, D died intestate.

3. **The best answer is (c).** The comment to UPC § 2–102 states that empirical studies "have shown that testators in smaller estates (which intestate estates overwhelmingly tend to be) tend to devise their *entire* estates to their surviving spouses, even when the couple has children." The comment further states that "[t]he theory of this section is discussed in Waggoner, "The Multiple-Marriage Society and Spousal Rights Under the Revised Uniform Probate Code," 76 Iowa L. Rev. 223, 229–35 (1991)." Professor Waggoner's law review article itself at p. 232 explains: "The 1990 UPC is predicated on the notion that decedents . . . see the surviving spouses as occupying somewhat of a dual role, not only as their primary beneficiaries, but also as conduits through which to benefit their children. If [the intestate decedent] died prematurely, at a time when their children were still minors, [the surviving spouse] would be better equipped than their children to use [decedent]'s property for the benefit of their children as well as for herself. If [the decedent] was older at death, when their children were middle-aged working adults, [the surviving spouse] would probably be older and have greater economic needs than their children. In this latter case, the conduit theory assumes that [the decedent]'s children will eventually inherit any unconsumed portion of his property from [the surviving spouse] upon her death." The conduit theory breaks down, however, when the decedent and the surviving spouse had "non-joint" or "non-mutual" children. If the couple had joint children and the surviving spouse also has children not of the decedent, one should expect that the surviving spouse will share the intestate property with both the joint children and her non-joint children. Thus, an intestacy statute might give more of the intestate estate to the joint children, who are children of the intestate decedent. The conduit theory breaks down further when the decedent had children not of the surviving spouse. One might expect that the surviving spouse would be more likely to disinherit the decedent's non-mutual children. Thus, an intestacy statute might give even more of the intestate estate to the non-joint children of the intestate decedent. In sum, an intestacy statute grounded in the conduit theory should give the largest share to the surviving spouse when the decedent and the surviving

spouse have "joint children" and neither the decedent nor the surviving spouse has any other children. Thus, **answer (c)** is the best answer.

4. **The best answer is (b).** In order to answer this question, you must understand what a pourover will is. A pourover will is a will that devises property to the trustee (as trustee) of an inter vivos trust to be distributed in accordance with the terms of the inter vivos trust. Today, legislation (in most states a version of the Uniform Testamentary Additions to Trusts Act ("UTATA")) validates pourover wills in each state. Prior to statutory validation, however, the issue arose of whether a pourover will violated the wills act in that it sought to dispose of property at death by means of a document that had not been executed with the formalities for execution of a will (the trust instrument). Both the doctrine of incorporation by reference and the doctrine of acts of independent significance could be used to overcome this objection and validate a pourover will. Under the doctrine of incorporation by reference as it existed at common law, a document that has not been executed with the formalities for the execution of a will can be given effect as part of the will provided that (1) the document was in existence at the execution of the will, (2) the will manifests the testator's intention to incorporate the document into the will, and (3) the will sufficiently identifies the document to be incorporated. A problem arose with the incorporation by reference approach to validating a pourover will, however, if the trust instrument was not in existence at execution of the will or was amended after execution of the will. In such a case, the incorporation by reference doctrine was unavailable since the document to be incorporated was not in existence at execution of the will. The acts of independent significance doctrine provides that the identification of the person who shall receive a devise or the property covered by a devise (or both) can be determined by an act or event outside the will provided that the act or event has a significance apart from passing property under the will. For example, the taker of a devise "to my oldest sister alive at my death" will be determined by events—the continuation or expiration of the testator's sisters' lives—that has a significance apart from passing property under the will. The execution of an inter vivos trust instrument can have a significance apart from passing property under the will: The trust instrument's independent significance is that it governs the management of property in the inter vivos trust. A problem arose with the acts of independent significance approach to validating a pourover will, however, if the trust was not funded during the life of the testator (and, therefore, the trust instrument was not governing the management of any property). Under the modern version of UTATA, a pourover devise will not be invalid merely because the trust instrument was executed or modified after execution of the will or because the trust was not funded during the testator's life.

   Republication by codicil only applies to a prior instrument that was itself valid as a will. A revocable trust is signed by the trustor, but generally not otherwise executed consistent with Wills Act formalities. Nor is it likely to indicate "testamentary intent" since the trust is intended to govern the management of assets during the life of the trustor. As a result, the republication by codicil doctrine cannot apply. That is why the other three alternative answers to this question are incorrect.

5. **The best answer is (b).** For a testator to revoke a will, he must (1) have the intent to revoke the will and (2) while he has that intent to revoke, he must either execute a subsequent will revoking the earlier will or perform a sufficient physical act upon the will he wishes to revoke. The doctrine of dependent relative revocation (DRR) works to negate the first element (T's intent to revoke) in certain cases where the court concludes that such negation actually would promote T's intent. The doctrine of DRR provides that where T purports to revoke a will while laboring under a mistake of fact or law, the court will disregard the revocation if T would have preferred that result had he known the truth about the mistake he was making. For example, as set out in the hypothetical, if T purports to revoke a will while mistakenly believing that by doing so he will revive an earlier will, the court will disregard the revocation (by concluding that T did not really have the absolute intent to revoke). To apply DRR, the court would need to find that T would not have revoked the later will had he known that the earlier will would not be revived by his revoking the later will.

   There are three general approaches to the issue of revival: (1) when a will that revoked an earlier will is itself revoked, the earlier will automatically is revived; (2) when a will that revoked an earlier will is itself revoked, the earlier will is not revived unless the testator re-executes the earlier will with the formalities necessary for the execution of a will (and this is the common law rule, sometimes described as "once revoked, always revoked"); and (3) when a will that revoked an earlier will is itself revoked, the earlier will is revived if the testator intended for the earlier will to be revived when he revoked the later will. The UPC adopts the third approach and employs a series of presumptions intended to lead the court to the correct conclusion regarding the testator's intent in more cases than not.

   Given that the legatees under Will #2 are arguing that the court should apply the doctrine of DRR, and the court agrees, T must have been mistaken in his belief that revoking Will #2 would revive Will #1. **Answer (a) is not correct.** If the jurisdiction applied the rule that when a will that revoked an earlier will is itself revoked, the earlier will automatically is revived, then Will #1 would have been revived when T revoked Will #2 and the legatees under Will #2 would not have a winning argument. **Answer (c) is not correct.** If the jurisdiction applied the rule that when a will that revoked an earlier will is itself revoked, the earlier will is revived if the testator intended for the earlier will to be revived when he revoked the later will, then Will #1 would have been revived when T revoked Will #2 because (as the facts expressly state) T intended for Will #1 to be revived. **Answer (b) is correct.** This jurisdiction must apply the remaining approach to revival—when a will that revoked an earlier will is itself revoked, the earlier will is not revived unless the testator re-executes the earlier will with the formalities necessary for the execution of a will. This is the general rule at common law (in absence of a revival statute). The rule is often described as: "once revoked always revoked."

6. **The best answer is (a).** Ademption by extinction is the nullification of a bequest because the item devised is not found in the testator's estate at his death. Ademption by extinction applies only to specific gifts. There are two approaches to ademption. Under the identity theory of ademption, a gift of a specific item is adeemed if it cannot be found in the testator's estate at his death. In general, under the identity approach, whether or not the testator intended to adeem the gift, in theory, is not relevant. Under the intent theory of ademption, a gift of a specific item that cannot be found in the testator's estate at his death is adeemed only if the testator intended for the gift to be adeemed. UPC § 2–606 adopts an intent theory of ademption.

   The question asks you to assume an identity theory jurisdiction. In the hypothetical, the testator devised "My house to my sister Susan" at a time when he owned the house at 1307 W. James St. That house cannot be found in the testator's estate at his death because the testator sold that house and bought a new house—the house at 11 Shawnee Lane—a year before his death. One might conclude, therefore, that the gift to Susan is adeemed and Jeff takes the house at 11 Shawnee Lane as the residuary devisee. **But answer (b) is incorrect.** Susan takes the house because a court will apply a "time of death **construction**" to the devise. Wills are generally construed at death. When the language "my house" is applied to the testator's circumstances at his death, the language refers to the house at 11 Shawnee Lane. That house is found in the testator's estate at his death, and so the gift to Susan is not adeemed. Had the testator instead devised "My house at 1307 W. James St. to my sister Susan," a court would not be able to apply a time of death construction to prevent ademption of the gift to Susan. In that case, answer (b) would be correct. The gift to Susan of the house at 1307 W. James St. would be adeemed because not found in the testator's estate at his death, and Jeff would take the house at 11 Shawnee Lane as the residuary devisee.

   Awarding the recently acquired house at 11 Shawnee Lane is also supported by reference to the Acts of Independent Significance Doctrine. Buying the new home as the testator's residence is an "act of independent significance." He did not purchase it for testamentary purposes, i.e., primarily to give it to sister Susan at his death. He bought it presumably to live in himself. That is an "act of independent significance." Yes, it changed his testamentary disposition to his sister Susan, but that is not *why* he purchased the house.

   Many have argued that the identity theory of ademption too often undermines the most likely intent of the testator. The "time of death construction" is just one of several techniques and exceptions that courts apply to avoid what many consider to be the unfortunately harsh consequences of the identity theory of ademption. Others include "reclassifying" an arguably specific devise as general (since ademption applies only to specific devises), finding that the property devised is in the estate in a changed form (for example, securities acquired in a merger in exchange for devised securities might be held to be the devised securities in a changed form), and allowing the devisee of property later involuntarily transferred out of the estate (for example, by a conservator) to take the proceeds resulting from the transfer.

7. **The best answer is (c).** The court should probate the first will but impose a constructive trust on Marc for the benefit of Fred even though Marc was wholly innocent of the fraud committed by Jake. While it may seem unusual to give the property to a beneficiary named in a will that has not been executed, there are cases to support this outcome. See *Pope v. Garrett*, 211 S.W.2d 559 (Tex. 1948)(some but not all of T's heirs prevented her from executing a will in favor of her friend, Claytonia Garrett; court held that even the innocent heirs would be "unjustly enriched" unless Garrett could receive the property as T intended). A constructive trust is really not a trust at all. Rather, a constructive trust is a remedy imposed in order to prevent unjust enrichment, particularly in cases of fraud, duress, or undue influence. **Answer (a) is not the best answer.** Even though Marc is innocent of any fraud, he still would be unjustly enriched if allowed to keep the property devised under T's first will because, absent Jake's fraud, T would have executed a new will revoking Marc's gift and devising his estate to Fred.

   Answer (b) is not the best answer. Since T never executed the second will revoking the first will, the court should not find that T died intestate. **Answer (d) is not correct.** T never executed the second will. Therefore, it cannot be probated.

8. **The best answer is (b).** Under a traditional purging statute, an interested witness to a will (a witness who otherwise would take a devise under the will) loses (is purged of) his gift and, thereby, (so the theory goes) becomes disinterested. The will, therefore, will not fail for lack of sufficient disinterested witnesses due to the circumstance that one or more witnesses also is a beneficiary under the terms of the will. Modern purging statutes also have the effect of preventing the will from failing for lack of sufficient disinterested witnesses due to the circumstance that one or more witnesses also is a beneficiary under the terms of the will. **Answer (a), therefore, is not the best answer** whether we are in a jurisdiction with a traditional purging statute or a jurisdiction with a modern purging statute. Such statutes purge the gift to BW, thereby making BW an uninterested witness as to the rest of the will. Since the will is otherwise valid, T does not die intestate.

   Under a modern purging statute, the interested witness does not necessarily lose his entire gift and does not necessarily lose any portion of his gift. Rather, the interested witness loses that portion of his gift that is in excess of what he would have taken from the testator's estate had the will he witnessed as an interested witness not been executed. Applying this approach of the modern purging statute to the facts of the hypothetical, however, BW should be purged of his entire gift in Will #2. The problem tells us that BW is unrelated to T. We know, therefore, that

BW was not an heir and would not have taken any portion of T's intestate estate had T died intestate. When BW acted as a witness to Will #1, therefore, all of the $170,000 devise of Google stock was "excess" and BW was entitled to take nothing under Will #1. (BW would take zero under intestacy. A gift worth $170,000 to BW under Will #1 would increase his take by $170,000. All of this $170,000 is excess, therefore, over what BW would have taken had Will #1 not been executed.) Given that BW was entitled to take nothing under Will #1, all of the $70,000 gift of real property to BW in Will #2, to which BW also was a witness, is excess. The purging statute purges BW of this excess, and he takes nothing under Will #2.

Note that UPC § 2–505(b) does away with the purging of gifts to witnesses: "The signing of a will by an interested witness does not invalidate the will or any provision of it."

9. **The best answer is (d).** Answer (d) states the standard for the harmless error principle (such as that of UPC § 2–503). Under the harmless error principle, a document that has not been executed with the formalities prescribed for execution of a will may nonetheless be probated as a will if the court finds that there is clear and convincing evidence that the testator intended the document to be his will. Thus, an unattested holographic will can be probated in a harmless error jurisdiction even if the jurisdiction does not otherwise recognize holographic wills. **Answer (a) is not correct.** It states the predominant standard in jurisdictions that recognize holographic wills for what material must be in the handwriting of the testator for a holographic will to be valid. The question states, however, that Nirvana does not recognize holographic wills. **Answer (c) is not correct.** It states the standard for substantial compliance with wills formalities. Even in a substantial compliance jurisdiction, however, T's attempt at a will should not be probated as an attested will. T has made no attempt to obtain witnesses for his will. He has not substantially complied with the witnessing requirement. If the jurisdiction does recognize the doctrine of substantial compliance, it might be worth making the argument on these facts, but **answer (c)** cannot be the **best** answer because **answer (d)** is absolutely correct.

10. **The best answer is (d).** Under the doctrine of administrative deviation, a court may modify the administrative terms of a trust, such as a restriction on the trustee's investment power, if, due to circumstances the settlor did not foresee, the administrative direction threatens the primary purposes of the trust. This is in theory an intent-promoting doctrine. The thinking is that the settlor would not want a direction of secondary importance (here, the settlor's direction that the trustee may not sell the buildings) to threaten the primary purpose of the trust—which must be to benefit the beneficiaries. **For this reason, answer (c) is not the best answer.** It should be noted that the court may not modify the administrative terms of the trust merely because to do so would likely produce a better return for the beneficiaries. Rather, the administrative direction must seriously threaten the purposes of the trust for the court

to apply the doctrine of administrative deviation. **Answer (a) is not the best answer** because generally the trustee has a duty of impartiality between the life tenant and the remainderman. The trustee should petition for administrative deviation, therefore, if the decline in value of the buildings threatens to seriously erode the remainderman's interest in the trust.

11. **The best answer is (a).** A testator may revoke a will by performing a sufficient physical act on the will with the intent to revoke it. The performance of the physical act and the intent to revoke must coincide in time. Marking the words of the will in such a way as to indicate an intent to revoke the will, such as by placing an "X" on each page of the will, is a sufficient act. This is called cancellation. In most jurisdictions, the mark of cancellation must touch the words of the will. Other sufficient physical acts include burning the will, tearing the will, and obliterating the will. In general, the burning, tearing, and obliterating need not touch the words of the will. The physical act may be performed by someone other than the T if done at T's direction and in T's presence. That person performing the physical act at T's direction need not be an attorney. **(Answer (d), therefore, is incorrect.)**

    The will in the hypothetical is not revoked, however, because Mark marked a copy of the will. In most jurisdictions, a physical act performed on a copy of the will is to no effect even if T performs the act with the intent to revoke the will. In contrast, a sufficient physical act performed on a duplicate of the will is effective if performed with the intent to revoke the will. A duplicate is created when the testator executes two identical documents with the formalities needed for execution of a will. Both documents are an original. Both documents are a duplicate. A copy is a photocopy of an executed will and, therefore, is not an original.

12–14:

General comments on questions 12–14: There are a few universal rules for applying an intestacy statute: The first rule to keep in mind is that only persons who survive a property owner are eligible to take a portion of the property owner's intestate estate. What counts as survival depends on what the state's Simultaneous Death Act provides. The Revised Act in the UPC requires survival by 120 hours.

A second rule to keep in mind is that no descendant who is a member of a lower generation (e.g., a grandchild of the Intestate) can take if that person's parent is alive.

A third rule to keep in mind is that if a descendant of the intestate property owner predeceases the intestate property owner, leaving issue who survive the intestate property owner, those issue will take a portion of the intestate property owner's intestate property by representation. The portion that those issue take by representation will be determined by the specifics of the intestacy scheme. At this point, it becomes necessary to know if the scheme is classic per stirpes, modern per stirpes, or per capita at each generation.

Given the fact pattern, we first should address the issue raised by the near simultaneous death of Scott and Zelda. Under the Revised Uniform Simultaneous Death Act and the UPC, one must survive a property owner by at least 120 hours in order to take from that property owner by intestacy. Otherwise we treat the survivor as having predeceased the property owner. Zelda survived Scott, but by only 72 hours. Therefore, under the Revised Uniform Simultaneous Death Act, we treat Zelda as having predeceased Scott for the purposes of distributing Scott's intestate property. Zelda takes nothing. Therefore, **answer (d)** is not correct in questions 12–14. And Victor and William do not take any of Scott's property through Zelda. Moreover, Victor and William will take nothing in their own right because they are only stepchildren. Therefore, **answer (a) is not correct** in any of the questions 12 through 14.

12. **The best answer is (b).** Under the classic per stirpes approach, (1) we begin dividing the intestate property into shares at the generation level immediately below the intestate decedent. (2) We assign a share to (a) any living descendant in that generation and (b) any predeceased descendant in that generation who left issue who survived the intestate property owner. A, B, and C did not survive, but they all left issue who did survive. Therefore, we divide Scott's estate into thirds. A's one-third goes to her two children, so E and F take 1/6 each. B's one third goes to his three children, so G, H, and I take 1/9 each. And C's one third goes to his two children, so they take 1/6 each.

13. **The best answer is (c).** The modern per stirpes approach has one major difference from the classic per stirpes approach: Rather than begin dividing the intestate property into shares at the generation level immediately below the intestate decedent, we begin dividing the intestate property into shares at the first generation level below the intestate decedent where we find a living descendant. In the facts of this question, that is at the grandchild stage. Otherwise, the modern per stirpes approach is the same as the classic per stirpes approach. Under the modern per stirpes approach, therefore (1) we begin dividing the intestate property into shares at the first generation level below the intestate decedent where we find a living descendant. (2) We assign a share to (a) any living descendant in that generation and (b) any predeceased descendant in that generation who left issue who survived the intestate property owner. (3)(a) Any share assigned to a living descendant of the intestate property owner goes to that living descendant of the intestate property owner. (3)(b) Any share assigned to a predeceased descendant of the intestate property owner who left issue that survived the intestate property owner passes by representation to the descendants of the predeceased descendant. (4) In dividing property among those descendants of the predeceased descendant, we essentially repeat steps 1 3 above.

    We apply the above rules to the fact pattern as follows:

    (1) Scott's children—A, B, and C have all predeceased Scott. Therefore, we begin dividing the intestate property into shares at the generation

level that contains Scott's grandchildren—the first generation of Scott's descendants where we find someone alive.

(2) All of the grandchildren survived. There are 7 of them and so they take per capita, or 1/7 each.

14. **The best answer is (c).** The per capita at each generation approach has one major difference from the modern per stirpes approach: Property that is assigned for calculation purposes to an individual who has predeceased the intestate property owner but left issue who survive the intestate property owner is not necessarily distributed to the descendants of the predeceasing individual. Rather, the property is gathered back and brought down to the next generation, where the assignment of shares begins anew. (This should become clearer with an illustration.) Under the per capita at each generation approach, therefore (1) we begin dividing the intestate property into shares at the first generation level below the intestate decedent where we find a living descendant. (2) We assign a share to (a) any living descendant in that generation and (b) any predeceased descendant in that generation who left issue who survived the intestate property owner. (3)(a) Any share assigned to a living descendant of the intestate property owner goes to that living descendant of the intestate property owner. (3)(b) Any share assigned to a predeceased descendant of the intestate property owner who left issue that survived the intestate property owner is gathered back up and becomes available for assignment in the next generation according to the same steps 1–3.

    We apply the above rules to the fact pattern as follows:

    (1) Scott's children—A, B, and C—have all predeceased Scott. Therefore, we begin dividing the intestate property into shares at the generation level that contains Scott's grandchildren—the first generation of Scott's descendants where we find someone alive.

    (2) F, H, I, J, and K are living and E and G have predeceased, but left surviving issue. That means we divide into 7 shares. The 5 grandchildren who are alive (F, H, I J, and K) each take 1/7. The remaining estate (2/7) is gathered back and brought down to the next generation where assignment of shares starts anew using the same rules as above, i.e., per capita if they are alive at the next generation.

    (4) As to this final 2/7: In the generation below the grandchildren, we find four people, M, N, O and P who are alive. They will share in this 2/7 of the estate equally and therefore each will receive 1/14 of the estate.

15. This one is hard because it will depend on whether or not the gift to Eric and State U is viewed as a residuary. Since Doug went to the trouble to execute a will, the better argument is that he intended to die testate and therefore this gift to Eric and State U is intended to dispose of all of his property. That makes the gift appear to be a residuary gift instead of two separate gifts of a portion of his estate, although there is some case law to support this latter characterization. Assuming the gift is in a residuary clause, **the best answer is (b).** When Eric predeceases Doug, Eric's

devise lapses. The anti-lapse statute does not apply to the devise to Eric because Eric is not among Doug's issue and, therefore, he does not fit within the relationships the statute sets out between the testator and the devisee in order for the anti-lapse statute to apply. The devise to Eric (and to State U) is a residuary devise. (A residuary devise is a devise of what is left over after all of the specific, general, and demonstrative gifts are paid. In the hypothetical, there are no specific, general, or demonstrative devises.) At common law, there was no residue of a residue. This meant that, a residuary devise that lapsed passed by intestacy. The hypothetical provides, however, that the jurisdiction has abolished the no-residue-of-a-residue rule. The effect is that a lapsed residuary gift will pass to and be divided among the remaining residuary devisees, if any. State U is the only other residuary devisee. State U, therefore, takes the 90% of the residuary devised to Eric as well as the 10% of the residuary devised to it.

On the other hand, it seems likely that Doug's intent would be to benefit his children over State U. One could argue that a gift of 10%, coupled with a gift of 90%, is not a true residuary. The California Probate Code provides that for purposes of determining whether or not there is a lapse in the residuary, "a transfer of 'all my estate' or words of similar import is a residuary gift for purposes of this section." 10% and 90% are not such words.

16. **The best answer is (a).** In general, one may disclaim an inheritance to avoid having one's creditors seize the property. Under the "relation-back" doctrine, the theory is that disclaimer relates back to the time of the decedent's death. Thus, the theory goes, the property passes directly from the decedent to the person or persons who take as a consequence of the disclaimer. For the purposes of creditor's rights, it is as though the person disclaiming predeceased the decedent. There is one creditor who can reach the disclaimed property and that is the federal government, provided a valid tax lien is in effect. See *Drye v. United States*, 528 U.S. 49 (1999) (holding disclaimer does not defeat federal tax liens). But as a general matter, all other creditor claims will be defeated. An heir or devisee also may disclaim to avoid adverse estate and gift tax consequences. A disclaimer allows the heir or devisee to, in effect, give the property to another without incurring gift tax liability or, at the subsequent death of the person disclaiming, estate tax liability for the estate of the person disclaiming. **Answers (b), (c), and (d) are not correct.** In general, one may not disclaim to avoid ineligibility for public assistance. One who qualifies for public assistance or seeks to qualify for public assistance may still disclaim. The state, however, will impute the property to the person disclaiming for the purposes of determining that person's eligibility for public assistance.

17. **The best answer is (a).** The traditional approach to delegation is reflected in the non-delegation doctrine. Under this doctrine, the trustee must not delegate duties that the trustee reasonably can be expected to perform himself. As a general rule, this approach forbids the trustee from delegating discretionary duties. Discretionary duties are those that

require the exercise of judgment. The investment function certainly is a discretionary duty. The Uniform Prudent Investor Act abrogates the nondelegation doctrine. Under the modern rule (also as reflected in the Restatement (Third) of Trusts), the trustee may delegate investment decisions. In fact, under the modern approach, the trustee has a duty to delegate investment decisions under some circumstances. The trustee must exercise care in the selection of the agent to whom he is delegating, must instruct the agent with respect to the trust's investment objectives, and must monitor the agent's actions. **Answers (b) and (c) are not correct.** The traditional approach to evaluating the trustee's investment decisions looked at each investment in isolation from others. Moreover, the traditional law forbade the trustee from investing in "speculative" investments even if an individual investment that was "speculative" in isolation reduced the risk of the investment portfolio when evaluated in the context of the entire portfolio. In contrast, the modern approach evaluates the investment portfolio as a whole rather than evaluating each investment in isolation. Relatedly, the Uniform Prudent Investor Act also abandons the view that the trustee must avoid "speculative" investments. A "speculative" investment may be entirely proper when viewed in the context of the entire portfolio. **Answer (d) is not correct.** Today, all states have adopted the prudent investor rule and all but a handful of states follow the Uniform Prudent Investor Act.

18. **The best answer is (b).** A provision in a will that purports to devise property to a devisee who shall hold the property as trustee, but which fails to specify the beneficiary of the trust or important terms of the trust is a semi-secret trust. In most American jurisdictions, a semi-secret trust fails (because the terms of trust are unknown from the terms of the will and not in compliance with the requirements for the execution of a will) and a resulting trust arises by operation of law channeling the property back to the testator's estate to pass to the testator's residuary devisees or (as in the case of a residuary clause that sets out the semi-secret trust) to the decedent's intestate heirs. Here the semi-secret trust was in the residuary, so Frank holds the property in a resulting trust for the benefit of intestate heirs. In some jurisdictions, in the case of a semi-secret trust, the court will impose a constructive trust in favor of the intended (but not named in the will) beneficiaries.

19. **The best answer is (a).** A reversion is the interest that is created in the transferor (or, perhaps more precisely, retained by the transferor) when he transfers an estate that is less than the estate that he had at the time of the transfer. A reversion can only be created in the transferor. A reversion can never be created in a transferee. (A transferee, however, might come to own a reversion that previously arose in the transferor.) **Answers (b), (c), and (d) are not correct.** Vested remainders, contingent remainders, and executory interests are future interests that can only be created in a transferee.

20. **The best answer is (a).** At the time of the original grant Ben was given a vested remainder subject to divestment. The condition that could have

divested Ben was Ben's death without issue surviving him. Issue did in fact survive him (i.e., Seth) and so he is not divested. He is, however, dead, and so we have to figure out where his vested interest went. It went to Ben's estate. Thus, answer (a) is correct.

Answer (b) is not the best answer. There is no language giving Seth anything. Seth might inherit from Ben's estate, but there is nothing in the stated facts that tells you that is the case. Therefore, option A is preferable since answer (b) might not be true. You might think that Seth was an intended beneficiary of this gift because the gift to Ben was conditioned on his being survived by issue. Could there perhaps be an implied gift to Seth in the event Ben is survived by issue—or more correctly an implied gift to Ben's issue? The implied gift argument is certainly worth making on behalf of Seth if Ben's estate is going to someone other than Seth. Common law courts, however, are more likely to opt in favor of the preference for construing language to create vested remainders, in which case answer (a) remains the better answer.

Answer (c) is incorrect because there is no longer any divesting event. Carol had an executory interest at the time of the original transfer from Ollie, but now she has nothing because the condition precedent to her ability to take will never happen. We know that the minute Ben dies survived by issue. **Answer (d) is incorrect** because Carol does not and never did have a contingent remainder. She had an executory interest which is extinguished at Ben's death.

21. **The best answer is (a).** This is a gift of a future interest, but the gift is not in trust. UPC 2–707 creates an implied condition of survival only when the future interest is in trust. If UPC 2–707 had applied, then both answers (b) and (c) would have been true. But since there is no implied condition of survival, **answers (b) and (c) are incorrect.** The remainder interest in Ben is vested and it stays vested since Ben died survived by issue. Thus, **answer (d) is incorrect** because the gift did not fail and there is nothing to fall into the residuary.

22. **Answer (c) is the best answer. Answer (d) is not the best answer** because it is not clear from these facts that Linda did enough to constitute an intentional and felonious killing. She does provide him with the means of ending his life and with full knowledge that he is likely to use the pills for this purpose, but her state of mind may fall short of the "intent" requirement for intentional and felonious killing. In fact, Ben may not win at all on his argument since this looks like a mercy killing and the law is currently unsettled on the level of culpability for someone like Linda. But, if Ben is to succeed, he will need one of the four arguments outlined. So, the point is to pick the best one. **Answer (c) is the best answer** because, even if Linda is not criminally liable, Ben can argue that what she did was "wrong." This characterization could trigger the equitable principle that a person should not benefit from his or her own wrongdoing. **Answer (a) is not correct** because Ben doesn't own any interest in Brent's estate. There is nothing in the eyes of the law that is "rightfully" his. **Answer (b) is plausible, but it is not the best answer** because the facts do not

provide enough information to conclude that Brent (solely because of his terminal illness) lacked testamentary capacity. Testamentary capacity is a low level of competence and presumably if he had the wherewithal to understand his fate, ask Linda for her help, and administer to himself a lethal dose, he was sufficiently conscious of his surroundings and of who his relatives and friends were to meet the level of capacity required to execute a will.

23. **The best answer is (a).** No one is under an affirmative obligation to offer the will for probate unless requested to do so by an interested person. See UPC 2–516. Failure to probate does not create a transfer for gift tax purposes. The property simply passes by intestacy to the heirs. Since Mary has no part in *directing* who those heirs are, she is not making a transfer. Thus, **answer (b) is incorrect. Answer (c) is also incorrect** because, absent a request by an interested party, there is no responsibility to probate. The estate can be administered without a will. **Answer (d) is incorrect.** This answer may appear to be correct because UPC 1–201 includes creditors as "interested persons." But that section also says that the meaning of "interested person" may vary depending on the circumstances. Case law generally holds that a person is not interested for purposes of forcing probate of the will unless he or she has an interest that might be lost for failure to probate the will. Arthur's estate is liable to his creditors whether the will is probated or not. Administration of the estate can occur without probate of the will. That is, intestate estates are often administered and, in cases where there are creditors, ought to be administered because that will normally provide a shorter period of limitations to creditors. If the estate is not administered, then the distributees of the deceased (in this case, the intestate heirs) take the property subject to creditors claims. See UPC 3–901.

24. **The best answer is (c).** Under UPC 2–102, the spouse receives the entire estate only if all of Harold's surviving descendants (Kate, Kim, and Ronald) are also descendants of Elizabeth (or if no descendants or parents survive). Since Ronald is not a descendant of Elizabeth, she does not qualify under 2–102(1) as the sole taker. Thus, **answer (d) is wrong.** Under subparagraph (2) of UPC 2–102, she takes the first $300,000 only if Harold has no surviving descendants. Since he clearly has surviving descendants, **answer (a) is wrong.** Under subparagraph (3) of UPC 2–102, she takes the first $225,000 only if all of Harold's descendants are also her descendants (which they are not) and so **answer (b) is wrong. Answer (c) is correct** because even though Ronald is not her descendant, the surviving spouse is always entitled to the first $150,000. These dollar amounts were included in the 2008 revisions to the UPC to account for inflation that had occurred since the original adoption of the UPC. Today, there is a separate provision, which if adopted by a state, would automatically increase the dollar amount based on the increase in the CPI index. See UPC 1–109. But the question assumes that there have been no such adjustments.

25. **The best answer is (b).** UPC § 2–101(b) specifically authorizes a "negative will" such as this one. If Ned survives Thomas, the effect of this negative will is to treat Ned as though he disclaimed his share of the estate. **Option (a) might work.** A good way to disinherit an intestate heir is to leave a valid will that gives all the testator's property to someone else. The facts state this is a valid will. If Sarah and Susan survive Thomas, they will take. But if they predecease Thomas, the gift will lapse and if they do not have issue to take as substitutes, then Thomas will die at least partially intestate and Ned will take his intestate share. **Option (c) could work** as well. But under the UPC the sisters would have to survive Thomas in order to take and thus option (c) runs the same risk as option (a). The gift to the sisters could lapse if they fail to survive. **Option (d) might work** as well, but Thomas would have to put all his future property holdings into joint tenancy as well. That might be hard to do. For example, if Thomas died before collecting his last paycheck, that claim would be a debt owed to him and his estate and not a joint tenancy piece of property. **After comparing all the options, answer (b) seems the most certain.** Even if Thomas does die intestate, Ned cannot take. If there are no other heirs, the estate will escheat to the state rather than pass to Ned.

EXAM II
ANSWER KEY AND EXPLANATIONS

1. **The best answer is (d).** Section 505(a)(2) of the Uniform Trust Code provides that "[w]ith respect to an irrevocable trust, a creditor or assignee of the settlor may reach the maximum amount that can be distributed to or for the settlor's benefit." This is in accordance with the traditional rule. The rule applies regardless of whether the trust contains a spendthrift provision. **Answer (b)**, therefore, is not correct. Moreover, the comment to Section 505(a)(2) of the Uniform Trust Code explains that "[i]f the trustee has discretion to distribute the entire income and principal to the settlor, the effect of this subsection is to place the settlor's creditors in the same position as if the trust had not been created." **Answer (c)**, therefore, is not correct.

2. **The best answer is (d).** Ademption by extinction is the nullification of a bequest because the item devised is not found in the testator's estate at his death. Ademption by extinction applies only to specific gifts. There are two approaches to ademption. Under the identity theory of ademption, a gift of a specific item is adeemed if it cannot be found in the testator's estate at his death. In general, under the identity theory, whether or not the testator intended to adeem the gift, in theory, is not relevant. Under the intent theory of ademption, a gift of a specific item that cannot be found in the testator's estate at his death is adeemed only if the testator intended for the gift to be adeemed. UPC § 2–606 adopts an intent theory of ademption.

   The question asks you to assume a jurisdiction that has adopted UPC § 2–606. Under the intent theory of ademption adopted by § 2–606, in theory, the gift to Susan will be adeemed if T intended to adeem the gift when he sold the house at 1307 W. James St. And the gift to Susan will not be adeemed if T did not intend to adeem the gift when he sold the house at 1307 W. James St. To help courts arrive more times than not at the correct finding with respect to T's intent, the UPC adopts a presumption against ademption when "replacement" property for the specifically devised property is found in T's estate at his death. Here the newly acquired property at 11 Shawnee Lane appears to be replacement property because it is being used for the same purpose, a primary residence. Alternatively, the UPC would adopt a presumption in favor of ademption when no replacement property for the specifically devised property is found in T's estate at T's death. See UPC § 2–606(a)(5)(6) and comment. Replacement property is property that is a "mere change in form" from the specifically devised property. Ask yourself whether the property in question serves the same function as the specifically devised property. If so, it likely is replacement property. In the hypothetical, the house at 11 Shawnee Lane serves the same function as the specifically devised house at 1307 W. James St. It is the testator's residence. It would seem to be a "mere change in form" from the specifically devised house. Thus, it likely is replacement property. Under § 2–606(a)(5), a devisee of a specific gift is entitled to "any real property or tangible personal property owned by the testator at death which the testator acquired as a replacement for specifically devised real property or tangible personal property." Susan presumptively is entitled, therefore, to the house at 11 Shawnee Lane.

Answer (b) is not the best answer. UPC § 2–606(a)(6) adopts a mild presumption in favor of ademption when the specific property devised is not found in T's estate at T's death and also there is no replacement property for the specifically devised property found in T's estate at T's death. If there were no replacement property in the hypothetical, then there would be a mild presumption in favor of ademption and Susan presumptively would be entitled to nothing. But the house at 11 Shawnee Lane is replacement property for the house at 1307 W. James St. UPC § 2–606(a)(6), therefore, is not applicable. The answer might be different if the testator had purchased the Shawnee Lane property as rental property rather than as a personal residence for himself.

Answer (c) is not the best answer. UPC § 2–606(a)(6) provides that where there is no replacement property, and certain other provisions [UPC § 2–606(a)(1) through (a)(4)] are not applicable, and where the claimant has overcome the mild presumption in favor of ademption arising because there is no replacement property, a specific devisee is entitled to "a pecuniary devise equal to the value as of its date of disposition of other specifically devised property disposed of during the testator's lifetime." If there were no replacement property in the hypothetical, therefore, Susan might be entitled to the value of the house at 1307 W. James St. at the time it was sold. But the house at 11 Shawnee Lane is replacement property for the house at 1307 W. James St. UPC § 2–606(a)(6), therefore, is not applicable.

3. **The best answer is (c).** Abatement is the reduction of a testamentary gift in order to satisfy an estate obligation of a higher priority. For example, testamentary gifts may be subject to abatement so that the estate can satisfy obligations to creditors. If there is not enough property in the estate to pay all of the creditors and satisfy all of the testamentary gifts, some or all of the testamentary gifts will be subject to abatement. In general, the order in which testamentary gifts abate is determined by the classification of the gifts. A common order of abatement is—first, residuary gifts abate; second, if necessary, general gifts abate; third, if necessary, specific gifts abate. Within a class, generally gifts abate pro rata. Gifts to certain devisees, however, might be given a preferred order of abatement. For example, a general gift to a relative might abate only after all general gifts to non-relatives have fully abated, or a gift to a spouse might abate last regardless of the class of gift.

The gift of "$100,000 to A, to be paid from the sale of my home, or from other sources if the sale is insufficient" is a demonstrative gift. A demonstrative gift is a gift of a type or quantity of property (here—$100,000) to be paid out of a specified asset in the estate (here—the testator's home) if that specified asset is available and sufficient to satisfy the gift, and to be paid out of general assets of the estate if that specified asset is not available and sufficient to satisfy the gift. Demonstrative gifts abate with specific gifts to the extent that the specified asset identified in the gift is available to satisfy the gift, and they abate with general gifts for amounts beyond that. In the hypothetical, the specified asset identified in the gift—the home—is available and sufficient to satisfy the gift. The home sold for $500,000. These proceeds are more than sufficient to pay the $100,000 gift. Therefore, if A's gift is subject to abatement, it will abate with the specific gifts. See generally UPC § 3–902.

4. **The best answer is (d).** An irrevocable trust created prior to the marriage is not subject to the elective share, even if the decedent spouse was the life beneficiary. See UPC § 2–205 (not including within the augmented estate an irrevocable trust created prior to the marriage). The other types of property listed would be included within the UPC's augmented estate. Property passing from the decedent to one other than the surviving spouse by a payable-on-death account would be included under UPC § 2–205(1)(C). Property passing from the decedent to the surviving spouse by means of an inter vivos revocable trust would be included under UPC § 2–206(3). Certain inter vivos transfers from the surviving spouse within two years of the decedent's death would be included under UPC § 2–207(a)(2).

5. **The best answer is (c).** When applied, the doctrine of republication by codicil brings the date of execution of the will up to the date of execution of the codicil. Thus, if the doctrine is applied on the facts of the hypothetical, the date of the will (executed in Year 1) will, in effect, become Year 3. The doctrine of republication by codicil should be applied only to a validly executed will and only if doing so will carry out the intent of the testator. The court should apply the doctrine on the facts of this hypothetical, therefore, only if it believes that T would not have wanted child C to take a portion of his estate as a pretermitted heir. This is so because the effect of applying the doctrine in this case would be to destroy child C's status as a pretermitted heir under the statute of this jurisdiction.

   A pretermitted heir statute is intended to protect a child from unintentional disinheritance. When the statute applies, typically, the pretermitted child receives the share of his parent's estate that he would have received had his parent died intestate. It should be noted, however, that there are many variations across jurisdictions on how to determine what portion of the estate the pretermitted child will receive. Most pretermitted heir statutes apply only to a child of the testator born after execution of the will. (Other pretermitted heir statutes protect any child of the testator from unintentional disinheritance regardless of when the child was born.) The theory behind such a statute is that the testator who has a child after execution of the will but does not then revise the will to provide for the child probably overlooked the fact that his extant will did not provide for his child born after execution of the will. The statute, in essence, fixes this mistake for the testator by providing the pretermitted child with a share of the estate.

To answer this question, you must keep in mind that, indeed, applying the doctrine, will disinherit C. A "no" answer would allow C to take his pretermitted share (typically his intestate share). Based on the facts of the question, you might conclude that most testators would prefer for their afterborn children to take instead of the testator's mother. And you are probably right about that. But that option was not available. There are two "no" options. **Answer (b)** says "no but only if Maude agrees." Maude's opinion is irrelevant. It is T's intent that matters. If T intended C to take instead of Maude then the court should not apply the republication doctrine *period* (i.e., no matter what Maude thinks). The other "no" option is **Answer (d).** But if T intended to disinherit C, then not applying the doctrine would do the *opposite*: it would give C a share of the estate. And **answer (a)** is wrong (or at least not the *best* answer) because having no other children still leaves open the question of whether or not T intended to disinherit C. The court should apply the doctrine of republication by codicil in this case only if T would have wanted to disinherit C. That makes **answer (c) the best answer.**

6. **The best answer is (d).** To create a trust, a settlor must have the intention to create a trust, he must place property in the trust, he must name a beneficiary, and the trust must have a trustee. One person may serve as the settlor, the trustee, and the beneficiary. **Therefore, answer (b) is incorrect.** Where the settlor is also the trustee, there need not be delivery of the property from the settlor to the trust. **Therefore, answer (c) is incorrect.** To be valid, however, the trust must have at least one beneficiary who is not also the sole trustee. The justification for this rule is that the trustee must owe duties to someone other than himself so that there is some beneficiary who can insist that the trustee perform his duties as trustee. **Answer (a) is incorrect** because the trust is not valid. It would be valid if the Settlor had named a subsequent beneficiary to take at his death. This is the way most revocable inter vivos trusts are structured. Since there is no other beneficiary, **answer (d) is the best answer.**

7. **The best answer is (d).** Ultimately, this is a question of T's intent. If the court concludes that T intended for his will to be effective only if he did not return from this trip to the jungle, then the court should not probate the will. But it is likely that T spoke of his trip to the jungle only because this event prompted him to consider his mortality and that prompted him to execute a will. If there is no evidence that T would want his estate to be distributed as set forth in his will only if he died in the jungle, but would want his estate to be distributed in a different manner if he returned from the jungle, then the court should ignore the conditional language in order to give effect to T's true testamentary intent. The

seminal case of *Eaton v. Brown,* 193 U.S. 411 (1904), is in accord with this reasoning.

8. **The best answer is (a).** First, the power is an inter vivos power of appointment. The donor of the power did not specify when the holder of the power could exercise it. Since the holder's authority with respect to a power is presumptively unlimited, the holder can exercise it at any time unless the donor says otherwise when he creates the power. Therefore, Daniel can exercise this power at any time. An inter vivos power is one that can be exercised during the life of the holder of the power. It might also be exercisable by the donee's last will, but so long as it is exercisable during the life of the donee as well, it is an inter vivos power. A testamentary power is one that is exercisable only by the donee's last will. The fact that a power is created by a testator's will is irrelevant to its classification. Since Daniel can exercise the power during his lifetime (as the donee of the power did not limit when Daniel could exercise the power), the power is an inter vivos power. Even though Daniel can exercise the power by his will, the power is not testamentary since it is not a power that can be exercised only by will. Moreover, the fact that Testator created this power in his will does not make this a testamentary power. Since this is not a testamentary power, **answers (b) and (c) are not correct.**

   Second, the power is a general power of appointment. A general power of appointment is one that includes within the class of permissible appointees at least one of the following: the donee, the donee's creditors, the donee's estate, or the creditors of the donee's estate. In contrast, a non-general (special) power of appointment does not include within the class of permissible appointees the donee, the donee's creditors, the donee's estate, or the creditors of the donee's estate. In the hypothetical, Testator gave Daniel the power to appoint "to such person or persons as Donee shall appoint." Daniel may appoint to himself, his creditors, his estate or the creditors of his estate. Therefore, Daniel holds a general power of appointment. Since this is not a non-general (special) power, **answer (d) is not correct.**

9. **The best answer is (c).** An heir is free to disclaim her inheritance (as is a devisee). Generally, today the law treats one who disclaims her inheritance (whether an heir or a devisee) as having predeceased the decedent (at least for purposes of distributing the disclaimed property). But this approach gives rise to issues of potential unfairness under both a modern per stirpes intestacy approach and a per capita at each generation intestacy approach. The UPC has modified its approach to calculation of the intestate share in cases of disclaimer to address these issues of potential unfairness. To see both the problem of potential unfairness and the UPC solution to the problem, it is helpful to begin by doing the intestacy calculation as though the disclaimant had not disclaimed.

   Under the per capita at each generation approach, (1) we begin dividing the intestate property into shares at the first generation level below the intestate decedent where we find a living descendant (2) We assign a share to (a) any living descendant in that generation and (b) any predeceased descendant in that generation who left issue who survived the intestate property owner. (3)(a) Any share assigned to a living descendant of the intestate property owner goes to that living descendant of the intestate property owner. (3)(b) Any share assigned to a predeceased descendant of the intestate property owner who left issue that survived the intestate property owner is gathered back up and becomes available for assignment in the next generation according to the same steps 1–3. We apply the above rules to the fact pattern in the question as follows: B is alive and is in the first generation below the intestate decedent. We begin dividing the intestate property, therefore, at that first generation below the intestate decedent. We assign 1/2 the property to B (who is alive) and 1/2 the property to A (who has predeceased the intestate decedent but left issue who survive the intestate decedent). B takes her 1/2. A's 1/2 is gathered back up and carried to the next generation. At that generation, A's three children are alive and will split his 1/2. Thus, E, F, and G each will take 1/6 of the intestate estate. C is alive in that generation as well, but he is not eligible to take because he has a living ancestor (B) who is also a descendant of the intestate decedent. In sum, absent B's disclaiming, B will take 1/2 of the property, and E, F, and G each will take 1/6 of the property.

If B disclaims and we treat her as having predeceased the intestate decedent, the calculation would change as follows: No one remains alive at the generation level immediately below the intestate decedent. In the next generation, E, F, G, and C all survive. We begin dividing the intestate property, therefore, at the generation level that contains E, F, G, and C. Each takes 1/4 of the intestate property.

The issue of unfairness is now apparent. By disclaiming, B has cost her branch of the family 1/4 of the intestate estate. (If B does not disclaim, she takes 1/2 of the intestate estate; if B does disclaim, her child takes only 1/4 of the intestate estate.) The issue of unfairness sometimes runs the other way in that the disclaimant's act of disclaiming increases the portion of the estate passing to his branch of the family. (To see an example of this, assume that A had survived the intestate decedent but disclaimed, and B did not survive the intestate decedent. The result of A's disclaimer would be to increase the portion of the intestate estate passing to his side of the family from 1/2 to 3/4.)

UPC § 2–1106(b)(3)(B) & (C) remedies this issue of unfairness. This section provides that only the disclaimed property is affected by the disclaimer. Moreover, where the disclaimed property would have passed by representation to the disclaimant's descendants had the disclaimant actually predeceased the intestate decedent, that disclaimed property passes only to the descendants of the disclaimant. A helpful way to apply this provision is to calculate the intestate distribution as though the disclaimant had not disclaimed, and then pass the disclaimant's portion of the intestate estate (that is, the disclaimed property) to his descendants by representation.

Applying this provision to the hypothetical, had B not disclaimed, she would have taken 1/2 of the intestate estate (see the calculation above). Only the property B would have taken but for the disclaimer is affected by the disclaimer. B's disclaimed property passes to her child C. Thus, C takes 1/2 of the intestate property and E, F, and G split the other half of the intestate property. Notice that under UPC § 2–1106(3)(B) & (C), B's disclaimer does not affect the amount of property which passes to her branch of the family (or to A's branch of the family).

10. **The best answer is (c).** Under the Revised Uniform Simultaneous Death Act, one must survive a property owner by at least 120 hours (five days) in order to take from that property owner by intestacy or by will (unless the will provides a different rule). Otherwise, we treat the survivor (who survives the decedent by less than five days) as having predeceased the property owner. Carol failed to survive Mike by five days. We treat her, therefore, as having predeceased Mike for the purposes of interpreting Mike's will and distributing his estate. Mike's will expressly provides that if Carol fails to survive him, Greg, Peter, and Bobby take his estate.

11. **The best answer is (c).** Section 502(a) of the Uniform Trust Code, in accordance with the traditional rule, provides that "[a] spendthrift provision is valid only if it restrains both voluntary and involuntary transfer of a beneficiary's interest." If a beneficiary's interest is subject to a valid spendthrift provision, the beneficiary may not assign his interest in the trust, and his creditors may not attach his interest prior to the beneficiary receiving the distribution from the trust. (Certain "exception creditors," such as a child owed child support by the beneficiary, might be able to attach the beneficiary's interest despite an otherwise valid spendthrift provision.)

12. **The best answer is (c).** That the transaction was fair and reasonable is not alone a defense to self-dealing. Self-dealing in the context of a trust occurs when the trustee buys property from the trust in his personal capacity or sells property to the trust in his personal capacity. In a case of self-dealing, most courts will apply the "no-further-inquiry" rule. Under the no-further-inquiry rule, the court only asks whether the trustee engaged in self-dealing; the court does not inquire into the fairness or reasonableness of the transaction. If the court finds that the trustee has engaged in self-dealing, the court may set aside the transaction and order the trustee to disgorge any profits regardless of whether the transaction was fair to the beneficiaries at the time of the transaction. There are, however, three defenses to self-dealing. Those defenses are set out in answers (a), (b), and (d). The first defense is that the settlor authorized the self-dealing, and the transaction was fair and reasonable. The second defense is that the beneficiaries consented to the self-dealing after full disclosure, and the transaction was fair and reasonable. The third defense is that the court approved the transaction before-hand. **Answers (a), (b), and (d), therefore, are not correct.**

13. **The best answer is (a).** Under the doctrine of incorporation by reference as it existed at common law, a document that has not been executed with the formalities for the execution of a will can be given testamentary effect under a will provided that (1) the document was in existence at the execution of the will, (2) the will manifests the testator's intention to incorporate the document into the will, and (3) the will sufficiently identifies the document to be incorporated. Technically, the document that is being incorporated by reference does not become a part of the will. The memorandum entry with respect to Ginny did not exist at the execution of the will. The common law doctrine of incorporation by reference alone, therefore, will not validate the devise to Ginny. In conjunction with the doctrine of republication by codicil, however, the devise to Ginny should be given effect. When applied, the doctrine of republication by codicil re-executes an earlier will and brings the date of execution of the earlier will up to the date of execution of the codicil. The doctrine of republication by codicil is properly applied only to a validly executed prior will and only if doing so will carry out the intent of the testator. Applying the doctrine in this case would carry out the intent of the testator—that Ginny take the home on Di Lido Island. If the date of the will is brought up to the date of the codicil (Year 9), the memorandum entry in favor of Ginny (made in Year 5) was in existence at the execution of the will. Since the will sufficiently identifies the document to be incorporated by reference ("a memorandum that I will title 'Distribution of My Real and Personal Property' ") and sufficiently manifests an intention to incorporate that document into the will ("Certain of my real and personal property shall be distributed to such person or persons as I will designate in a memorandum that I will title 'Distribution of My Real and Personal Property' "), the prerequisites for application of the doctrine of incorporation by reference are satisfied. **Answer (d) is not correct.** Given the effect of the doctrine of republication by codicil, it is not controlling that the memorandum entry in favor of Ginny was not in existence in Year 1 when the will originally was executed.

    Answers (b) and (c) are not correct. Under the common law doctrine of incorporation by reference, the document to be incorporated need not be signed by the testator. Moreover, the common law doctrine of incorporation by reference is not limited to devises of personal property. It is not correct, therefore, to say that the doctrine does not apply to devises of real property. UPC § 2–510 is in accord with the common law doctrine of incorporation by reference. ("A writing in existence when a will is executed may be incorporated by reference if the language of the will manifests this intent and describes the writing sufficiently to permit its identification.") The UPC also has a second incorporation by reference provision: UPC § 2–513 allows for incorporation by reference of a document that was not in existence at the execution of the will. UPC § 2–513 requires, however, that the testator must have signed the document to be incorporated by reference. Moreover, UPC § 2–513 applies only to devises of tangible personal property. On the facts of the hypothetical, however, UPC § 2–513 is not needed since the devise to Ginny can be given effect under the common law doctrine of incorporation by reference in conjunction with the republication by codicil doctrine.

14. **The best answer is (d).** A constructive trust is really not a trust at all in the sense of contemplating an on-going fiduciary relationship between the "constructive trustee" and the beneficiary. Rather, a constructive trust is a remedy a court imposes in order to prevent unjust enrichment, particularly in cases of fraud, duress, or undue influence, which appears to have occurred in this fact situation. Commonly, the court orders as a constructive trust remedy that the holder of certain property transfer the property to another. With no valid will, Anna died intestate and her heirs, her cousins, become owners of her property. They should be ordered to hold the property under a constructive trust that requires them to transfer the legal title to the animal shelter. **Answer (a) is not correct.** Where the donor transfers property and expresses his "desire," "hope," or "wish" (or uses similar precatory language) that the transferee use the property to benefit a third party, the court will have to decide if the donor intended to impose a legal obligation on the transferee to hold the property in trust (in which case a true trust arises), or whether the donor merely intended to impose at most a moral obligation on the transferee. In the latter case, the donor has created a mere "precatory trust." Despite the name, this is no trust at all, as it is not a fiduciary relationship with respect to the property. And while Anna expressed her desire to give her property to the animal shelter she did not express that desire in connection with any actual transfer. **Answer (b) is not correct.** An honorary trust is a trust-like gift that is not intended to benefit the transferee and does not have any specific beneficiary who can enforce the trust as a gift, but has a specific non-charitable purpose. The honorary trust lacks the "for the benefit of another" element of a trust. Honorary trusts are often imposed on gifts for the benefit of animals (there is no actual trust because animals as beneficiaries cannot enforce the trust terms of the trust). Besides, here the intended beneficiary was an organization, presumably tax-exempt, which could own the property and carry out the testator's wishes, according to its own mission. **Answer (c) is not the best answer.** When a trust fails or terminates of its own terms and the settlor has not directed what is then to happen to the property (or the settlor's direction cannot be carried out) a resulting trust arises by operation of law channeling the property back to the settlor (or the settlor's estate). A resulting trust does not involve the on-going management of property or a fiduciary relationship with respect to property. And, as a remedy, it can arise even in the absence of wrongdoing. Here we have wrongdoing by the cousins and a constructive trust is the best way to provide a remedy to counter that wrongdoing.

15. **The best answer is (d).** The testator's "then surviving issue" have a contingent remainder. A remainder is contingent if it is subject to a condition precedent or if it is given to takers who are not ascertained at the time of its creation. The remainder in the problem is contingent either because (with respect to issue alive at the testator's death) it is subject to a condition precedent of survival or because (with respect to unborn issue

at the time of the testator's death) it is given to unascertained persons. In sum, it is contingent because we cannot presently ascertain who will qualify as "then surviving issue" until the death of the last of Kevin, Brian and Danny to die. The testator's estate retains a reversion. The reversion will become possessory if no issue of the testator survive Kevin, Brian, and Danny. The reversion will be divested (all reversions are vested) if issue of the testator survive Kevin, Brian, and Danny.

16. **The best answer is (c).** As a general rule, joint tenancy real assets cannot be reached by creditors after death because the deceased joint tenant's property interest ceases at his death. See UPC § 6–102. A creditor can always reach whatever interest the debtor owns in the property before death. Thus, before death, Bob's creditors could have pressed their claims and caused a partition of the joint tenancy (because Bob himself had the right to partition as a joint tenant). In that case, the creditor would have been able to reach 50% of the joint tenancy property to satisfy the claim. However, after death, Bob owns nothing. His estate owns nothing. So, there is nothing for a creditor to attach. Thus, **answer (a) is incorrect. Answer (b) is incorrect** because these are creditors of Bob, not of Ellen. Thus, they have no right to pursue her property to pay off Bob's debt. In a community property state, creditors might be able to reach community assets for payment of a community debt, but this fact situation does not occur in a community property state. In some states, a spouse could be held liable for a deceased spouse's debts provided the debt was for certain expenditures such as living expenses or necessaries. But this loan was made for Bob to pay off a gambling debt, a debt that was his own, not his wife's. Nor did Bob engage in a fraudulent transfer as to Klare since the property was already in joint tenancy when Klare made the loan. **Thus answer (d) is incorrect.**

    [Note: Rules vary from state to state regarding a creditor's right to reach assets in a joint bank account after the death of a joint tenant. In most states, joint bank accounts are viewed differently from true joint tenancies because the depositor usually has the right to withdraw the funds up until the moment of death. Thus, they more closely resemble revocable transfers, which creditors can usually reach. The general rule under the UPC is that the funds of the depositor are presumed to belong to the depositor even after they are deposited in a joint bank account. So, Klare might have been able to reach funds in a joint bank account had Bob created the account with his own funds.]

17. **The best answer is (b).** A lawyer does have an affirmative obligation to acquire relevant facts about a client's family and assets before giving estate planning advice, but it is unlikely that a court would expect a lawyer to do an independent investigation of a client's claims about family status. If Larry Lawyer asked Ted about his family and Ted declined to mention his wife, then Larry should be justified in relying on Ted's representations. **Answer (a) is not correct** because a spouse can waive a right to an elective share under UPC 2–213. The waiver may not be effective if it fails to comply with the provisions of 2–213. Nonetheless, a

spouse CAN waive the right. **Answer (c) would be correct in some states, since a minority of states still require privity.** The growing trend is to allow claims of malpractice by disappointed beneficiaries despite the lack of privity between them and the lawyer who drafted the will so long as the testator's intent to benefit the disappointed beneficiary is made clear to the lawyer. Here the testator's intent to benefit Pam was clear. So she has standing. **Answer (d) is incorrect** because it is not against public policy to leave property to a paramour. Ever since *Marvin v. Marvin* was handed down by the California Supreme Court in 1976, holding that contracts between paramours could be enforced and were not against public policy, so long as they were not contracts providing for payment of sexual services, almost every other state has upheld the *Marvin* principle. While wills are not contracts, provisions in wills have sometimes been struck down on the basis of public policy. Nonetheless, the *Marvin* principle that contractual transfers to paramours are not against public policy should extend to testamentary transfers such as the one in this problem.

18. **The best answer is (a).** UPC 2–102 gives everything to the surviving spouse if "all of the decedent's surviving descendants are also descendants of the surviving spouse and there is no other descendant of the surviving spouse who survives the decedent." The question is whether or not Ronald, who was adopted by Elizabeth, is a descendant of Elizabeth. UPC 2–118(a) provides that "[a] parent-child relationship exists between an adoptee and the adoptee's adoptive parent." Thus, Ronald is Elizabeth's child and Elizabeth meets the requirement of being the parent of all of Harold's children. She will inherit the entire estate no matter what its size.

19. **The best answer is (b).** An attorney-in-fact has the power to disclaim under the UPC provision and under similar provisions in most states. Thus, **answer (a) is incorrect.** Disclaimers do not avoid estate taxes in the estate of the testator. Rather they avoid gift taxes that otherwise be imposed on the beneficiary. If Evelyn, the beneficiary, accepted the bequest and then gave it to Evan the property would be the subject of two transfers, one at Testator's death which is subject to the estate tax (and perhaps the generation skipping tax) and a second one which is a gift from Evelyn to Evan and is subject to the gift tax. The disclaimer creates a single transfer from Testator to Evan and thus avoids the gift tax. **Answer (c) is incorrect** because the disclaimer does not avoid estate taxes. **Answer (d) is incorrect.** If Evelyn is still at the nursing home when her insurance runs out, she will presumably be entitled to Medicaid. So, **option (d)** raises the issue of Medicaid coverage. While Medicaid may not be able to access the disclaimed funds, it can count the disclaimer as a transfer from Evelyn which is subject to Medicaid lookback rules. Thus, the disclaimer may affect her eligibility for Medicaid. That makes **option (d)** untrue. Evan has the power to disclaim, but he should realize it may affect Evelyn's right to uninterrupted nursing home care and he should be prepared to cover any costs that arise during the applicable lookback period (typically five years).

20. **The best answer is (b).** There are a handful of reported cases in which testators have ordered their executors to destroy a certain piece of property. The majority rule is that destruction of a house is against public policy so long as the house is in good condition and there is no reason to destroy it other than the whim of the testator. **Answers (c) and (d) are incorrect.** Arguments are sometimes made that since the testator could have destroyed the house during his lifetime he ought to have that right at death. But courts hold that the right to destroy the property ends at death. The harm to the beneficiaries and the neighbors is more important as a matter of policy than the carrying out of the direction to destroy. This is true even though American law recognizes a strong policy in freedom of testation. The public policy interest in maintaining valuable property for the benefit of the living is likely to trump the policy in favor of freedom of testation where the direction to destroy was included merely to satisfy a whim of the testator. Finally, so long as Bill and the executor agree that the property should not be destroyed, no one has standing to enforce the request. Thus, **answer (a) is incorrect.** Litigation is not possible is no one has standing to bring the case to court.

21. **The best answer is (d).** A videotape is not a writing and a holographic will must be in writing to be effective as a will. Thus **answer (a) is wrong.** A nuncupative will is an oral will, but nuncupative wills statutes require that the will be made in the last sickness of the decedent. Here, Frank died two years later. In addition, nuncupative wills require witnesses and here there were none. Thus **answer (b) is wrong. Answer (c) is also wrong.** The harmless error statutes only apply to wills in writing and this is not a will in writing.

22. **The best answer is (b).** The statute is clear. The divorce revokes the gift and distributes it as though Lon were dead. In that event, Ted takes. If she really wanted Lon to take despite the divorce, she'd have to include that language in a testamentary instrument. Remaining friends is not sufficient to overcome the statute. Thus, **answer (a) is incorrect.** While the UPC revokes gifts to the relatives of the ex-spouse, this state's statute is silent as to that matter. Thus, only Lon's gift is revoked and **answer (c) is incorrect. Answer (d) is also incorrect** because the statute is sufficient to provide a "constructive" death. The property is to be distributed as though Lon had predeceased and the will provides that, in that case, the property goes to Ted.

23. **The best answer is (d).** Historically, a person had little to no control over the disposition of his own body after death. **Option (a) will not work** because the body is not property that can be willed to anyone. **Option (b) will not work** because a power of attorney is revoked upon the death of the principal. A durable power of attorney can survive the principal's disability, but it still is revoked upon Van's death. **Option (c) will not work** because living wills are merely directives to physicians to restrain from resuscitation where appropriate. They have nothing to do with burial arrangements or cremation. In some states (e.g., California and Illinois) a durable power of attorney for health care will include a

provision that allows the attorney in fact to make disposition of body decisions. But these documents are not called living wills. Also, a number of states have adopted power of attorney statutes that specifically provide for the attorney in fact to make decisions regarding disposition of the body. But, again, these documents are not called living wills.

24. **The best answer is (d).** Answer (d) is false because Zoe does have a basis for claiming part of the estate. She can claim as a putative spouse. Whether she will get a distribution or not depends on the state law regarding putative spouses and their inheritance rights, but she at least has a basis for a claim. The facts in this problem are based on the facts in *Reed v. Campbell*, a Texas case in which the nonmarital child claimed a share in the estate but under state law was prevented from inheriting because nonmarital children could only inherit from their fathers if their parents subsequently married. See 476 U.S. 852 (1986). The statute was struck down on the basis of equal protection, thereby allowing the child of Prince Ricker to proceed with her claim. By analogy, Clarissa should inherit in this fact situation as a child of Prince. Thus, **answer (c) is true. Answer (a) is wrong** because it is true that Minnie will be considered the only legal spouse of Prince. **Answer (b) is wrong** because it is true that Clarissa will be considered a nonmarital child since her parents' marriage is not legal.

25. **The best answer is (b).** The rule applied to omitted spouses is based on the assumption that most testators favor their spouses in their testamentary plans. In the absence of a rule that revokes a will upon marriage, a premarital will remains valid and can prevent the surviving spouse from getting anything. The omitted spouse statute creates the same result with respect to a spouse as a rule that revokes a premarital will upon marriage. A surviving spouse who married the testator after the will was executed will be entitled to a spousal intestate share under either rule. In turn, the spousal intestate share, which can amount to 100%, is crafted to reflect the distribution scheme that most testators favor. Thus, the omitted spouse statute is justified on grounds that it is most likely to carry out testator's intent. The purpose of the elective share statute, by contrast, is to protect a spouse who has been disinherited by the testator. The limit to one-third of the estate may not seem fair in cases of a long-term marriage. That is why the UPC has adopted a sliding scale, under which the share available to the electing spouse increases in amount with the age of the marriage. Some states, however, still embrace the old dower-driven elective share which typically gives the surviving spouse a one-third interest. **Answer (a) is incorrect** because, even though the one-third elective share can be traced to dower, that is not a sufficient explanation for why the two provisions are different. **Answer (c) is incorrect** because frequency of use should have nothing to do with the size of the spousal share in the two statutes. **Answer (d) is incorrect** because the difference does matter to a surviving spouse who does not qualify as an omitted spouse as that spouse can only claim an elective share. In other words, the spouse does not always have an election. If she

or he is disinherited, the only claim is to an elective share unless the will was executed before the marriage.

EXAM III
ANSWER KEY AND EXPLANATIONS

1. **The best answer is (c).** The elective share percentage is employed to implement the marital-sharing theory that grounds the UPC's elective share. The marital-sharing theory holds that the surviving spouse is entitled to end up with one-half of the marital property accumulated during the marriage, even if the deceased spouse held title to the property and did not name the surviving spouse in the will. To carry this out, UPC 2–202 gives the surviving spouse an elective share equal to 50% of the marital property.

   To determine the amount of marital property, one first calculates the amount of the "augmented estate."

   > The augmented estate includes the couple's combined assets, not merely the value of the assets nominally titled in the decedent's name. The application of the "elective-share percentage" to the "augmented estate" yields the "elective-share amount"—the amount to which the surviving spouse is entitled. Inclusion in the "augmented estate" of the couple's combined assets is absolutely essential for the system to implement a marital-sharing theory. If the elective-share percentage were to be applied only to the decedent's assets, a surviving spouse who has already been overcompensated because of the manner that the couple's marital assets have been nominally titled would receive a further windfall under the elective-share system.

   Lawrence W. Waggoner, The Multiple-Marriage Society and Spousal Rights Under the Revised Uniform Probate Code, 76 Iowa L. Rev. 223, 248 (1991).

   Next, UPC 2–203 assumes that the portion of the augmented estate that is marital property is likely to depend on the length of the marriage. According to the table in 2–203, the portion of the augmented estate that is presumed to be marital property is 30%. Since the surviving spouse is entitled to half of that amount, that spouse can claim 15% of the augmented estate.

2. **The best answer is (a).** To create a trust, a settlor/testator need not use the word "trust" or "trustee." But the settlor/testator must manifest an intent that one person hold the property for the benefit of another. The testator in the hypothetical has not stated clearly an intention that Susan hold the property in trust for the benefit of Jeff. Rather, the testator has used words of desire but not words of direction. The testator has created a "precatory trust." Despite the name, this is no trust at all. Susan may have a moral obligation to use the profits from the ranch to benefit brother

Jeff, but she does not have a legally enforceable obligation to do so. Susan owns the ranch outright.

3. **The best answer is (a).** The UPC's harmless error principle (UPC § 2–503) provides that a document may be probated as T's will if there is clear and convincing evidence that T intended the document to be his will. Note that the UPC does not dispense with the formalities for execution of a will. Rather, the UPC maintains formalities for execution of the will as a safe harbor for those who comply, yet adopts the harmless error principle so that a document might still be probated as a will even if the testator failed to comply with the specified formalities, provided that the court is convinced by clear and convincing evidence that the testator intended the document to be his will.

4. **The best answer is (b).** The *Claflin* doctrine (named after the leading case of *Claflin v. Claflin*, 149 Mass 19, 20 N.E. 545 (1889)), which is followed in most American jurisdictions, provides that the beneficiaries of a trust may modify or terminate the trust provided that all of the beneficiaries consent to the modification or termination of the trust (and are capable of doing so), and such modification or termination of the trust will not defeat a material purpose of the settlor. The question asks you to assume that all of the beneficiaries have consented to early termination of the trust. The issue, therefore, is which of these trusts has a material purpose of the settlor that would be defeated by early termination of the trust. In general, a spendthrift trust, a discretionary trust, a support trust, and a postponement-of-enjoyment trust all are considered to have a material purpose of the settlor that would be defeated by early termination. A mere successive interest trust (also known as a bypass trust) generally is thought not to have a material purpose of the settlor that would be defeated by early termination.

   Trust 1 is a support trust: The amount of income that is paid to A is measured by A's need for support. Trust 2 is a postponement-of-enjoyment trust: The settlor likely postponed Son's access to the principal until age 35 because the settlor felt that Son should have a certain level of maturity before he enjoyed the freedom to control this property. Trust 5 is a spendthrift trust: A's interest is not assignable and is not attachable by his creditors. The settlor's purpose in setting up a spendthrift trust generally is thought to be to protect the beneficiary from his own ineptitude at financial management. Trusts 1, 2, and 5 each have a material purpose that would be defeated by the beneficiaries' early termination of the trust. Each is not destructible, therefore, under the *Claflin* doctrine.

   Trust 3 is a mere successive interest trust. Trust 4 also is a mere successive interest trust. Trust 4 is not a support trust regardless of the language "to be used for A's support" because, under the terms of the trust, A receives all of the income, not just an amount of the income measured by his need for support. Mere successive interest trusts are destructible under the *Claflin* doctrine.

5. **The best answer is (c).** Steven holds a power that he can exercise at any time and that he can exercise to benefit himself. Therefore, a court likely will enforce his contract to exercise the power in the future in favor of Harriet's children even if the contract also benefits Steven. When the holder of a power that is not presently exercisable (for example, a testamentary power) contracts to exercise the power, a court will not enforce the contract. The best reasoning supporting this approach is that the donor of the power intended for the holder of the power to be able to change his mind about who to benefit by exercise of the power up until the time that the power becomes exercisable. For example, the donor of a testamentary power (a power that is exercisable only by the will of the holder of the power) intended for the holder of the power to be able to change his mind about who to benefit by exercise of the power up until the time of the holder's death. To enforce a contract in which the holder of a testamentary power has agreed to exercise the power in a certain manner, therefore, would defeat the intent of the donor of the power. If Steven held a power that was not presently exercisable, therefore, a court would not enforce the contract. In the hypothetical, however, Steven holds an inter vivos power of appointment, which is presently exercisable. For this reason, **answer (a) is not the best answer.**

   In cases in which a general power is not presently exercisable (usually because it is a testamentary power), some courts will enforce a contract to release the power, even though they would not enforce a contract to exercise the power. When the holder of a power contracts to release the power, he agrees not to exercise the power and to allow the appointive property to pass to the takers in default. The power in the hypothetical, however, is an inter vivos power and is most likely presently exercisable. **Answer (b), therefore, is not the best answer.**

   Moreover, a holder of a special power commits "fraud on the power" when he exercises the power to benefit someone who is not an object of the power. When the holder of the power contracts to exercise the power, he presumably receives consideration for agreeing to exercise the power in a certain way. Thus, the holder benefits himself by contracting to exercise the power. If the power is a special power, by definition, the holder may not benefit himself, his creditors, his estate, or the creditors of his estate. Therefore, when the holder of a special power contracts to exercise the power in favor of someone who is not an object of the power, he commits a "fraud on the power." In the hypothetical, however, Steven holds a general power of appointment. By definition, Steven is an object of the power. It is not an obstacle to enforcement of the contract, therefore, that Steven benefits when he contracts to exercise the power. For this reason, **answer (d) is not the best answer.**

6. **The best answer is (d).** Benny is not entitled to anything under T's will. **Answer (c) is not the best answer.** T's crossing out of the $50,000 gift is a sufficient partial revocation by physical act (the physical act is cancellation) such that the gift is revoked, provided that T had the intent to revoke the gift when he performed the physical act. The question asks

that you assume that this jurisdiction does not apply the doctrine of dependent relative revocation. Therefore, that doctrine is not available to undo the partial revocation pursuant to the legal fiction that T did not have the intent to revoke when he performed the act of cancellation on the will. The $50,000 gift, therefore, should be held to be revoked. **Answer (b) is not the best answer.** The handwritten notation—"$60,000"—would not be a valid holographic codicil to the typed will even though T signed and dated the notation. A typed attested will can have a holographic codicil. But a holographic will (and a codicil is a species of will) is not valid unless, at a minimum, the material provisions of the will are in T's handwriting. (In a minority of jurisdictions that recognize holographic wills, the entire will must be in T's handwriting for the will to be valid as a holographic will.) At a minimum, the names of the beneficiaries and the property they are to receive under the will are material provisions. The name of "Benny" is typed in the document in question. Therefore, the material provisions of the attempted holographic codicil are not all in T's handwriting, and the purported codicil is not valid. The net result is that Benny is devised $0 under the will.

7. **The best answer is (b).** Benny is entitled to $60,000. To be clear, the handwritten notation—"$60,000"—would not be valid as a duly executed holographic codicil to the typed will even though T signed and dated the notation. A typed attested will can have a holographic codicil. But a holographic will (and a codicil is a species of will) is not valid in a strict compliance jurisdiction unless, at a minimum, the material provisions of the will are in T's handwriting. (In a minority of jurisdictions that recognize holographic wills, the entire will must be in T's handwriting for the will to be valid as a holographic will.) At a minimum, the names of the beneficiaries and the property they are to receive under the will are material provisions. The name of "Benny" is typed in the document in question. Therefore, the material provisions of the attempted holographic codicil are not all in T's handwriting, and the purported codicil is not valid as a duly executed holographic will.

   Under the harmless error principle (see UPC § 2–503), however, a document that has not been executed with the formalities prescribed in a jurisdiction for execution of a will may nonetheless be probated as a will if the court finds that there is clear and convincing evidence that the testator intended the document to be his will. The UPC harmless error principle applies equally to written attested wills and holographic wills. The hypothetical arguably presents clear and convincing evidence that T intended by crossing out the "$50,000" figure and writing in its place "$60,000 for Benny to receive $60,000 under his will. Thus, in short, Benny is entitled to $60,000 under the will because there is clear and convincing evidence that T intended for Benny to take $60,000 at his death pursuant to the document which he intended to be his will.

   Because the harmless error principle is available in this jurisdiction to give effect to T's intent, the doctrine of dependent relative revocation (which can be used to give effect to T's second preference when he has made a mistake of fact or law which precludes a court from recognizing his first preference) is not relevant on the facts of the hypothetical.

8. **The best answer is (c).** First, Bennie will not receive the $60,000 gift that T attempted to leave him under the purported codicil. **Answer (b), therefore, is not the best answer.** The handwritten notation—"$60,000"—would not be a valid as a holographic codicil to the typed will even though T signed and dated the notation. A typed attested will can have a holographic codicil. But a holographic will (and a codicil is a species of will) is not valid unless, at a minimum, the material provisions of the will are in T's handwriting. (In a minority of jurisdictions that recognize holographic wills, the entire will must be in T's handwriting for the will to be valid as a holographic will.) At a minimum, the names of the beneficiaries and the property they are to receive under the will are material provisions. The name of "Benny" is typed in the document in question. Therefore, the material provisions of the attempted holographic codicil are not all in T's handwriting, and the purported codicil is not valid.

   Second, the $50,000 gift to Bennie will be revoked, and Bennie will get nothing, unless the revocation can be "undone" pursuant to the doctrine of dependent relative revocation. T's crossing out of the $50,000 gift is a sufficient partial revocation by physical act (the physical act is cancellation) such that the gift is revoked, provided that T had the intent to revoke the gift when he performed the physical act. The doctrine of dependent relative revocation (DRR), however, may negate T's intent to revoke.

   For a testator to revoke a will, he must (1) have the intent to revoke the will and (2) while he has that intent to revoke, he must either execute a subsequent will revoking the earlier will or perform a sufficient physical act upon the will he wishes to revoke. The doctrine of dependent relative revocation works to negate the first element (T's intent to revoke) in certain cases where the court concludes that such negation actually would promote T's intent. The doctrine of DRR provides that where T purports to revoke a will while laboring under a mistake of fact or law, the court will disregard the revocation if T would have preferred that result had he known the truth about the mistake he was making. For example, as set out in the hypothetical, if T purports to revoke a will while mistakenly believing that he simultaneously is executing a new will (or, as in this case, a codicil), the court will disregard the revocation (by concluding that T did not really have the intent to revoke) if the court concludes that T would not have revoked the earlier will had he known that the subsequent will he was attempting to execute would not be valid. The intent to revoke is "dependent" or "conditional" on the new holographic will being valid. If the condition is not satisfied then the intent is not effective.

   On the facts of the hypothetical, DRR should be applied to undo the revocation of the $50,000 gift to Bennie. It seems clear that T's intent to revoke the $50,000 gift to Bennie was premised on his mistaken belief that his notation "$60,000" would be effective to devise Bennie an even larger gift. If DRR is not applied, Bennie will receive nothing. As T wanted to leave Bennie $60,000 but failed to properly execute the codicil, T certainly would prefer that Bennie receive $50,000 rather than nothing. Therefore, the court should conclude that T's intent to revoke the $50,000 was premised on a mistake of law (believing that the new codicil would be effective) and under the doctrine of DRR should be negated. Without the intent to revoke, the physical act (the cancellation) is of no effect. Bennie, therefore, should receive $50,000.

9. **The best answer is (c).** As a preliminary matter, whenever dealing with the issue of potential advancements, the first issue to address is whether there is sufficient evidence that the intestate property owner intended for a lifetime gift to be an advancement of an heir's intestate share. The question, however, asks you to assume that the lifetime gifts listed qualify as advancements. The only issue then is to calculate how the advancements affect the intestate shares of the heirs (that is, to calculate the "hotchpot").

   In calculating how one or more advancements affects the intestate distribution: (1) add the value of the advancements (generally, calculate the value of each advancement as of the time the donee came to enjoy the advancement) to the value of the net intestate estate; (2) calculate an intestate distribution as though the intestate estate were valued at that figure arrived at in Step 1; and (3) subtract each heir's advancement from the amount they otherwise would take under step 2 to arrive at that heir's intestate share. Applying these rules to the facts of the hypothetical: First, we add the $150,000 (home), $100,000 (boat), and $25,000 (car) advancements to the $800,000 net probate estate. We get a total figure of $1,075,000. We divide this figure by five (the number of children who, putting advancements aside, would split the intestate estate equally—each taking 1/5) and arrive at a preliminary intestate share of $215,000 each. Because E and F did not receive an advancement during D's lifetime, E and F will each take $215,000. To calculate the final intestate share of each of the other children, we must subtract that child's advancement from this figure. Doing that, we arrive at $65,000 for A ($215,000 - $150,000); $115,000 for B ($215,000 - $100,000); and $109,000 for C ($215,000 - $25,000).

   Notice that if you have done the calculation correctly, the total value of the intestate shares should add up to the value of the actual net intestate estate. Note also that if an heir's advancement is larger than his preliminary intestate share, he does not have to repay the estate for any amount of the advancement, but he gets no portion of the intestate estate. In that case, we ignore that heir (and his advancement) when re-calculating the hotchpot.

10. **The best answer is (b).** The facts in the question support a claim of fraud in the inducement. In contrast, fraud in the execution exists where a person intentionally makes a misrepresentation concerning the content or character of a document that is intended to and does in fact cause the testator to believe that the document is that which the testator wishes to be his will. For example, if Frank had handed his father a document and

represented that it was the will that the father had asked Frank to prepare, and the father signed it, that would constitute fraud in the inducement, if, in fact, the document was not the will the father had wanted. **Answer (a), therefore, is not correct.**

11. **The best answer is (b).** The law of the marital domicile at the time that property is acquired determines the characterization of that property as separate or community. While some experts have advised married couples domiciled outside of Alaska to create Alaskan trusts of personal property in order to have the trust property classified as community, the general rule is that the marital domicile will determine the character of personal property acquired during marriage. Thus, B is clearly the best answer. **Answer (a) is not correct.** Even if the property is placed in a trust or a bank account outside of the marital domicile, the domicile generally controls the title. **Answers (c) and (d) are not correct.** In general, the law of the decedent's domicile at death provides the choice of law rules with respect to the survivor's right, if any, to an elective share. And it is the domicile at death that generally determines who inherits under intestacy.

12. **The best answer is (c).** A provision in a will that purports to devise property to a devisee who shall hold the property as trustee, but which fails to specify the beneficiary of the trust is a semi-secret trust. **Answer (a) is not correct.** An honorary trust is a trust-like gift that is usually intended to benefit some cause (e.g., the care of the transferor's pet cat), but does not have an identifiable beneficiary who can enforce the trust. Care of the transferor's cat is not a charitable purpose, because the purpose is private. But such gifts are sometimes enforced as honorary trusts. **Answer (b) is not correct.** A secret trust exists when a will purports to make an absolute gift, but there is an undisclosed agreement between T and the legatee that the latter will hold the property in trust for another. This differs from a semi-secret trust in that, in the case of a secret trust, the face of the will does not reveal that the testator/settlor intended to make a gift in trust. **Answer (d) is not correct.** To create a trust, a settlor must manifest an intent that one person hold the property for the benefit of another. Where the donor transfers property and expresses his "desire," "hope," or "wish" (or uses similar precatory language) that the transferee use the property to benefit a third party, the court will have to decide if the donor intended to impose a legal obligation on the transferee to hold the property in trust (in which case a true trust arises), or whether the donor merely intended to impose at most a moral obligation on the transferee. In the latter case, the donor has created a mere "precatory trust." Despite the name, this is no trust at all.

13. **The best answer is (a).** A person's heirs are those who would take that person's property in intestacy if the person died intestate. In general, we determine a person's heirs at that person's death. Thus, ordinarily we would determine the testator's heirs at the testator's death. **Nonetheless, (b) is not the best answer.** That is because the question involves a rule of construction, not a rule of law. What did Testator mean when he said,

"to Elizabeth for life and then to my heirs?" The will speaks at Testator's death. If Elizabeth is his only heir (as she appears to be from the facts stated), then the devise is to Elizabeth for life, then to Elizabeth. This result appears incongruous. See Restatement (Second) of Property: Donative Transfers § 29.1 through § 29.5. While the general rule is that a gift over to Testator's heirs is to be construed as a gift to the heirs of Testator determined as of Testator's death, evidence of a contrary intent, will change this result. The issue is whether or not the incongruous result of devising to the same person a life estate and a vested remainder is sufficient evidence of a contrary intent. The Restatement (Second), cited above, adopts the position that the incongruity is sufficient evidence. The rationale is that the testator likely did not intend for Elizabeth to be both the life tenant and a taker of the remainder. Most states follow the Restatement principle and thus would determine Testator's heirs as of Elizabeth's death in order to avoid the incongruity. Some states adopt the Restatement position only if Elizabeth is the only heir and some adopt it if Elizabeth is merely one of the heirs. Based on the statement in the question that Elizabeth is his only child, she is likely his only heir. A few states may construe the language to mean "Testator's heirs, other than Elizabeth, determined at his death." But since that option was not offered in this question, that position is irrelevant to the answer. **Option (a) is the best answer** because many states have a statute that requires this result. See UPC Section 2–711 for an example of applicable statutes. In states without a statute, it is the preferred result under both the Restatement (Second) cited above and in the Restatement (Third) Property: Wills and Other Donative Transfers at § 16.1 (gift over to T's heirs means heirs of T at time of distribution rather than at T's death).

14. **The best answer is (d).** See UPC § 3–312. All of Jerry's assets pass outside of probate except for the $30,000 of stock and personal items. Since most of the property passes outside of probate, she will not need to initiate a formal administration to clear up title to most of the property. **Thus, option (a) is incorrect.** While Samantha may be able to claim ownership of the personal items solely because of possession, she will need to take some action to transfer title of the Rockwell stock from Jerry to her. **Thus, option (c) is incorrect.** She cannot use the affidavit process because the value of the estate, even after accounting for debts, exceeds $25,000. See UPC § 3–1201. **Thus, option (b) is incorrect.** In some states this process is available for estates larger than $25,000. But as a general rule, the availability of an affidavit process in lieu of administration would not require that there be no minor children. As a result, **option (b) is still incorrect.**

15. **The best answer is (a).** There is no sufficient evidence to prove whether Larry survived Jane and so the statute says that his property will be distributed as if he did survive her. And since he named Esther as the beneficiary upon his death, Esther should take. For Jane (or Jane's estate) to take as beneficiary under the policy she would have to survive Larry because beneficiaries must survive in order to take. **Thus, answer (b) is incorrect.** Similarly, **answer (c)** is incorrect. Mildred can only inherit

through Jane, but Jane did not survive long enough. Since Jane did not survive, the contingent beneficiary provision kicks in and gives the insurance proceeds to Esther. If Larry had not named a contingent beneficiary, the proceeds would have gone to his estate (option (d)). But **option (d) is incorrect** because he did name a contingent beneficiary.

16. **The best answer is (a).** The trust creates a contingent interest in Lawrence's heirs. The only contingency is that Dorothy die without any surviving issue. That contingency occurs at Dorothy's death and vests the heirs or their distributees at that time. Lawrence's heir, i.e., the person who would have inherited as his intestate heir if had died intestate, is his brother Benjamin. This would be true under the UPC intestacy scheme and the scheme of states generally. Some states provide for stepchildren to inherit, but typically not before siblings and their issue. Heirs are determined as of the moment of death and as of the Lawrence's death, his only heir was Benjamin. Benjamin's contingent interest was not destroyed by his death. Instead, it passed under his will to his wife, Millie. Thus, at Dorothy's death, Millie becomes vested and takes the full trust corpus. Note that a different result would occur under the UPC. Under UPC § 2–711 or a similar statute requiring that any gift over to heirs goes to the heirs determined at the time of Dorothy's death. The question also assumes there is no modern case law, which might change the traditional common law rule. The traditional common law rule is that Lawrence's heir, Benjamin, had a contingent interest, but contingent only upon Dorothy dying without surviving issue.

17. **The best answer is (d).** UPC § 2–711 provides that a gift over to heirs such as the remainder in Lawrence's trust should be distributed to "those persons, including the state, and in such shares as would succeed to the designated individual's intestate estate under the intestate succession law of the designated individual's domicile if the designated individual died when the disposition is to take effect in possession or enjoyment." The gift in the trust was to "my heirs" and so Lawrence is the designated individual. The persons who would take as his heirs if he had died at the time the trust ended (i.e., at Dorothy's death) are the children of his deceased brother Benjamin. Luke is the only child and so he is the person who will take the remainder interest.

18. **The best answer is (d).** UPC § 2–804 revokes all testamentary gifts to an ex-spouse and to the ex-spouse's relatives. Thus the will cannot give property to either Willa or Stella. The property passes as if the spouse and all her relatives disclaimed. That leaves no one to take the property so the property escheats to the state. UPC § 2–804 applies to any revocable gift in favor of an ex-spouse. Life insurance beneficiaries can be changed by the owner. That makes it a revocable gift. Thus 2–804 applies to life insurance and so the gift of the life insurance proceeds to Willa is revoked as well. Since none of her relatives can take either, the life insurance proceeds go to the estate and escheat to the state along with the rest of the probate estate.

19. **The best answer is (d),** all of the above. The problem is that the description of the property is not very specific. Had Truman said, "I give Annie the Ansel Adams photograph located in my desk drawer," there would be no problem. But the word "contents" is not very specific. The contents of a desk drawer probably often change without Truman giving much thought to his actions. That makes desk drawers different from safety deposit boxes, which do have independent significance. **Thus, answer (c) is certainly a viable argument,** because it distinguishes desk drawers from safety deposit boxes. (There is case law supporting gifts of contents of a safety deposit box.) Also, there are no testamentary formalities (e.g., witnesses) to the act of putting things in the desk drawer. **Thus, answer (b) is also a good argument.** Finally, we allow changes that occur after the execution of a will to affect its meaning, but we generally require that those changes constitute acts of independent significance. The act of storing a valuable photograph in a drawer may be significant but it doesn't stand on its own—so it isn't ***independently*** significant. In fact, most people do not store valuable photographs in their desk drawers. If Truman had a photography gallery and was constantly changing what was hanging there, one might argue that hanging an Ansel Adams photograph on the wall of the gallery was an act of independent significance. In any event, the argument outlined in **answer (a) is certainly viable in this case. Thus (d) is the best answer.**

20. **The best answer is (c).** Trustees generally do not have standing to contest a will and it would certainly make no sense for a trustee named under the will to contest the will that names him (or her). If the trustee did not like the terms of the trust in the will, the trustee could resign and a successor trustee would be named. As a rule, trustees do not have a sufficient enough interest in the estate to allow them to challenge the will. **Answer (a) is clearly wrong** since adopted children are heirs and heirs can challenge. **Answer (b) is incorrect** because any beneficiary in an earlier will, contingent or otherwise, can argue that harm will result if the current will revoking that earlier will is admitted to probate. **Answer (d) is incorrect.** The testator's divorced spouse has no intestate interest in the estate and so challenging the will would not produce any benefit to her. Besides she is claiming that her sister should have been included in the will. She makes that claim on the basis of an alleged contract. If she can prove that the contract is valid, she will have a contract claim that she can assert against the estate. But that is not a "contest" of the will. It is a claim against the estate just like all other claims, e.g., claims by creditors of the estate.

21. **The best answer is (d),** the state of M. When Will predeceases Betsy, the gift to him lapses. His estate cannot take. **Thus, answer (a) is incorrect.** The antilapse statute, UPC § 2–603, would save the gift for Will's son, Darwin, if Will had been related to Betsy as required by the statute. He would have to be a grandparent or descendant of a grandparent of Betsy or, alternatively, a stepchild of Betsy. He isn't, and **so answer (b) is wrong.** As a result, Betsy died intestate. Her closest relative is Colin, a grandchild of Betsy's mother's great aunt, Sarah. Sarah

and Colin are descended **not** from Betsy's grandparents, but from her great-grandparents, who would have been the parents of great aunt, Sarah. The UPC intestacy statutes stop at descendants of grandparents. More remote relatives, such as Colin, are not heirs. UPC § 2–103. Thus, **answer (c) is wrong.** The property escheats and goes to the state of M.

22. **The best answer is (d).** The conveyance is irrevocable and so the interests are fixed upon delivery of the deed. Ellen has a vested life estate and a contingent remainder should she survive Harvey. If she does in fact survive him, she is certain to get the property. **Answer (a) is wrong** because Harvey can unilaterally sever the joint tenancy thereby destroying the survivorship right. A unilateral severance can occur without Ellen's knowledge (e.g., Harvey transfers his interest in the property to his brother). The severance will convert the title into a tenancy in common. **Answer (b) is wrong** because the tenancy in common gives her only a 50% interest in the property and although the will leaves her the other 50% interest, a will can be revoked or amended at any time. The tenancy by the entirety is a better option than the first two options because there is no possible unilateral severance. Still, the tenancy will be revoked upon divorce since it is only available for married couples. Upon divorce the tenancy would convert to a tenancy in common. Thus, **answer (c) is not the best answer.**

23. **The best answer is (a).** While there is no doubt that Decedent is the genetic father according to these facts, the amendment of the Probate Code as late as 2005 means that the legislature must have had cases of conception after death in mind when they drafted this language. By 2005, at least three states had reported cases involving the question of whether or not a child conceived after death could be an intestate heir. Several states have adopted statutes providing for inheritance in such cases provided there was written consent before death on the part of the Decedent. Several states, however, have rejected the possibility by amending their probate codes to provide that such children, conceived after death, will not inherit unless they are named in a will. The statute of State G, modeled on a Georgia statute, presents two problems: (1) It requires that the child be conceived before death, which was not the case, and (2) It requires that the child be born within 10 months of the decedent's death, which is not likely to occur since impregnation did not occur until 6 months after death.

    Some courts have been willing to construe language that appears to limit afterborn heirs to those conceived before the father's death liberally so as to include afterborns conceived after death. A liberal construction is in keeping with legislative intent to include afterborn heirs generally and is possible in cases in which the legislation was enacted long ago before legislators knew anything about new reproductive technologies. But in this case, with an enactment date of 2005, this afterborn child would have a very difficult time asking a probate court to construe the statute in a way that totally ignores its plain meaning.

Could the afterborn child attack the statute on constitutional grounds? Yes, the child could make an argument that the statute violates equal protection by invidiously discriminating against afterborn children who are conceived after death as compared with those conceived before death. But the state could defend based on its interest in seeing that estates are settled timely and that title to property is determined soon enough to ensure stability. If conception can occur at any time, then estates would have to be held open for lengthy periods of time to ensure that all children conceived post-death could receive an intestate share. Similar arguments were made in cases like *Trimble v. Gordon*, 430 U.S. 762 (1977), which challenged probate statutes that disinherited a father's children if born out of wedlock. The *Trimble* Court recognized the state interest in timeliness and stability, but held that the statute in that case was overbroad because it excluded nonmarital children from inheriting from their fathers even when paternity had been established during the father's lifetime. In similar fashion, a court could apply *Trimble* and hold that the G statute is overbroad in excluding too many after-conceived children. The lines could be redrawn to include a time limit that would sufficiently protect the after-conceived child and the interests of the state. If the statute were struck down on these grounds, then the child could make a claim, but would nonetheless still have to prove that he or she was a child of Decedent. The definition of parent and child, usually contained in the family law statutes, is not included in the facts of this problem. If the woman was inseminated after the death of decedent, it is possible under certain versions of the UPA that the sperm donor will not be considered a parent. He probably will not be considered a parent in any state unless there was some evidence of intent to become a parent. In any event, the question asks what the *Probate Court* is likely to do. The Probate Court is likely to follow the plain meaning of the statute and rule that the afterborn child is not an heir. In many states, the jurisdiction of the Probate Court is limited and so that Court would not have jurisdiction to hear a constitutional challenge to the statute. As a result of all of these considerations, the Probate Court is likely to distribute the full estate to Decedent's mother as his intestate heir.

Answer (b) is incorrect because the UPC intestacy statute recognizes the surviving parent as heir to the exclusion of siblings. **Answer (c) is incorrect** because the child is excluded by the plain meaning of the statute. **Answer (d) is not the best answer** because the child is excluded by the plain meaning of the statute and for the fiancé to take as "guardian," the child would have to be entitled to take. As explained above, under the plain meaning of the statute, the child cannot take.

24. **The best answer is (c).** These facts present a classic purchase money resulting trust hypothetical. Gene provided the money for the purchase and the land was supposed to be his, but record legal title is vested in Frank. A resulting trust acknowledges Frank's legal title, but declares that the beneficial interest is vested in Gene. If all Frank owns is legal title and no beneficial interest, the property should not be part of his probate estate and Rose has no claim to it. **Answer (a) is wrong** because

record title is only prima facie evidence of ownership. The facts indicate that Gene can rebut Frank's ownership by proving that he (Gene) provided the funds to purchase the property. **Answer (b) is incorrect** because a constructive trust is an equitable remedy to be used in cases in which a person in Frank's shoes has defrauded Gene or done something wrong. The constructive trust prevents the wrongdoer (or others) from benefiting from the wrong. But here Frank has done nothing wrong. Courts sometimes confuse constructive trust theories and resulting trust theories. Both produce the same end result and give the property to the person who ought to have beneficial ownership. But since you are asked to pick the best answer, the "resulting trust" solution is more accurate than "constructive trust."

Answer (d) is wrong because even though courts often presume gifts in cases such as this where the monetary transfer occurs between family members, there appears to be enough evidence to rebut that presumption here and thus it is unlikely that Rose will win.

25. **The best answer is (c),** the doctrine of integration. The will that is offered for probate is the amended will which includes the revised Article V. The Testator never signed that will. Instead he signed the original will at a time before the revised Article V was included as part of the will. The doctrine of integration requires that all pages of the will be present and together when the testator executes the will. That requirement is not met in this case. **Answer (a) is incorrect** because there is no state that requires the testator to sign each page. Lawyers often ask the testator to initial each page at the time of execution, but that is to prove that all the pages were present and together at the time of execution (i.e., that the doctrine of integration had been satisfied. **Answer (b) is incorrect.** While it is true that an amendment to a will is invalid if there is no testamentary intent as to the amendment, based on the fact of this question, there was in fact testamentary intent. The testator did intend to amend his will. The failure here was not of testamentary intent, but rather the failure of testamentary formalities. The testator did not sign the amendment or have it witnessed. **Answer (d) is not the best answer.** It is true that stock is not tangible property. Therefore, any argument that these gifts of stock are made via a memorandum disposing of tangible property will fail. But the reason that the Charities in the new list take nothing is because of the doctrine of integration. One does not even reach the question of "disposition by memo" unless and until the amendment to the trust has been found invalid under the integration doctrine. Thus, **answer (c) is the best answer.**

EXAM IV
ANSWER KEY AND EXPLANATIONS

1. **The best answer is (b).** When the holder of a power of appointment fails to exercise the power, the property passes to the takers in default, provided that the donor of the power named takers in default. Where the holder of a power of appointment fails to exercise the power and the donor of the power of appointment failed to name takers in default, the rules for passing of the appointive property are as follows: Where the power is a general power, the appointive property passes back to the donor or the donor's estate. Where the power is a special power, a court may imply takers in default if the class of permissible appointees is a defined limited class. In such a case, the appointive property will be divided equally among the implied takers in default. The class of permissible appointees is a defined limited class if the class is not very large and it is easy to identify the permissible appointees and divide the property among them. An example where this would not be the case is where the special power could be exercised in favor of anyone except the donee, the donee's creditors, the donee's estate, and the creditors of the donee's estate. Where the power is a special power, the appointive property passes back to the donor or the donor's estate if the class of permissible appointees is not defined as a limited class.

   In the hypothetical, Harold died intestate. He failed, therefore, to exercise the testamentary power that he held. Gary, the donor of the power of appointment, failed to name takers in default. The power is a special power: The class of permissible appointees does not include the donee, the donee's creditors, the donee's estate, or the creditors of the donee's estate. The class of permissible appointees consists of three identified individuals—Oscar, Oprah, and Andrew. This is an example of a defined, limited class of permissible appointees. A court, therefore, is likely to imply that Oscar, Oprah, and Andrew are the takers in default. The appointive property will pass, therefore, to Oscar, Oprah, and Andrew in equal shares.

   Answer (a) is incorrect. Property subject to a special power of appointment that the holder of the power does not exercise does not pass to the estate of the holder. (Where the holder of a general power of appointment makes an ineffective appointment, as opposed to failing to exercise the appointment, the appointive property might pass to the holder or his estate under a doctrine called "capture" if the donee manifested an intent to assume control of the appointive property for all purposes. The issue is whether the holder would prefer that, given an ineffective exercise, the property pass to her estate or would prefer that the property pass to the takers in default or back to the donor.) Here, since

Harold held a special power of appointment, by definition, he could not exercise the power in favor of his estate. Thus, answer (a) would not make sense at all.

Answer (c) is not correct. An appointee is one in whose favor a power has been exercised. In the hypothetical, Harold did not exercise the power. Therefore, there were no appointees and no class of appointees. Rather, there was a class of permissible appointees.

Answer (d) is not correct because the rule implying default takers can apply to these facts. Had the list of permissible appointees not been a limited, identifiable group, then Harold's failure to appoint would leave Gary's estate with a reversionary interest following Harold's life estate. Therefore, **answer (b)** is the best option.

2. **The best answer is (c).** Abatement is the reduction of a testamentary gift in order to satisfy an estate obligation of a higher priority. For example, testamentary gifts may be subject to abatement so that the estate can satisfy obligations to creditors. If there is not enough property in the estate to pay all of the creditors and satisfy all of the testamentary gifts, some or all of the testamentary gifts will be subject to abatement. In general, the order in which testamentary gifts abate is determined by the classification of the gifts. A common order of abatement is—first, residuary gifts abate; second, if necessary, general gifts abate; third, if necessary, specific gifts abate. Within a class, generally gifts abate pro-rata. Gifts to certain devisees, however, might be given a preferred order of abatement. For example, a general gift to a relative might abate only after all general gifts to non-relatives have fully abated, or a gift to a spouse might abate last regardless of the class of gift.

   The gift of "$100,000 to A, to be paid from the sale of my home, or from other sources if the sale is insufficient" is a demonstrative gift. A demonstrative gift is a gift of a type or quantity of property (here—$100,000) to be paid out of a specified asset in the estate (here—the testator's home) if that specified asset is available and sufficient to satisfy the gift. If the identified fund for payment (the home) is not sufficient, then the gift is to be paid out of general assets of the estate. Demonstrative gifts abate with specific gifts to the extent that the specified asset identified in the gift is available to satisfy the gift. See UPC § 3–902.

   In the hypothetical, the specified asset identified in the gift—the home—is available and is sufficient to satisfy the gift. The home sold for $200,000, which is enough to satisfy a gift of $100,000. Therefore, this gift will abate with specific gifts.

3. **The best answer is (d).** This gift will abate in part with the general gifts and in part with the specific gifts. Demonstrative gifts abate with specific gifts to the extent that the specified asset identified in the gift is available to satisfy the gift, and they abate with general gifts for amounts beyond that. See UPC § 3–902.

   In this hypothetical, the specified asset identified in the gift—the home—is available but is not sufficient to satisfy the gift. The home sold for only

$80,000. These proceeds are not sufficient to pay the $100,000 gift to A. General assets of the estate will be used to pay the $20,000 of the gift in addition to the $80,000 of the gift payable out of the proceeds of the house sale. If the gift to A is subject to abatement, it will abate with the specific gifts to the extent that the specified asset identified in the gift—the house—is available to satisfy the gift, and will abate with general gifts for amounts beyond that. That is—$20,000 of the gift will be treated as a general gift and will abate with the other general gifts; the remaining $80,000 of the gift will be treated as a specific gift and will abate with the other specific gifts.

4. **The best answer is (d).** Under the per capita at each generation approach, we divide at the first generation containing a person who is alive. Classic or strict per stirpes would divide at the first generation containing a descendant who was survived by issue, whether or not there are any descendants then alive at that generation. Modern per stirpes would also divide at the first generation containing a person who is alive, but from there, divisions would be made per stirpes. Therefore, if the deceased (D) is survived by a child and also by two predeceased children who left issue, the modern per stirpes approach would divide at the child level into thirds. Issue of a deceased child (i.e., grandchildren of D) would then share the one-third share of their parent. This could result in grandchildren (all related to D in the same degree) taking different shares. For example, if one predeceased child was survived by one child and another survived by two children. By contrast, the per capita at each generation approach, would group the two-thirds of the estate left after distributing one-third to the surviving child of D and would distribute that two-thirds per capita (i.e., equally) among the three grandchildren.

   A necessary result of this per-capita-at-each-generation calculation is that persons who take a share of the intestate estate will take the same proportion of the estate as others in the same generation as themselves who take a portion of the estate. That is to say—persons who are equally related to the intestate decedent and who take a share of the intestate estate, take the same proportion of the estate.

5. **The best answer is (d).** Section 503 of the Uniform Trust Code provides that an otherwise valid "spendthrift provision is unenforceable against . . . a beneficiary's child, spouse, or former spouse who has a judgment or court order against the beneficiary for support or maintenance." This is in accordance with the rule in many jurisdictions. The Uniform Trust Code does not provide an exception to a valid spendthrift provision for tort judgment creditors. This also would seem to be in accordance with the prevailing rule, although there is not much case law on point.

6. **The best answer is (d).** Section 505(a)(1) of the Uniform Trust Code provides that "[d]uring the lifetime of the settlor, the property of a revocable trust is subject to claims of the settlor's creditors." This is not the traditional rule, but it is the prevailing rule today. Answers (a) and (b) reflect the traditional rule, but do not reflect the Uniform Trust Code position and do not reflect the rule in most American jurisdictions today.

Furthermore, the creditors of a settlor of a revocable trust can reach the trust assets regardless of whether the trust contains a spendthrift provision. Therefore, **answers (a), (b), and (c) are not correct.**

7. **The best answer is (b).** UPC 2–702 requires beneficiaries under a life insurance policy (a governing document) to survive by 120 hours in order to be treated as surviving. Since Jane did not survive Larry by 120 hours, she is deemed to have predeceased him. As a result, the contingent beneficiary provision in the life insurance policy kicks in and the proceeds should be paid to Esther.

8. **The best answer is (a).** Under the UPC, a joint survivorship account cannot be changed by will. The only question, therefore, is whether or not this was a valid joint survivorship account when it was opened. There are cases that hold the form of the account (joint) can be rebutted by evidence that the depositors intended some other form of account, such as an agency account. But there are no facts in this hypothetical to suggest anything other than a true joint account was intended from the beginning. Therefore, since this is a true joint account, the survivor is entitled to all the funds at the death of the joint owner.

9. **The best answer is (d).** Stella did not name her daughter, Donna, as the beneficiary of her own estate for the purpose of making her the beneficiary under Carson's will. She had an independent reason for naming Donna, i.e., to make her the beneficiary of her estate. The gift to Donna is saved under the doctrine of facts (or acts) of independent significance. As a result, you do not have to rely on incorporation by reference. If incorporation by reference were to be the justification for the validity of this gift, the gift would fail because the document mentioned by Carson, Stella's will, was not in existence when Carson executed his will. Thus, **answer (a)** would be correct IF we had to rely on the doctrine of incorporation by reference. But that doctrine is not determinative because the doctrine of facts (acts) of independent significance saves the gift.

10. **The best answer is (a).** At common law, when a specific gift, general gift, or demonstrative gift lapsed, the gift passed to the residuary taker or takers. Answers (b), (c), and (d), therefore, are not correct. At common law, however, there was no residue of a residue. This meant that, a residuary devise that lapsed passed by intestacy.

11. **The best answer is (d).** Under UPC 2–103, the lineal descendants take by representation. UPC 2–106 defines representation to require dividing the estate at the first generational level where there are surviving descendants entitled to take. In this fact situation, that is at the grandchild level, since three of the grandchildren are alive. There are three grandchildren alive and two grandchildren who are predeceased but left issue. That includes William, a child of Joan and Kathy's parent who was a child of Gary's son, Harry. As a result, the estate will be divided at the grandchild level into 5 equal parts. Three parts will be distributed to the three living grandchildren, (1/5 each). The other 2/5 is available to then be distributed equally at the great grandchild level, Kim, Karl, and

Kathy. They each take one-third of that 2/5 portion, which results in 2/15 to each of them. The UPC applies a per capita at each generation approach. That means the grandchildren share equally and anything left over (in this case the 2/5) must be distributed equally among the great grandchild generation.

12. **The best answer is (b).** While many jurisdictions continue to refuse to correct scrivener's errors, this case involves an ambiguity rather than a mistake. Thus, **option (a) is incorrect.** The rule regarding latent ambiguities is that the court will allow extrinsic evidence to help clarify the ambiguity. The clause in Maureen's will contains two latent ambiguities. We don't know the ambiguity concerning the property description until someone points out that she doesn't own 214 Dover Street. That makes **option (d) incorrect** since it describes this ambiguity as a patent one (i.e., ambiguous on the face of the will). And we don't know that the gift to Annie is uncertain until we know that there are three people who claim to be the intended beneficiary. **Option (c) cannot be correct** because the testator's intent was clearly stated: the house was to go to one person named Annie, not three. That leaves **(b) as the best answer** and it is in fact what most courts will do.

13. **The best answer is (b).** In general, the standard for mental capacity to execute a will is thought to be not as high as the standard for mental capacity to deal with one's property during life, at least insofar as irrevocable inter vivos transfers are concerned. One rationale for this distinction is that the property owner who imprudently manages his property interests during life might consequently lack the resources needed for his own support. Lifetime support is not an issue that arises out of a decedent having improvidently executed a will. Given that the standard for mental capacity to manage one's property during life is higher than the standard for mental capacity to execute a will, we cannot conclude from the fact that Marc has been adjudicated incompetent to manage his property that Marc lacks the capacity to execute a will. **Answers (a) and (c), therefore, are not correct. Answer (d) is not correct.** The standard for mental capacity to revoke a will is the same as the standard for mental capacity to execute a will.

14. **The best answer is (c).** The trust creates a future interest in Susan's then living heirs. Susan's heirs, determined at the time of her death, are her two sons, Thomas and Samuel. For either of them to take, two things must happen: (1) Thomas must die with no surviving issue and (2) the heirs must be then living. #1 did occur, but #2 did not. Neither of the heirs was then living. Thus the interest fails and the remainder reverts to Susan's estate. Since the gift was in the residuary clause of her will, this reversionary interest passes via intestacy to Susan's heirs—who only had to survive Susan to become heirs. Susan's heirs were Thomas and Samuel so the trust assets must be divided between their estates. **Answer (a) is incorrect** because Thomas cannot inherit to the exclusion of Samuel. **Answer (b) is incorrect** because Samuel cannot inherit to the exclusion of Thomas. **Answer (d) is also incorrect.** Rachel can't take in her own

right because she was not literally one of Susan's heirs. Her father, Samuel, was alive at Susan's death and his existence prevented Rachel from being an heir. She may ultimately be the distributee of Samuel's estate, but we don't know that. Samuel may have left a will naming someone else as beneficiary. If so, that is the person who will take from Samuel's estate. Similarly, we don't know who will take from Thomas's estate.

15. **The best answer is (b).** While the witnesses can sign after the testator's death, they must sign within a reasonable time. Six months later does not seem reasonable. Both the lawyer and Clara were aware of the fact that the execution of the codicil had not been completed. Clara was sufficiently healthy for a while. There are no facts that suggest it was reasonable for everyone to wait six months to finish the signing ceremony. **Option (a) is wrong** because the witnesses do not have to witness the signing of the codicil for it to be effective. Witnessing her acknowledgement of her signature is sufficient. **Option (c) is wrong.** The lawyer witnessed Clara's acknowledgement and there is nothing to prevent him from being a witness. **Option (d) is wrong** because the witnesses must sign within a reasonable time.

16. **The best answer is (d).** While this is a joint will, all that means is that the single document can be probated twice, once at Hank's death and then again at Wilma's death, if she hasn't revoked it. UPC § 2–514 deals with contracts concerning succession, in which joint and mutual wills are sometimes used in connection with a contract not to revoke. Section 2–514 makes it difficult to prove that there was a contract not to revoke unless the terms of the contract are spelled out in the will. Here, we simply have a joint will and not a contract not to revoke. **Thus option (a), while true, is irrelevant.** The point is that Wilma did not revoke. The will is still available to be probated as her will. This fact situation is no different from a situation in which Hank executes a will leaving everything to Wilma if she survives and if not, to his children, and then Wilma executes a will leaving everything to Hank if he survives, and if not, to her children. Hank dies and his will operates to give everything to Wilma. Then Wilma dies never having revoked her will. It leaves everything she owns to her children. **Option (b) is wrong** because under the UPC the witnesses do not need to witness the signing of the will if they witness instead the acknowledgement of the signature by the testator. **Option (c) is wrong** because UPC § 2–301 does not give anything to a pretermitted spouse if the premarital will leaves all the property to children of the testator. Since Wilma's will leaves everything to the children, Henry gets nothing under this provision. Henry can claim his elective share, however. Under UPC § 2–202, if they were married two years, he can claim 6% of the augmented estate. The children will get the rest. Thus, **the best answer is (d).**

17. **The best answer is (d).** Most states have a slayer rule that will prevent Mary from inheriting from Henry since she is responsible for his death. But before there were slayer statutes, courts formulated an equitable remedy in such cases to prevent a wrongdoer (a slayer) from benefiting

from the wrong (here, the killing). Thus, **answer (a) is not the best answer** since, in the absence of a statute, the state is likely to apply the equitable remedy. **Answer (b) is not the best answer** because, even though ERISA pre-empts state law, there is likely a federal common law rule that would prevent a killer from inheriting in these circumstances. The *Egelhoff* case, decided by the Supreme Court in 2001 (see 532 U.S. 141), held that ERISA pre-empted a state law that revoked upon divorce a life insurance and pension plan benefit in favor of the ex-wife. But the Court stated in dicta that ERISA was not likely to pre-empt the state slayer statute. Cases decided after *Egelhoff* have overwhelmingly held that ERISA does not protect a slayer who is a named beneficiary of the victim's pension plan or related life insurance policy. See, e.g., *Atwater v. Nortel Networks, Inc.*, 388 F. Supp. 2d 610 (M.D.N.C. 2005). **Answer (c) is incorrect** because Mary is only entitled to her half of the community property. She cannot receive Henry's share because of the slayer statute, the equitable doctrine under state law, or because the life insurance is covered by ERISA and federal common law which also adopts an equitable remedy to prevent slayers from benefiting. **Answer (d) is best** because application of the slayer rule would give the assets to the alternative beneficiaries, in this case the children. There is nothing to prevent them from then gifting the assets to their mother.

18. **The best answer is (d).** The questions asks for statements that are *not* true, i.e., that are false. The best way to answer a question like this is to mark each option as true or false. The false options are the correct answers. A survivor can disclaim the joint tenancy property at the death of the first joint tenant. See § 2–1107 UPC. The IRS has in the past questioned whether a disclaimer of the property that comes to the survivor as a result of the survivorship right is valid for tax purposes since the disclaimer must occur within 9 months of the creation of the interest in the property. The argument is that the survivorship right and thus all interests that flow from it are created at the moment the joint tenancy is created. At common law there is no real transfer of anything at the death of the first joint tenant. Instead the surviving joint tenant merely continues to enjoy the same estate as before although now it is enlarged. But current state probate law (as indicated in the UPC) and tax law both recognize the right of the survivor to disclaim the interest that is at least "constructively" being transferred at death. So, if there's a joint tenancy between A and B, presumptively 50/50, and A dies, then B can disclaim the 50% additional share that is constructively transferred to B at the time of A's death. **Thus, answer (a) is false.** But it is not the best answer. **Answer (b) is true.** The primary reason to use a joint tenancy arrangement is to avoid probate. The title passes to the survivor outside of probate. **Since the question asked for untrue answers, answer (b) is wrong.** Answer (c) also contains a non-true (false) statement about joint tenancies. Joint tenancies can be unilaterally severed into tenancies in common. The tenants do not all have to agree. **Thus, answer (c) is false, but it is not the best answer. Answer (d) is best because both (a) and (c) are false** (i.e., not true).

19. **The best answer is (c).** Putting burial instructions in the will is generally a bad idea. Burial often happens before the will is read by the people closest to the decedent. **That makes both options (a) and (d) unattractive. Option (b) is incorrect** because the power of attorney is revoked at her death. That leaves option (c). A present gift in trust would put the beneficiary on notice that if he carried out her wishes, he would be rewarded. If this person is someone who is not even named in the will, the trade off between burying the jewelry and giving it to beneficiaries does not exist. But the sum must be substantial enough to make it worth the person's time to carry out and it must be substantial enough to resist being bought out by the beneficiaries who would otherwise be entitled to the jewelry.

    Instructions like this are often challenged by the heirs or beneficiaries who claim that following the instructions would be against public policy. Here, the instructions require the removal of otherwise valuable property from current benefit or use by people who are still alive and would enjoy such property. Some have argued that burying jewels or other valuable property with the deceased would encourage gravediggers. But in 1977, millionaire heiress Sandra West was buried in a San Antonia cemetery, seated in her baby blue Ferrari. The judge who ordered that the instructions be followed also ordered that the grave containing the Ferrari be buried underneath cement to thwart any would-be gravediggers.

20. **The best answer is (d).** In general, to have standing to challenge a will one must have a direct pecuniary interest in the success of the will contest. That is to say, a successful outcome of the will contest must positively affect how much of the decedent's estate the contestant will take. The rationales for such a rule are first to ensure that one who has standing to challenge a will has an incentive to litigate diligently, and second to limit the number of lawsuits. Mary has standing to challenge the second will because she would take more under the first will if the second will is held invalid. Paul has standing to challenge the second will because he would take 1/3 of the estate by intestacy if the second will is held invalid and the first will also is held invalid, but he will take nothing under the second will. Peter does not have standing to challenge the second will because he will take more under it than if it is held invalid and Father's property passes either under the first will, where he gets nothing, or by intestacy, where he takes one-third.

21. **The best answer is (b).** See § 2–511 UPC, which codifies the Uniform Testamentary Additions to Trusts Act. At common law a problem arose if a Testator left property to a trust that was either created after the execution of the will or was modified after the execution of the will. The common law doctrine of incorporation by reference could validate such gifts only if the trust was in existence at the time the will was signed. Answer (d) looks like it might be correct at common law. But these facts occur in a UPC state. Thus, **answer (d) is incorrect. Answer (a) is incorrect.** The creation of an irrevocable trust funded with $1.0 million should satisfy the "acts of independent significance" doctrine. **Answer (c)**

is incorrect because § 2–511, which has been adopted in most states, applies to trusts created by persons other than the testator.

22. **The best answer is (d).** In 1977 the Supreme Court ruled in *Trimble v. Gordon*, 430 U.S. 762, that a statute that prevented nonmarital children from inheriting from their fathers violated the equal protection clause. One year later, in *Lalli v. Lalli*, 439 U.S. 259 (1978), the Court ruled that a New York statute survived an equal protection challenge when it limited the right of nonmarital children to inherit from their fathers to cases in which paternity had been established during the father's lifetime by a court of competent jurisdiction. *Lalli* would thus seem to bar S's claim. However, *Lalli* can be distinguished because the child in that case, despite having plenty of time to establish paternity, had not done so. S, by contrast has not had a reasonable time in which to establish paternity since the father died before S was born. Even assuming that paternity could be established before birth, the amount of available time to do so was less than 9 months. Cases addressing the constitutionality of limitations on the rights of nonmarital children tend to be very fact sensitive. In cases involving the establishment of paternity for child support payments, the Court has struck down state statutes of limitations in a number of cases, holding that there must be a reasonable amount of time for a child to bring a paternity action. See generally *Clark v. Jeter*, 486 U.S. 108 (1988), striking down a Pennsylvania six year statute and discussing earlier cases that struck down a two year statute (Tennessee) and a one year statute (Texas). While these cases can be distinguished because they involved child support and liability for child support does not generally survive a father's death, they do suggest that each case focusing on a nonmarital child's treatment under state statute must be analyzed on the basis of the particular facts. Furthermore, it can be argued that for children in S's position, who are given no opportunity to seek a paternity order at any time after their birth, they are completely excluded from the right to inherit, which violates equal protection. Despite the fact that *Lalli* can be cited against S, answer D is still the "best" answer. See also *Daniels v. Sullivan*, 979 F.2d 1516 (11th Cir. 1992) (holding that a Georgia intestacy statute requiring proof of paternity during the lifetime of the father was unconstitutional as applied and interpreted by the Social Security Administration because the child was just over two years old at the time of the death of the father and thus did not have a reasonable time to establish paternity before the father's death).

    Answer (a) is wrong because there is no such thing as constructive marriage. Some states recognize common law marriage. But that doctrine only applies to cases in which the couple has agreed to be presently married and is holding themselves out as married. M and F, by contrast, were intending to be married in the future. **Answer (b) is wrong** because no matter how unfair it may be, S will have to establish a legal claim in order to succeed in court. **Answer (c) is wrong** because no one has a fundamental right to inherit. American law allows testators to disinherit their children, even their minor children to whom they owe a duty of support.

23. **The best answer is (c).** It is very difficult to prove abuse of discretion by a trustee, but bad faith, animus toward the beneficiary, and similar improper motives will establish abuse. Here the Trustee is making the decision in order to protect a potential competitor of Tim, which seems a total abuse of discretion since the direction in the trust is to make decisions that are in the best interest of the beneficiaries. If Tim can prove that the Trustee's decision was in fact based on a desire to protect a non-beneficiary of the trust, then the decision will be considered a breach of the duty of loyalty, which in turn is a breach of trust. The remedy for this breach may not be to reverse the decision, but rather to remove the trustee and have a new trustee consider the request. Since Tim is not guaranteed that a different trustee will distribute the requested income, **answer (b) is incorrect. Answer (d) is also incorrect since it includes option (b). Answer (a) is incorrect** because a trustee never has absolute discretion. The discretion must be exercised in good faith.

24. Both **answers (a) and (b) are possible** at common law and so the question is which one is best. **Answer (c) is clearly wrong.** If the doctrine of dependent and relative revocation applies, there is no way it could be used to probate Will #1. Will #1 was revoked by Will #2 unconditionally. Therefore, there is no way that Will #1 can be probated. If the state had a revival statute, it might be applied to "revive" Will #1, but the facts state this is a non-UPC jurisdiction, applying general principles of common law. Revival is only possible under a statute that would change the common law principle of "once revoked always revoked." **Answer (d) is wrong** as well. Or, at the least, it is not best. First there is the question of whether or not a document that revokes a prior will is a valid testamentary document itself. In most states, revocation of an existing will by a document executed with testamentary formalities is sufficient to revoke the existing will. So, yes, the revoking document is a valid testamentary document so long as executed with testamentary formalities, which the facts say you are to assume was the case. Also, while the UPC does validate negative wills by statute, there is insufficient evidence to conclude whether or not other states would or would not recognize a negative will. There just are two few cases to establish any principle.

    A strict application of the common law principle, "once revoked, always revoked," would support option (a). That is because Will #2, if valid, did revoke (always) Will #1 and Will #3 did revoke (always) Will #2. BUT, if dependent and relative revocation did apply, as option (b) assumes, then the Will #2 beneficiaries could argue that Will #2 was revoked on condition and therefore not absolutely revoked. The condition, attached to the intent to revoke Will #2, was that Will #1 be revived. And that is impossible without a revival statute. The facts matter here as well. Will #1, if revived, gave a large gift to friend Anna. That can't happen. But if T dies intestate Anna will get nothing. On the other hand, if Will #2 is probated, Anna will take half of a fairly large residuary gift. These facts are likely sufficient to succeed on an argument that T did not mean to revoke Will #2 if it meant he would die intestate, with nothing for Anna. If dependent and relative revocation is applicable, and option (b) assumes that it is, then yes, Will #2 might be probated. That makes **option (b) preferable to option (a).**

25. **The best answer is (d).** In order for a testator to execute a valid will he must have the intent to execute a will and he must comply with the formalities required for the execution of a will. In the hypo, Frank did not have the intent to execute a will. His intent was otherwise. The purported will, therefore, is not a will and **answer (b) is not the best answer.** Formalities are not enough for a valid will. There must also be testamentary intent. **Answer (c) is not correct** because the intent to execute a will and the execution of the will must coincide in time. Thus, it is not sufficient that Frank change his mind about leaving his estate to Mary prior to his death. And **answer (a) makes no sense** in this fact situation. If Frank committed a fraud, it was a fraud against Mary, lying to her to get her to sleep with him. Fraud in the inducement in the wills context is a fraud committed by a third party against the testator resulting in the testator signing a will that, absent the fraud, he would never have signed.

EXAM V
ANSWER KEY AND EXPLANATIONS

1. **The correct answer is (a).** Sonny takes all because he is related to the decedent in the 6th degree, while both Buddy and Happy are related to the decedent in the 7th degree. In a degree of kinship system, each surviving relative is assigned a degree of kinship with respect to the decedent. The surviving relative with the nearest degree of kinship takes the intestate property. (Note that the degree of kinship system is not a representative system; takers take only in their own right, not as representatives of a predeceasing relative.) If two or more surviving relatives are related to the decedent in the same degree, in most jurisdictions, they will divide the property. In some jurisdictions, however, a parentelic preference is applied so that of those surviving relatives related to the decedent in the same degree, the relative (or relatives) in the lowest parentela takes the property.

   To calculate the degree of kinship between the decedent and a surviving relative: (1) find the first ancestor in common between the decedent and the surviving relative; (2) count generations up from the decedent to the common ancestor; and (3) count generations down from the common ancestor to the surviving relative. Adding the number of generations in steps 2 and 3 will give you the degree of kinship. Repeat this process for each surviving relative who might take an intestate share. The surviving relative (or relatives) with the lowest number (the nearest degree of kinship) wins.

   Applying these steps to the hypothetical:

   Sonny is related to the decedent in the 6th degree. We count 4 generations up from the decedent to the decedent's great-great grandparents (the first common ancestors between the decedent and Sonny). We then count down 2 generations to Sonny. 4 + 2 = 6.

   Buddy is related to the decedent in the 7th degree. We count 3 generations up from the decedent to the decedent's great grandparents (the first common ancestors between the decedent and Buddy). We then count down 4 generations to Buddy. 3 + 4 = 7.

   Happy is related to the decedent in the 7th degree. We count 2 generations up from the decedent to the decedent's grandparents (the first common ancestors between the decedent and Happy). We then count down 5 generations to Happy. 2 + 5 = 7.

   Because Sonny is related to the decedent in the 6th degree, while Buddy and Happy are both related to the decedent in the 7th degree, Sonny takes the entire intestate estate.

2. **The correct answer is (c).** Happy takes all because she is a second-line collateral, while Buddy is a third-line collateral, and Sonny is a fourth-line collateral.

 The first step to understanding how the parentelic system works is to understand what a "line" (aka a "parentela") is. A line (in relation to any individual) is an ancestor and all of the descendants of that ancestor, excluding any descendants who are included in a lower line. For example, a decedent's first-line relations would be that decedent's parents and any descendants of the parents (excluding the decedent and descendants of the decedent). The decedent's second-line relations would be the decedent's grandparents and any descendants of the grandparents, excluding the first-line relations (decedent's parents and any descendants of the parents) and also excluding the decedent and descendants of the decedent. And so on. Notice that we can figure out which line any particular relative is in by counting generations up from the decedent to the *first* common ancestor between the decedent and that relative. Thus, the first-line relations are descended from the decedent's parents (one generation up), the second-line relations are descended from the decedent's grandparents (two generations up) but not the decedent's parents, the third-line relations are descended from the decedent's great-grandparents (three generations up) but not the decedent's parents or grandparents, and so on. A parentela is conceptually practically the same as a line, except that because we begin numbering parentelas with the decedent and his issue, the number for a parentela is always one less than the number for the corresponding line. Thus, the first line is the second parentela, the second line is the third parentela, the third line is the fourth parentela, and so on. (The decedent and his issue are in the first parentela but not in any line.)

 A second important point to understand about the parentelic system is that a living relative in a lower line takes to the exclusion of any relative in a higher line. For example, if a second-line collateral is alive, no collateral from the third-line or any higher line will take any of the intestate estate.

 Finally (although it is not relevant to resolution of the hypothetical presented in this question), it is important to know that the parentelic system generally is a representational system. That is, under the parentelic system, a relation of the decedent in the lowest line in which any relation of the decedent is alive may take by representation from a predeceasing ancestor in the same line. To demonstrate this point, assume that the decedent is survived not only by Happy (say, she is a lineal descendant of decedent's maternal grandparents), but also by Lucky, who is a lineal descendant, a great-great grandchild of decedent's paternal grandparents. In that case both Happy and Lucky would take, equally, because they are both descendants of grandparents, even though Lucky is more closely related than Happy.

 To answer the question, we need to figure out which line each of the claimants is in. The intestate and Happy have as their first common ancestor the intestate's grandparents (two generations up from the intestate). Happy, therefore is a second-line collateral. The intestate and Buddy have as their first common ancestor the intestate's great-grandparents (three generations up from the intestate). Buddy, therefore, is a third-line collateral. The intestate and Sonny have as their first common ancestor the intestate's great-great-grandparents (four generations up from the intestate). Sonny, therefore, is a fourth-line collateral. Happy takes all because she is a second-line collateral, while Buddy is a third-line collateral, and Sonny is a fourth-line collateral.

Another way to state this rule is that the heir(s) who is related to the decedent through the nearest common ancestor (e.g., grandparents as opposed to great grandparents) is the heir who will take.

3. **The best answer is (d).** Abatement is the reduction of a testamentary gift in order to satisfy an estate obligation of a higher priority. For example, testamentary gifts may be subject to abatement so that the estate can satisfy obligations to creditors. If there is not enough property in the estate to pay all of the creditors and satisfy all of the testamentary gifts, some or all of the testamentary gifts will be subject to abatement. In general, the order in which testamentary gifts abate is determined by the classification of the gifts. The most common order of abatement is—first, residuary gifts abate; second, if necessary, general gifts abate; third, if necessary, specific gifts abate. Within a classification, generally gifts abate pro rata. Gifts to certain devisees, however, might be given a preferred order of abatement. For example, a general gift to a relative might abate only after all general gifts to non-relatives have fully abated, or a gift to a spouse might abate last regardless of the class of gift.

   Testator has given Anthony a specific gift. A specific devise is a gift of a particular item that can be identified as part of the estate. Testator has given Brittany a general gift. A general devise is a gift of a type or quantity of property, and it does not refer to any particular item that can be identified as part of the estate. Testator has given Carlos a residuary gift. A residuary devise is a gift of whatever is left over after all of the general, specific, and demonstrative gifts have been paid (and, in practice, after all the creditors have been paid). The most likely order of abatement is Carlos's gift (a residuary gift) will abate first, Brittany's gift (a general gift) will abate second, and Anthony's gift (a specific gift) will abate third.

4. **The best answer is (c).** To answer this question, it would be wise to read each statement and determine whether it is true or false. The correct answer will be a false statement, i.e., one that is not true. A will substitute is an inter vivos transfer that avoids probate yet has the effect of passing property at the donor's death. Because the transfer is inter vivos, not testamentary, the transfer need not comply with the formalities for the execution of a will. Answer (c), therefore, is not true. The other statements are true.

5. **The best answer is (b).** These are general gifts. A general gift is a gift of a certain quantity or type of property, but it does not refer only to, and

is not payable only out of specific property found in the estate at T's death. A gift of $10,000 is a gift of a certain quantity or type of property (in this case money) and the gift can be paid even if the estate does not contain $10,000 in cash at the death of T. This is not a residuary gift. A residuary gift is a gift of whatever remains in the estate after the payment of specific, general and demonstrative gifts. **Answer (a), therefore, is not correct.** This is not a specific gift. A specific gift is a gift of a particular thing that can be identified as part of the estate. For example, a gift of "the $10,000 I have stashed in my mattress" would be a specific gift. **Answer (c), therefore, is not correct.** This is not a demonstrative gift. A demonstrative gift is a quantity or type (but not a specific item) of property to be satisfied out of a specific asset if available, otherwise from general assets of the estate. **Answer (d), therefore, is not correct.**

6. **The best answer is (a).** Testamentary fraud involves an intentional misrepresentation that is intended to deceive the testator and influence the testator's will, and that does in fact deceive the testator and influence the testator's will. Testamentary fraud is of two types. When the misrepresentation relates to the contents of the will or purported will, the fraud is in the execution of the will. When the misrepresentation relates to facts that cause the testator to want to include a provision in a will (or refrain from including a provision in a will, or revoke a provision already in a will, or refrain from revoking a provision already in a will) the fraud is in the inducement. **Answer (b), therefore, is not correct.** Constructive fraud, also known as technical fraud, may arise even without an intent on the part of the speaker to mislead. Constructive fraud arises where one speaks of a supposed fact that is susceptible of knowledge as though one has actual knowledge of the fact, but in fact the speaker does not have actual knowledge of the supposed fact and the supposed fact turns out not to be true. **Answers (c) and (d), therefore, are not the best answers.**

7. **The best answer is (a).** Michael created a vested remainder in Jackie. The remainder is not defeasible and more specifically is not subject to the condition that Jackie survive Anna or anyone else to take. The holder of a future interest (one that has already been created) need not survive until the time of possession in order to take unless the grantor conditions taking on survival. Jackie did not need to survive Anna, therefore, in order to take possession of the property. Moreover, remainders (as well as executory interests and reversions) are both devisable and descendible. Jackie had the ability, therefore, to devise his future interest. He did devise that interest to Edward. Edward will take the property, therefore, when Jackie's interest becomes possessory (at the expiration of Anna's life estate). **Answer (b) is not correct.** Michael gave away a vested remainder in fee simple to Jackie. Michael, therefore, did not retain a reversion. **Answer (c) is not correct.** Anna never possessed a contingent remainder. **Answer (d) is not correct.** Lapse is a concept that traditionally has been applied only with respect to a devise where a devisee has predeceased the testator. Anti-lapse statutes, it follows, generally apply only to devises and only where the devisee has

predeceased the testator. **Note:** UPC § 2–707 is to the contrary. It requires any taker of a future interest in trust to survive until the date of distribution. It, therefore, reverses the common law, which is identified as the applicable law in this question.

8. **The best answer is (c).** The land is community property because it was acquired during marriage with marital wages. In Texas (and most community property states), all property is community if it is acquired during marriage except for property that is acquired by gift, bequest, or devise (and certain other limited exceptions). The stock was inherited so it is not community property. It is Harold's separate property. The estate tax rule is that only half of the value of community property at death is included in the decedent's gross estate. So, $1.0 million in value of the land is included together with the $1.0 million in stock. The gross estate is thus $2.0 million and that makes **answers (a) and (b) both incorrect. Answer (d) is incorrect.** The federal estate tax allows a 100% deduction for any property that is left to the surviving spouse. This is known as the unlimited marital deduction.

9. **The best answer is (b). Answer (a) can't be true.** There are numerous cases in which a testator or witness neglected to sign the will, but did sign the self-proving affidavit along with everyone else. If answer (a) were true, then those cases could have easily been dismissed on the theory that the self-proving affidavit proved the execution. Instead, most of these cases were litigated on the question of whether or not the signing of the affidavit could count as the signing of the will. Early cases held that signing the affidavit was insufficient to constitute the signing of the will. Those cases demonstrate that in many states the presumption of valid execution can be no more than rebuttable.

   Answer (c) is wrong. The affidavit, even with a duly executed will, cannot establish an irrebuttable presumption that the will is valid. If it did, there would be no will contests based on mental competence or undue influence or any of the grounds for challenging a will. Nor does the affidavit create even a rebuttable presumption about validity. **Answer (d) is wrong.** Will contests on grounds of undue influence and mental competence are controlled by the same substantive and procedural rules, whether or not there was an affidavit. Witnesses and notary publics signing an affidavit are not swearing to the absence of undue influence. Nor are they swearing to the mental competency of the testator. They may swear that the testator appeared to be of sound mind, and that might create a presumption of competence (since the testator appeared sane at the time), but that presumption would not be irrebuttable.

10. **The best answer is (b).** UTC 1008(a) provides that "A term of a trust relieving a trustee of liability for breach of trust is unenforceable to the extent that it . . . relieves the trustee of liability for breach of trust committed in bad faith or with reckless indifference to the purposes of the trust or the interests of the beneficiaries." The comment to Section 1008 explains, "Even if the terms of the trust attempt to completely exculpate a trustee for the trustee's acts, the trustee must always comply with a

certain minimum standard. As provided in [this section], a trustee must always act in good faith with regard to the purposes of the trust and the interests of the beneficiaries." The Restatement (Third) of Trusts is in accord. This minimal standard applies regardless of whether the trustee is a professional trustee, the settlor had independent legal advice about the exculpatory clause, or the terms of the trust give the trustee "absolute discretion." Thus, **answers (a), (c), and (d) are not correct.** The approach is grounded in the understanding that a purported trust is not a trust if the beneficiaries cannot hold the trustee accountable for her behavior as trustee.

11. **The best answer is (b).** The gift to Amir is valid because it vests immediately upon Ursula's death, but the contingent remainder "may" vest too remotely. As a result, it is void. The remainder is not to Sam, if he graduates from college. It is to the first child of Amir to graduate. That may or may not be Sam. It is possible that it will be to another child of Amir, a child yet to be born. Let's call him Seth. Since Seth cannot be used as the measuring life to validate the gift to him, the only way a gift to him would be valid would be if it were necessarily to vest within 21 years of the death of someone who was a life in being at the time the interest was created. We only have two possibilities, Amir and Sam. Yet it is hypothetically possible that both will die and Seth will graduate from college more than 21 years later. As a result, the remainder interest is void under the rule. It is void even if it turns out that Sam is the first child to graduate from college and even if it turns out that Amir has no more children. The rule looks at what is possible from the time of creation of the contingent future interest. If there is a possibility, no matter how slight or absurd, that the interest will vest too remotely, then the interest is void.

12. **The best answer is (d).** Since Amir is dead, he can have no more children. That means the remainder to Sam is valid under the rule. But **answer (b) cannot be the correct answer** because it says that Sam will in fact get the trust corpus. We will not know whether he will actually get the corpus until he has met the condition: graduation from college. **Answer (a) cannot be correct** because Amir was given only a life estate. Since he is now dead, his estate cannot collect anything. **Answer (c) is not correct** because the gift to Sam does not violate the rule. If he graduates from college, it will necessarily happen during his own lifetime and he can be the validating life, since he was alive at time of creation of the interest (i.e., at Ursula's death). **Thus answer (d) is correct.** His interest is valid and so he will collect the corpus provided he graduates from college.

13. **The best answer is (a).** The question is whether Mick intended to exercise the power even though he did not specifically make reference to it. Mick has a general power and the creator/donor of the power did not provide for takers in default. UPC § 2–608 provides that, in such a case, a general residuary clause expresses an intent to exercise the power. Of course, if Fred's will had required that the power be mentioned, then the

residuary clause standing along would be insufficient. But his will says nothing about how the power should be exercised. Thus, any action by Mick indicating an intent to exercise is sufficient and, in this case, the residuary clause does that.

14. **The best answer is (c).** The power of appointment was not exercised and since it is not a general power, it cannot be exercised by the residuary clause. **Thus answer (a) is wrong.** Also, since it is not a general power, it cannot go to Mick's estate. **That means answer (b) is wrong.** And since there are no takers in default or implied takers in default, the interest passes as a reversionary interest retained by Fred. Fred owned the property at his death subject to being divested if Mick exercised the power. Since Fred was never divested, whatever he owned at death passes to his successors in interest. The residuary clause in Fred's will is broad enough to capture the reversionary interest and it existed at that time since it was created in the devise of the trust property. Thus, the property goes to Yale. That makes **answer (c) the best option.** The trick is to determine who those successors are and following the general rule that a failed gift in a specific devise falls into the residuary, the conclusion is that the property goes to Yale.

15. **The best answer is (d).** Under the harmless error principle (see UPC § 2–503), a document that has not been executed with the formalities prescribed in a jurisdiction for execution of a will may nonetheless be probated as a will if the court finds that there is clear and convincing evidence that the testator intended the document to be his will. The writing on the back of the will and on the back of the codicil should be considered subsequent instruments that revoke the will and codicil, respectively. True, these writings are not executed with the formalities generally prescribed for execution of a will. Nor do these writings qualify as valid holographic wills because the material provisions ("null and void") are not in the handwriting of the testator. Moreover, these notations do not qualify as "cancellations" (revocations by physical act) under the majority approach because the marks of cancellation ("null and void") do not touch the words of the will. Nevertheless, if a court concludes that there is clear and convincing evidence that the testator intended for the signed notations to be her last will (revoking the earlier will and codicil), the court should find that the will and codicil are revoked by subsequent instrument. The testator's signature immediately below the notations "null and void" arguably should be sufficient for a court to find by clear and convincing evidence that the testator intended these notations to be her will. The lawyer's evidence should confirm this was her intent. **Answers (a) and (b), therefore, are not the best answers.** Moreover, the will cannot be considered revoked by physical act because the words of cancellation do not touch the words of the will. The UPC's harmless error principle does not apply to physical acts of revocation and, therefore, is not a means to cure this defect in the requirements of "physical act of revocation." The will and codicil, therefore, are not revoked by physical act. **Answer (c), therefore, is not the best answer.**

16. **The best answer is (d).** To answer questions like this, one should read through each statement and decide independents whether each statemen is true or false. It is probably wise to mark each statement with a T or F. Any answer that is marked T cannot be the correct answer. Option (a) is true and therefore **option (a) in incorrect as an answer. Both answers (b) and (c) are not true** (i.e., false). And that makes **(d) the best answer** since it includes both (b) and (c). The judicial doctrine of equitable adoption provides that for the purposes of intestacy, under certain facts, a person who is not the legal child of the intestate decedent may inherit from the intestate decedent the same as a child of the intestate decedent. Most jurisdictions that recognize equitable adoption hold that the doctrine of equitable adoption will not apply unless the decedent had contracted to adopt the child with a person legally capable of consenting to the child's adoption. The decedent must have acted as a parent to the child even though the decedent failed to legally adopt the child. Equitable adoption allows the child to inherit from the intestate equitable adoptive parent. In effect, it equitably estops the parent's estate from denying that there was no adoption. The doctrine, however, does not allow the equitable adoptive parent to inherit from the equitable adoptive child who dies intestate. The rationale is that given that the equitable adoptive parent failed to perform the adoption contract, the equitable remedy should not be available to him. Equitable adoption does not allow the child to inherit through the equitable adoptive parent from a relative of the equitable adoptive parent. The rationale is that because the relative of the equitable adoptive parent was not a party to the adoption contract, it is not appropriate to apply an equitable remedy against the relative's estate.

17. **The best answer is (c).** Because Peter and Paul have predeceased Tom, the gift of the residue to Peter and Paul lapses. A residuary gift that lapsed at common law passed by intestacy. The residue of Tom's estate, therefore, will pass by intestacy. Mary is Tom's sole intestate heir. It is of no moment that Tom's will expressed his intent that Mary not take any of his property. At common law and in most American jurisdictions today, the only way to disinherit an heir with respect to probate property is to effectively devise that property to someone else. The UPC, in contrast, provides for a "negative will." UPC § 2–101(b) provides that "[a] decedent by will may expressly exclude or limit the right of an individual or class to succeed to property of the decedent passing by intestate succession. If that individual or a member of that class survives the decedent, the share of the decedent's intestate estate to which that individual or class would have succeeded passes as if that individual or each member of that class had disclaimed his [or her] intestate share." Thus, if the jurisdiction had adopted UPC § 2–101(b), Mary would be treated as having disclaimed her intestate inheritance and her share would pass instead to her daughter Louise.

18. **The best answer is (c).** The putative spouse doctrine is not accepted in all jurisdictions. In those jurisdictions that do recognize a putative spouse doctrine, a court may award property to a person who in good faith

believed that she was married to the property owner. The doctrine may be applied when the parties break up or at the death of the property owner. The doctrine is an equitable remedy and the court has discretion to apportion the property at issue as the court believes justice requires. Some courts have given the putative spouse all of the marital property and some have split the property between the putative spouse and the legal spouse. Applying equitable principles, it is hypothetically possible that a judge would decide to give no property to the putative spouse. However, once a court recognizes the doctrine, it is likely that at least some of the property will go to the putative spouse. Option **(d) is also possible,** although not the best answer. That is because the legally married spouse, May, is actually entitled to all of Bill's share of community property. It is therefore unlikely that a judge would give all of that property to the putative spouse as contemplated in option (d). But it is very likely that a judge will give June some of the property acquired during her ten-year relationship with Bill.

See Uniform Marriage and Divorce Act § 209, which provides: "If there is a legal spouse or other putative spouses, rights acquired by a putative spouse do not supersede the rights of the legal spouse or those acquired by other putative spouses, but the court shall apportion property, maintenance, and support rights among the claimants as appropriate in the circumstances and in the interests of justice."

19. **The best answer is (c).** UPC § 6–213(b) specifically states that a POD designation may not be altered by will. That means **(a) is incorrect. Option (b) is also incorrect** because a codicil has the same power as a will and can therefore pass any kind of property. **Option (d) is also incorrect.** Although the $100,000 will pass outside of probate, it was nonetheless owned by the decedent at death and so will be included in his gross estate for estate tax purposes.

20. **The best answer is (a).** The gift to Sam and John is a residuary gift. John's death causes the gift to John to lapse. The antilapse statute does not apply to save the gift for John's daughter because Tony and John are not related. The antilapse statute only applies when the lapsed gift is a gift to certain relatives. See UPC § 2–603. **That makes (b) incorrect.** There are only two possible places John's lapsed gift can go. It will either go to the remaining residuary taker, Sam, or it will go to Tony's intestate heirs as property that was not disposed of under the will. Most states adopt a rule that a lapsed gift in the residuary clause goes to the other residuary clause beneficiaries. **That makes (a) the best answer.** A handful of states still apply the "no residue of a residue" rule and treat the lapsed residuary gift as one that falls outside of the residuary, which means outside of the will, and thus must pass as intestate property. **In such a state, (d) would be the correct answer.** But the question asks for the result in a UPC state. UPC § 2–604 provides that a lapse in the residuary passes to the other residuary takers. That makes **(a) the best answer** in a UPC state.

21. **The best answer is (b).** Under UPC § 2–607, a specific devise passes subject to any existing mortgage on the property. Thus, **answers (a) and (c) are wrong** since they say that Sally takes the property free and clear of the mortgage. After distributing the home to Sally, the executor should distribute the stock to Pat. The gift of the Rockwell stock is a specific bequest and so Pat should take the 100 shares of stock regardless of what the value is at time of death. **Option (d) is incorrect** because the gift was of the stock, not of the value of the stock. A will speaks at death. At death, the 100 shares were worth less. Pat takes the stock owned at death, not additional stock.

22. **The best answer is (a).** This is not a charitable trust. Gino's purpose is admirable in support of college educations, but these scholarships are really just private gifts to the children of his employees. That is not a sufficient enough public purpose to qualify as a charitable trust. As a result, the trust is subject to the rule against perpetuities and will likely be struck down. It is difficult to see how "wait and see" or the 90-year statutory provision will help this trust. We know that Gino's intent was to set up a perpetual trust fund, something that you cannot do under the rule against perpetuities. The trust provides that only income will be distributed to beneficiaries and so we cannot wait and see whether the assets will vest within the period of the rule. We cannot really wait 90 years to see whether they vest either because we know from the beginning that they will not. **Answer (d) is not the best answer.** If there is a *cy pres* statute in the jurisdiction that can be applied to rewrite an interest that violates the rule against perpetuities, a court might construe the trust as lasting only for the period of the rule. That means some future gifts of income would be possible, but they would have to stop once the period of the rule had run its course and the trust assets would have to be distributed to someone at that time—either the then living potential beneficiaries (if the court construed the trust solely for the benefit of future issue of the three managers) or as a reversionary interest in Gino. Such a rule could prevent future generations from receiving scholarships even though the intent was for them to benefit. But because of the rule against perpetuities, such a statute might "save" the gift. It would not "threaten" the gift. **Answer (b) is not correct.** The issue of three individuals may grow to be a large class, but they are certainly identifiable and so the trust will not fail for lack of identifiable beneficiaries. **Answer (c) is not correct.** A trust never fails for want of a trustee. The court will appoint a successor.

23. **The best answer is (b).** Under UPC § 2–507 tearing up the will is sufficient to revoke the will provided the testator so intended and provided further that the testator was the one doing the tearing. The testator can ask someone else to perform the act of tearing, but the act will not revoke the will unless it is done in the "conscious presence" of the testator. "Conscious presence" is discussed further at UPC § 2–502 (comment to subsection (a)). It includes an act that is done within one of the senses of the testator. Thus, it need not be within the testator's line of sight if it is close enough for the testator to hear what is going on. Here, however, the

act was done at Blanche's home, miles away from the hospital and, thus, not within her conscious presence. Therefore, the will was not property revoked and may be probated.

24. **The best answer is (b).** The trustee is likely to be judged imprudent because her investments are subject to excessive firm risk and excessive industry risk. A trust portfolio is subject to various kinds of risks, only some of which can be reduced through diversification. Firm risk is the risk that factors specific to a particular firm will negatively impact an investment. Thus, an investment in First National Bank stock is subject to the firm risks particular to First National Bank. A trustee can reduce this firm risk by spreading the trust's investments over multiple firms. Industry risk is the risk that factors specific to a particular industry will negatively impact an investment. Thus, an investment in First National Bank stock is subject to industry risks particular to the banking industry. Similarly, an investment in Bank of the East stock also is subject to industry risks particular to the banking industry. A trustee can reduce this industry risk by spreading the trust's investments out over multiple industries. Finally, market risk is the risk that an overall market decline will negatively impact an investment. Nearly all investments are subject to market risk. Thus, investments in First National Bank stock and Bank of the East stock are subject to market risk. The trustee cannot reduce this market risk, however, through diversification. Under the Uniform Prudent Investor Act (UPIA), a trustee does not necessarily violate her fiduciary duty of prudence by investing in a risky investment. Rather, the trustee's central duty when it comes to investing is to balance the risk of an investment against its potential return in the context of the trust's entire portfolio and in light of the circumstances of the trust. Market risk is compensated risk because investing in the market affords a greater expected return. The problem with excessive firm risk and excessive industry risk is that the trust is not compensated for taking on this excessive risk. Thus, the trustee who fails to diversify by investing, for example, 70 percent of the trust portfolio in a single firm or 100 percent of the trust portfolio in a single industry is likely to be judged imprudent because she has created a portfolio that has excessive firm risk and excessive industry risk. Indeed, Section 3 of the UPIA provides that a trustee has a duty to "diversify the investments of the trust unless the trustee reasonably determines that, because of special circumstances, the purposes of the trust are better served without diversifying."

25. **The best answer is (b).** If Marvin adopts Samantha, she becomes his sole intestate heir. That would prevent his other current heirs apparent from having standing to challenge the will.

    Answer (a) is not the best answer even though it might look like a good option. Transferring current ownership to himself and Samantha is one way to protect against a will contest because none of the joint tenancy property will be in the probate estate. Samantha will take as the surviving joint tenant. Answer (a) is not as fool-proof as answer (b), however, because if Marvin were to die in the next few years, his heirs would have standing to challenge the inter vivos transfer on the same grounds they might have to challenge a testamentary transfer (e.g., lack of capacity, fraud, duress, undue influence). Answer (a) only works to defeat the claims of the heirs if Marvin lives beyond the statute of limitations for those claims. So, while answer (a) is not wrong, it is not as attractive and complete a solution to the problem as answer (b).

Answer (c) is of no help. The only way to draft an effective no-contest clause is to provide that the challenger will lose a bequest in the will. If the challenger challenges and wins, he/she will claim his/her intestate share. If he challenges and loses, then the will will be probated and the challenger will not be entitled to any intestate share that can be "lost." If the will doesn't make any provision for the challenger—e.g., a gift that will be lost—then the challenger has nothing to lose in pursing the challenge.

Answer (d) is not the best answer. While it may seem helpful for a testator to explain in detail why he is disinheriting certain family members, that tactic carries some risks. One of the heirs might be angered by the explanation and be more inclined to challenge the will. And sometimes explanations, if they are particularly detailed or emotional, are used by the challengers to prove that the testator was not of sound mind. In any event, including the reasons will not absolutely protect the will from challenge by the disinherited heirs.

EXAM VI
ANSWER KEY AND EXPLANATIONS

1. **Option (c) is the best answer** because Tony decided to make a gift causa mortis to Carmen in anticipation of death and he gave up all control over the necklace when he gave Johnny the claim check and he died from the cause he feared. It does not matter that Carmen was the ultimate recipient since Tony intended to make Johnny an agent for Carmen, and Johnny agreed by taking possession and control over the claim check. The key with any kind of inter vivos or causa mortis gifts is that the donor relinquish sufficient control and possession so that he cannot reclaim or revoke it. Since Tony had the intent and gave up possession of the claim check, without which the jeweler would not turn over the necklace, Tony had met the requirements of delivery and intent for a gift causa mortis. It was not necessary that Carmen take possession prior to Tony's death, so **option (b) is incorrect.** The **next best answer would be option (d),** because someone can give the keys to the safe deposit box, the car key, or the claim check and that would count as constructive possession so long as the donor did not retain another key or claim check or any way to control the disposition of the gift. **Option (a) is incorrect** because Tony did not intend to make a testamentary gift since he intended to relinquish possession during life.

2. **Option (d) is the best answer** under the UPC and even under most state statutes that demand strict compliance. A minor is permitted to serve as a witness so long as she understands what she is doing and most states do not void a will because the son was an interested witness. The test is that the witness be "competent" to testify. A notary is not prohibited from notarizing documents executed by family members. Thus, the granddaughter's challenge will likely fail. **Option (b) is the next best answer** because in some states an interested witness is disqualified. **Option (a) and (c) are both incorrect** because a minor can witness a will so long as she understands the meaning of her signature and a notary can notarize a document executed by a family member.

3. **Option (d) is the best answer** because the class closing rule requires that an open class closes when distribution of principal is made. At that time, it is important for the trustee to know how many shares the principal shall be divided into so that any distribution does not exceed that class member's share. Because Ashley reached age 18 and was therefore entitled to distribution from principal, the class closing rule would close the class at that time with the three grandchildren as class members. However, sometimes if the trust is sufficiently large so that a principal distribution like this one for education is trivial enough not to affect the final distribution shares, then prudence would suggest waiting

until the class closes naturally and final distribution is made. That means that **option (c) is the next best option.** If the trust contained $100 million, the small amount of distribution for college expenses would normally not require division of trust shares and all education expenses could be accounted for with the final distribution. But if the trust is relatively modest, the trustee will need to go ahead and divide the shares at the time the first distribution is made, which makes option (d) the best answer. **Option (a) is incorrect** because donors use class gift terminology to intentionally keep a class open to take in subsequently born members. Here Peter clearly intended to allow afterborn grandchildren to participate in the trust. However, the same argument could be made that the class should close at Peter's death if Ashely was already age 18 and entitled to a distribution of principal. In that case, the gift would be an immediate vested interest in the two living grandchildren and no additional class members would be allowed. **Option (b)** has the same class members as the correct option (d) but it is incorrect because the death of the spouse is not an event that vests an interest in the trust principal for the grandchildren.

4. **Option (c) is the best option** because unsecured debts (the credit card and the medical expenses) are paid from probate property first, and they reduce each class of property ratably. Under abatement rules, debts are paid first out of property passing by intestacy, then out of property that passes pursuant to the residue clause. If those are insufficient, the general and then the specific bequests are abated ratably, in that order. In this case, since there is no intestate property, and the property in the residue is sufficient to satisfy the credit card and medical debts, those assets will be reduced. In general, secured debts are not paid by the estate under nonexoneration rules. Thus, the car loan and the mortgage will not be paid out of other estate assets unless the decedent left clear instructions to do so. In most cases, the assets will simply pass to the designated beneficiaries subject to the debts. In some cases, however, a mortgage or a car loan may have a "due on sale" clause which requires that upon the sale or transfer of the asset (including at death), the debt must be entirely paid off. If that occurs, and the beneficiaries of that property are unable to pay the debt, the executor will have to sell the property and then the proceeds may become estate assets available to pay other debts. UPC § 2–607 states that a specific devise passes "subject to any mortgage interest existing at the date of death, without right of exoneration," but that does not bar "due on sale clauses." Without more information about the mortgage and car loan, the best option is (c). Most importantly, the non-probate property (the IRA and the securities account) both have beneficiary designations so that property will pass automatically to the named beneficiaries and will not be used to pay debts since there is sufficient probate property to pay them. **Option (d) is the second-best answer** and would possibly be correct had Darren devised his personal property to one beneficiary and the bank account was left to pass by the residue clause. Depending on Darren's will, it is possible that the unsecured debts would be paid from one or more specific assets first, even

if that depleted them. **Option (a) is incorrect** in the absence of an instruction to pay secured debts and an instruction to pay all debts from the IRA. Without both instructions, we do not pay debts out of the largest asset, but instead follow the abatement priorities of UPC § 3–902. **Option (b) is also incorrect** because the securities account is not used unless there is insufficient property to cover the debts in the probate estate. The key is that probate assets are used first to pay unsecured debts.

5. **Option (c) is the best answer.** The living will is an instrument that identifies whether someone wants to be placed on artificial life support in the case of terminal illness or accident. Sometimes a health care proxy will include this information, but the health care proxy is an instrument that identifies who the patient would want to make health care decisions in case the patient cannot make them herself. In this case, in the absence of a living will expressly stating the patient's wishes with regard to artificial life support, the health care surrogate designated by the health care proxy may make that decision. That means that **option (a) is the second-best option.** Both **options (b) and (d) are incorrect** because the durable power of attorney and the last will and testament are instruments that are used to make financial decisions about one's property, not about one's health care.

6. **Option (d) is the best answer.** The majority rule in most states is that no-contest clauses are unenforceable where the challenger has probable cause. See also UPC § 2–517. Since incapacity, failure to follow the will formalities, and undue influence would all render the will invalid, including the no-contest clause itself, these challenges are often permitted where there are grounds for these allegations. If the children simply don't like the bequests and think Calliope made them because she was mad at the children or was mistaken about their worthiness, the court is likely to enforce a no-contest clause in such instance. The best approach, however, would be for the children to seek a declaratory judgment from the probate court as to whether a challenge on the grounds of incapacity, undue influence, or failure to follow the will formalities would trigger the no-contest clause. No-contest clauses are unenforceable in Indiana and Florida, so it would not matter the grounds. And some states provide safe harbors for challenges, thus permitting challenges on the grounds of undue influence or failure to follow the will formalities. The majority rule, however, is a good cause rule, and if the children have the evidence to support any of the first three grounds, they are likely to be able to challenge Calliope's will. But dislike of the bequests is never good cause without a showing of undue influence or some other wrongdoing. This means that **Options (a), (b), and (c) are wrong** because they could be valid challenges to the will and, if successful, would negate the no-contest clause itself.

7. **Option (a) is the best answer.** Roughly half the states follow the UPC § 2–513 to permit a separate writing to dispose of tangible personal property even if the document is changed after the will is executed so long as it is signed by the testator. It is not necessary that the testator sign the

separate writing after each change so long as it is signed by the testator at some point. In this case, however, Holly clearly signed the appendix shortly before death. It could, therefore, be validated as a holographic codicil in a state that permit holographic codicils. **Option (b) is incorrect** because incorporation by reference does not permit changes to the separate document after the will is executed and Holly's dating of the appendix suggests changes were made after it was originally written. **Option (c) is incorrect but could be the second-best answer** because although the appendix page could be integrated as part of the original will, the changes were not made prior to execution. Thus, the changes on the appendix document are not validly executed with the will formalities. However, the harmless error doctrine, if applicable in your state, might permit the changes to serve as holographic codicils. **Option (d) is incorrect** because the appendix page has no independent significance except disposing of Holly's property, so the acts of independent significance doctrine would be inapplicable.

8. **Option (b) is the best answer.** This trust does not meet the requirements of a charitable trust which must be "created for the relief of poverty, the advancement of education or religion, the promotion of health, governmental or municipal purposes, or other purposes the achievement of which is beneficial to the community." See UTC § 405. When a private express trust fails for lack of ascertainable beneficiaries, and does not fit within the exceptions (pet trust, honorary trust, or charitable trust), then a resulting trust is imposed on Eric to transfer the property back to the settlor's estate to be disposed of as part of the estate. Because this trust likely fails, it is inappropriate to use the remedy of a constructive trust to give the property to the likely intended beneficiaries because we do not know who that would be. Thus, **option (c) is incorrect. Option (d) is the next best option.** The UTC § 409 permits a private express trust that does not meet the charitable trust requirements to be enforced but only for 21 years and only if a trustee is willing to undertake the obligations. Assuming Eric is willing to distribute the trust assets for the next 21 years (or a successor trustee is willing to do so), an honorary trust may be enforced, but any excess funds must be returned to the settlor in the form of a resulting trust. **Option (a) is incorrect** because this trust does not meet the terms of a charitable trust.

9. **Option (a) is the best answer.** Tom is mistaken as to the constitutionality of the estate tax as well as to his estate being subject to the tax. That mistake of law has caused him to write the will he did. Presumably he would not leave his estate in trust to a lawyer to use the proceeds to sue to declare the estate tax unconstitutional if he was not operating under the mistake about the law. Mistakes in the inducement are mistakes by the testator about facts or law that cause a will or devise to be made. Since this is not a mistake of fact, neither **options (b) nor (d) are correct.** Mistakes in the expression are evident from the face of the will and generally make provisions that either don't make sense or are expressed incorrectly. **Option (c) would therefore be the next best option,** but it is still likely incorrect since there is no indication from the

facts given that there is any mistake in the expression of the will itself. The words used in the will seem to comply with Tom's intent. In other words, he did not mis-express himself.

10. **Option (d) is the best answer** under the UPC § 2–606 which gives the devisee of a specific devise any specifically devised property (the Picasso and the furniture to Sabine and Griffin respectively), plus the proceeds from the sale of any specifically devised property (the $500,000 from the sale of the artwork to Sabine, and the $500 from the sale of the furniture to Griffin). The UPC does not distinguish between sale of property by the testator after execution of the will and sale by a guardian or conservator, so long as it is established that ademption would be inconsistent with the testator's manifested plan of distribution. That exception makes this a difficult question to answer. Most testators would want to provide for a surviving spouse, and if the non-ademption rule would result in Doris receiving nothing, that might go against Wilbur's general plan. On the other hand, he might have wanted his artwork to benefit Sabine, whether in its original form or even if it was sold and turned into cash because Doris is independently wealthy and needs nothing from him. The burden would be on Sabine to show that ademption would be inconsistent with Wilbur's general plan. Of course, if Doris is not otherwise provided for through probate or non-probate transfers, she would be entitled to an elective share in many states. But community property states do not guarantee a surviving spouse an elective share, which means that Wilbur could completely disinherit Doris (although he cannot dispose of her half of the community property). And if they had been married a short time, Doris' elective share under the UPC could be quite de minimis, or Wilbur might have provided for Doris through non-probate assets. Without more information, the straightforward application of § 2–606 makes option (d) the best answer. Further, a devisee of specifically devised property is also entitled to the proceeds from an insurance payout or condemnation award, which means Griffin would also get the $100,000 from condemnation of the house. **Option (b) would be the next best answer** in states that do not treat specific devises as adeemed when sold by a guardian, conservator, or are proceeds from insurance or condemnation (i.e., involuntary disposition of the property) but do treat sales by testator's of specifically devised property as adeemed. **Option (b) would also be correct** if it is proved that ademption is consistent with the testator's dispositive plan. **Option (a) would be correct** under the common law rules of ademption by satisfaction, but most states have adopted some form of non-ademption, especially when property is no longer in the estate through actions of someone other than the testator. **Option (c) would be incorrect** because more states permit a devisee to take the proceeds from involuntarily disposed of property than property disposed of by the testator.

11. **Option (c) is the correct answer** to the hotchpot calculation. Because Donald predeceased Roland, his advancement is ignored in the calculation under UPC § 2–109(c). Thus, we add together $500,000 from Roland's estate, plus the advancements to Abel, Bonnie, and Chelsea ($50,000 +

$100,000 + $30,000) for a total of $680,000. We divide that by 4 for each living child and deceased child with living issue, entitling each to $170,000. We then subtract the advancements each already received, so Abel takes $120,000 ($170,000 - $50,000); Bonnie takes $70,000 ($170,000 - $100,000); Chelsea takes $140,000 ($170,000 - $30,000); and Donald's 3 children split Donald's $170,000 share. **The other hotchpot calculations are incorrect.**

12. This is a very tricky question but **option (c) is the best answer.** The conflict arises in how we interpret the term "personal property" in the bequest to Sherry. If it means all personal property, it would include intangible as well as tangible property and would therefore include the stock, the cash, and the checking account (answer d). But there is a latent ambiguity because the residuary bequest to Kevin indicates that he was to get all the rest of her property "of every kind and character." Arguably this phrase would have no meaning if the bequest to Sherry included intangible personal property as well as tangible personal property. If Sherry were to get all personal property, that would leave only real property for Kevin, which makes the "every kind and character" unclear and likely ambiguous. This is a latent ambiguity in the meaning of the term personal property because it has a legal meaning, but it appears from the face of the will that Jocelyn possibly meant a different meaning, something more akin to tangible personal property. That is the best way to interpret the two clauses of the will together in light of the property that Jocelyn in fact owned. The term "personal property" is not patently ambiguous, so **option (a) is incorrect**. And **option (b) is incorrect** because cash in physical form in the house would not count as tangible personal property even though it can be held. The exception for money in hand would be gold bullion, but not bills or coins because the latter only represent money and value by virtue of the government's guarantee. Thus, if the ambiguity is resolved to give Sherry the tangible personal property, she would not get the cash, the stock, or the checking account, which makes **option (d) incorrect** as well. It may be likely that **option (b)** reflects Jocelyn's intent, however, so it would be **the second best answer.** For instance, if the bills in the mattress was Jocelyn's foreign money or coin collection, then it would be considered tangible personal property and option (b) would be better.

13. **Option (a) is the best answer.** A mistake in the inducement is one that exists in the testator's mind and causes a bequest to be made that would not otherwise be made. In this case, the mistake would be over a fact and not a matter of law—the fact that Jimmy had five children and not four. Roman would argue that because Jimmy was mistaken about the number of children he had, he did not provide for Roman. But that is a tough argument to make. Hence, if Jimmy had forgotten about Roman and would have included him in the will had he remembered, then we clearly have a mistake of fact in the inducement. Or, if Jimmy's lawyer misheard Jimmy when identifying Jimmy's children and in drafting the bequest to them, and Jimmy intended to include Roman, then we would have a mistake of fact in the expression. Unfortunately, Roman is unlikely to be

successful in either because there is no evidence that Jimmy wanted to include Roman in his estate. He could easily have believed that Roman was being taken care of through his mother's side and that he should provide solely for his four children with Rosa. Thus, if the mistake did not affect the bequest, Jimmy will be unsuccessful in his challenge. **Answer (b) is the next best option** because a mistake in the expression is a mistake on the face of the will as to a fact or a matter of law. Usually, mistakes in the expression consist of scrivener's errors or an incorrect statement of the law that are evident on the face of the will itself. It is possible that the mistake was made by the lawyer who misheard Jimmy and who drafted four when Jimmy had told him five, but that seems unlikely, especially if Jimmy read his will before executing it. Since Jimmy clearly knew he had five children, but stated in his will that he only had four, it seems that he intentionally omitted Roman. This is a tricky question because a successful challenge must show that the testator was under the influence of a mistake (in this case a mistake of fact) and that the mistake tainted the will in some way. **Options (c) and (d) are incorrect** because the mistake does not appear to have affected the bequests.

14. **Option (b) is the best answer** under the UPC anti-lapse statute (UPC § 2–603). Because Bettina provided for alternate bequests in the case of the death of her primary beneficiaries (her brother Sven and sister Eva), we first honor the alternate bequest. That means Klaus will take half the estate, making **option (d) incorrect.** The half that was to go to Sven or Olga is more difficult. Had Olga survived she would have taken, but since both the primary and alternate beneficiaries predeceased Bettina, the question is whether to apply the anti-lapse statute to save the gift for their issue. Since Sven and Olga do not have issue together, and Olga is not related to Bettina through grandparents, the anti-lapse statute cannot apply to the gift to Olga. Thus, Olga's issue are not entitled to take, making **option (c) incorrect.** Since Sven and Bettina are related, and the gift to Sven lapses because he predeceased, and he left issue, the anti-lapse statute will provide a substitute gift in his issue (option (b)). However, some states would not apply the anti-lapse statute at all if there is survivorship language or an alternate gift. Florida is such a state. The mere existence of an alternate gift in the event a beneficiary predeceases is sufficient evidence of contrary intent not to apply the anti-lapse statute. If that rule were applied, then **option (a)** would be the correct answer.

15. **Option (b) is the best option** under the Uniform Simultaneous Death Act which requires that a beneficiary survive the testator by at least 120 hours (5 days). Since Ophelia survived by six days, she is treated as having survived the testator and her estate is entitled to take the bequests. The fact that she had died by the time probate occurred is irrelevant, making **option (d)** incorrect. It also does not matter that Ophelia and Hamlet died of the same cause. Had Hamlet had a heart attack that killed him, but the heart attack led to the crash that killed Ophelia, they would have died from separate causes, but Ophelia would not inherit if she did not survive Hamlet by at least 5 days. Thus, **option**

(c) is also incorrect. Option (a) would be correct in a state that does not follow the UPC or the Uniform Simultaneous Death Act but requires merely evidence that one party survived the other. In that case, Ophelia would only have to have survived by a few minutes in order to take the bequests from Hamlet's will.

16. **Option (b) is the correct answer.** A pre-nuptial agreement can be used to waive rights to all statutory entitlements, such as elective share, pretermitted spousal share, family allowance, homestead, and exempt property. It can also waive the right to serve as a personal representative. But it cannot waive the right to disclosure of the other party's assets. A valid agreement requires a fair and reasonable disclosure of the property or financial obligations of the other party. See the Uniform Premarital Agreement Act and UPC § 2–213. Because option IV is the only one that cannot be enforced, the other answer options are incorrect.

17. **Option (b) is correct.** In the United States, a decedent has sufficient testamentary freedom to disinherit his children entirely. This means that he has no obligation to support his children after his death. As a result, Rupert does not have to provide for his children's future child support. But he does have to pay all debts and judgments that existed at the time of his death. Thus, he will owe on any delinquent child support, as well as any involuntary tort judgments and government fees and taxes. This means that **options (a), (c), and (d) are incorrect** because these are valid debts against Rupert's estate.

18. **Option (b) is the best option** in most states. In some states, including Florida, **option (c) is best.** The problem here is that the testator, Irving, did execute a codicil to his earlier will. There is a general rule that a codicil republishes the original will as of the time that the codicil is executed. If that rule is applied here, then the children are not pretermitted since they were born before the date of the codicil. See, *Azcunce v. Estate of Azcunce*, 586 So.2d 1216 (Fla. 3d DCA 1991)(so holding). But most states follow the Restatement approach which says that the doctrine of republication by codicil should only be used in cases that carry out testator's intent. See Restatement (Third) of Property: Wills and Other Donative Transfers, section 9.6 at comment e.

    > Republication by codicil. Under the doctrine of republication by codicil, a will is treated as if it were executed when its most recent codicil was executed, whether or not the codicil expressly republishes the prior will. The doctrine is not applied, however, if the effect of its application would be inconsistent with the testator's intent, as would usually be the case if its application would bar a share to an afterborn or after-adopted child under an omitted-child statute.

    Option (a) is incorrect. Charlene could claim a spousal share only if she were living in a state that recognized common law marriage. While a handful of states do, no state recognizes a common law marriage unless the partners themselves agreed to be married. It doesn't matter what the community thinks. Charlene and Irving would need to agree to be married before common law marriage could apply. And they never held themselves out as such.

Option (d) is also incorrect because mistake as to the efficacy of a will is not sufficient grounds to void it. Although mistake may be grounds to void a provision in a will that was tainted by the mistake, Irving was under no mistake when he executed his 2001 will. That means the 2001 will is valid, except to the extent it is trumped by the pretermitted child statute.

19. **The best answer is (d).** One must have capacity to revoke, which is similar to testamentary capacity. The mental ability needed both to execute a will and to revoke one is less than is needed to deal with one's everyday affairs. A person who has been adjudicated incompetent is presumptively not capable to execute or revoke a will. But that presumption can be rebutted if it can be proved that Vicki was in a lucid moment. Thus, **answer (a) is not the best** answer because the presumption about lack of capacity is rebuttable. **Answer (b) is simply incorrect.** Destroying a will by tearing it up, even if other documents are torn at the same time, is a sufficient revocatory act so long as Vicki has sufficient capacity and intent. **Answer (c) is not the best answer** because will #1 was revoked by will #2 and not by physical act.

20. **Option (d) is the best answer** because the devise to Bill was revoked by operation of law because of the divorce and Chelsea's gifts were revoked under the slayer statute (UPC § 2–803). Chelsea also could not serve as trustee if she was guilty in the death of her mother. A court would try to best approximate Hilary's intent, which was to keep the property in trust for the minor children, so a different trustee would be found. But Chelsea would not be entitled to serve as trustee or receive her share of the trust benefits because she failed to provide aid, which would satisfy the slayer statute's requirement of a felonious killing. **Option (c) is the second-best answer** because there may not be sufficient evidence to prove intentional or felonious killing, which means that Chelsea would not be knocked out of her mother's estate, nor would she be prohibited from serving as trustee. However, Bill's bequests are revoked because the divorce was finalized and the property was split. **Option (a) is incorrect** because Bill's gifts are revoked because of the divorce. Even though the bequests to Bill and Chelsea both might be revoked, the bequests to Hilary's other four children are not affected, which means that her will can still stand and she did not die intestate, meaning that **option (b) is also incorrect.**

21. **Option (d) is the best answer** but this is a very tricky question. David executed his will after Gregory's birth but before he knew of Gregory's existence, which would appear to suggest that Gregory is a pretermitted child. However, once David received a judgment of paternity, the date of parentage is set to the child's birth. Under this relation back principle, Gregory would not count as a pretermitted child because he was born before David made his will. Ginny, however, was born after the will and

would normally be entitled to a pretermitted child share. Unfortunately, both Ginny and Gregory are provided for in the will as alternate beneficiaries if Alison predeceases David so they do not count as *pretermitted* children. Therefore, under UPC § 2–302(a), because they are provided for in his will they are not entitled to pretermitted child shares, which omits **option (a).** The second best answer is **option (b),** since Ginny was certainly born after David executed his will, but the alternate bequest to his heirs at law would normally strike Ginny. And if it strikes Ginny, it will strike Gregory as well, even though he technically is not a pretermitted child since he was born before the will was executed. **Option (c) is clearly incorrect** because Gregory was born before the will was executed and Ginny was born afterwards. The fact that both Gregory and Ginny are non-marital children is irrelevant, especially since David acknowledged paternity of both children.

22. **Option (b) is the best answer,** although this is tricky. It is true that some people with brain injuries may lack capacity to write a will. But the test for capacity is whether the testator knows a) the natural objects of his bounty, b) the nature and extent of his property, and c) the disposition he is making and how it relates to the other two elements. Because Ben's will shows that he understands the natural objects of his bounty and is providing for his brother and sister-in-law who have been taking care of him, there is nothing to indicate that he is lacking mental capacity so **option (a) is incorrect.** And although Caleb took Ben to the lawyer and assisted with translating Ben's wishes, there is no indication that Caleb procured the will or influenced Ben in making the will, thus precluding any undue influence allegation. Ben initiated the will conversation and asked for help in getting it done. That means **option (d) is incorrect. Option (c) is the second best answer** because it does appear that Ben formed the intent to benefit Caleb, Jenny, and Newman. However, intent alone is insufficient if the testator lacks mental capacity. Thus, as between answers (b) and (c) the first question will be whether Ben had capacity. And if he did, then so long as the will reflects his intentions, it will be valid.

23. **Option (b) is the best answer.** A beneficiary of a gift of securities is entitled to any securities identified in the will, or any securities of another organization acquired as a result of a consolidation, reorganization, or merger (see UPC § 2–605). That is what happened when ABC corp bought out XYZ corp. The other answers are incorrect because a beneficiary is not entitled to different or additional stock purchased or acquired by the decedent, which eliminates **options (a) and (c). Option (d) is also incorrect** although Jason would be entitled to the remaining proceeds from the sale of the XYZ stock by a guardian through traditional ademption rules such as UPC § 2–606 but he is not entitled to the shares Janice inherited.

24. **Option (d)** is the best answer without additional facts. A trustee is entitled to compensation for her time and efforts as a trustee, which means that **options (a) and (c) are incorrect.** Thus, so long as Giana

is not taking an excessive fee, she is entitled to compensation. Similarly, Giana is entitled to establish an account for the trust assets, and so long as she does not commingle them, her actions are appropriate, which means that **options (a) and (b) are incorrect.** It is possible that Giana has breached her duty of prudent administration if the bank account is not paying sufficient interest and a reasonably prudent person would instead invest the funds in a different account that might generate more income. But that is not a breach of the duty of loyalty and those facts are not provided in the question.

25. **Option (c) is the best answer.** Persons with standing to participate in probate include anyone named in a will, including the personal representative, all creditors, and any legal heirs. Elsie does not have standing because her father, Jon, would take as heir instead of her. The New York Humane Society does have standing because they may have been the intended recipient of Abel's bequest if Abel had made a mistake, such as a scrivener's error in the description of the organization. Elsie is the only person who lacks standing because whether or not the will is judged to be valid, she would not be entitled to any of Abel's estate. **Options (a), (b), and (d) are incorrect** because creditors, legal heirs, and devisees do have standing.

EXAM VII
ANSWER KEY AND EXPLANATIONS

1. **Option (c) is the best answer.** Under class gift rules, a class remains open to take in additional members until it either closes naturally, which would be the death of both Aileen and Salvador, or until distribution of assets under the rule of convenience. When Louisa dies, the then-living nieces and nephews are entitled to distribution of principal. So, the trustee must determine the number of shares into which the trust assets must be divided. Under UPC § 2–707, class gift rules are changed from the traditional common law rule. Traditionally, a class member who dies before the time for distribution would lose their share, which would be redistributed to other class members. That is what would normally happen to the share of the niece who died. But under UPC § 2–707, all shares are deemed contingent until distribution, but a substitute gift is created for the living issue of any class member who predeceases. This means that the deceased niece's issue will be entitled to a share. If these interests of the nieces and nephews are considered to be vested subject to open, then the deceased niece's estate will take her share. Either way, the proper outcome is to divide the trust into ten shares. **Option (b) is the second best answer** because, under the common law, class gifts lapse and pass to other class members if they were contingent. Since the class closing rule would require closing of this class when it becomes possessory, then nine shares would be created for the living nieces and nephews. **Option (a) is incorrect** because Aidan used class gift terminology (i.e., he did not name his nieces and nephews by name) and delayed into the future when distribution would occur (at Louisa's death). Both of these imply that he would want to take in additional class members up until the point of distribution. **Option (d) is incorrect** since the rule of convenience requires the closing of an open class when the first taker is entitled to distribution. Salvador's desire to wait is not warranted as the rule of convenience requires that he close the class.

2. **Option (b) is the best answer.** While it might be true under state statutory law that a decedent has a legal right to give directions about his or her own burial (some states, including Florida, California, and Louisiana have such a statute), the normal remedy in cases where the wishes are not followed is specific performance of the stated wishes. See *Byrd v. Byrd*, 488 So.2d 1134 (La. App. 1986)(decedent's wishes, expressed only orally, authorized parents to exhume son's body from burial location chosen by wife and to bury him in parent's cemetery close to son's grandfather, which was the wish of the son). But, at common law, a decedent has no right to give binding instructions regarding disposition of his or her body. So to say that Robbie was legally entitled to have his

funeral wishes followed is simply not true under the common law, which the question states is the applicable law.

At common law, the human body is regarded as quasi property and is protected as such. See 22A Am. Jur. 2d Dead Bodies § 3 (2019). But it is not the sort of property than can be "owned" by anyone. The decedent does not own his body at time of death and so has no right to say what should happen with the body, whether it should be buried or cremated, for example. Some states have changed that by statue. A number of states have enacted statutes that authorize the appointment of an agent who can make binding legal decisions about the disposal of the body of the principal. Only a handful of states give that right to the decedent who has not appointed an agent. For a state by state analysis of a person's right to control their own burial or to name an agent to do so see the Funeral Consumers Alliance web page at:

https://funerals.org/your-rights/state-by-state-rights/state-by-state-assigning-an-agent-to-control-disposition/

States that do authorize a decedent by statute to direct the disposition of his remains do not say who can enforce that direction. There are no facts to suggest that a friend, like Shaggy, would have any such right. And even if he did have a right to enforce, that right would be to assert compliance with Robbie's instructions and not damages to Shaggy. He certainly has no standing to make a claim for damages. What is the specific harm to Shaggy for the failure to follow Robbie's instructions? There is none suggested by the facts.

As to Robbie's instructions, the general rule is that requests must be reasonable and legal. The instruction about the weed is questionable. It would depend on the applicable state law. But **option (c) seems enforceable.** The tattoos could have been removed. There does not seem to be any public policy affecting that. Of course, Robbie could not demand that they be displayed if no one wanted to have them hanging on their walls. And of course it is too late now to enforce that request because of the cremation. Since removal of the tattoos is likely permissible, **option (c) is incorrect** as an answer.

Option (d) is similarly incorrect, because there is no public policy against burial in a mushroom suit. A mushroom suit is a burial garment made from organic cotton and mushroom spores that is intended to help decompose the body and nourish the soil. Under state statutory law, burial in a mushroom suit may require a licensed professional, but it is not unreasonable or against the law generally. **Option (a) is also incorrect** because it does not state a legal rule, but rather a prudential standard. Wishes expressed in a will may have legal effect but, in most cases, they are unlikely to be followed since wills are not ordinarily probated or consulted before burial.

3. **Option (b) is the best answer** because the general rule on advancements is that any lifetime gift is NOT considered an advancement unless there is a contemporaneous writing by the donor (answer a), or an

acknowledgement by the donee that the gift is an advancement (**option (c)**). See UPC § 2–109(a). The UPC also treats lifetime gifts as advancements if there is a contemporaneous writing by the donor or a writing by the donee indicating that the gift is to be taken into account in computing the division and distribution of the decedent's estate (**option (d)**). Because the UPC, and most states, require a writing of some sort, the facts in **option (b)** are the most likely to be insufficient to treat the gifts as advancements.

4. This is a very tricky question but **option (a)** is the best. At the time Caroline drafted her will, she had a clear intention of devising $100,000 to ABC University and there was no ambiguity in the bequest itself. When she later changed the beneficiary designation and drafted the gift letter she could have stated that the money from her IRA was to be in satisfaction of the devise, but she did not do so. She simply said the money was for the scholarship fund and the fact that there was no scholarship fund until it was created with her money does not matter—the letter did not say the IRA designation was in satisfaction of the bequest nor did it refer to the bequest in any way. Thus, the gift letter does not meet the contemporaneous writing requirement under UPC § 2–609 which requires either that the will provides for deduction of the gift, the testator declared in a contemporaneous writing that the gift is in satisfaction of the bequest, or the devisee acknowledged in writing that the gift was in satisfaction of the bequest. None of these occurred, so **option (d) is incorrect. Option (b) is also inaccurate** because extrinsic evidence is admissible to resolve latent ambiguities in a will. **Option (c) is inaccurate** because the gift letter cannot show intent at the time Caroline drafted her will, which occurred earlier. Because all we are doing is interpreting Caroline's will, there is no ambiguity, but if there was, then extrinsic evidence could be admitted. The real problem here is that the gift letter does not meet the contemporaneous writing requirement for ademption by satisfaction and a simple beneficiary designation cannot clarify what Caroline's intent was when she drafted her will, months earlier (option (d)).

5. **Option (d) is the best answer.** Clearly Kevin formed the intention to make the gifts of the money to Lesley in anticipation of his death, and he died of the causes that motivated the gifts. That would normally make option (a) the correct answer, but the general rule on checks is that the gift is incomplete until they are cashed because, until then, the donor of the gifts could exercise control by contacting the bank and stopping payment on the checks. Since delivery was not complete, **neither option (a) nor (b) would be correct.** However, some states may treat delivery of the check itself as delivery of the money it represents since that would follow the donor's likely intent. But that would certainly be a minority view. **Option (c) is also incorrect** because Kevin formed the intent to make the gift during his life and followed through by attempting to deliver, thus, he was trying to make an inter vivos gift and not a testamentary gift.

6. **Option (c) is the correct answer** under a classic per stirpes distribution. Under classic per stirpes, the estate is divided into shares for each living child and for each deceased child leaving issue. Since there were three children, and each left issue or survived Cynthia, we do our initial distribution into 3 shares. So, Anabelle takes her 1/3. Then Michael left 2 surviving children and 1 deceased child who left living issue, so his share is divided into 3 shares for 1/9 of Cynthia's estate. Britney and Cleo each take 1/9 and Imogen and Kristina share Herman's 1/9 for 1/18 each. Nadine's 1/3 is divided into 4 shares for her living children, Darren, Ernestine, Flaco, and Gabby, so each of those grandchildren received 1/12 of Cynthia's estate. **Option (d) would be correct** in a state that follows the per capita by generation rule of the UPC. **Neither Option (a) nor (b) is correct** because the fractional shares do not add up to 1. And **Option (a)** is incorrect because Herman did not survive Cynthia. He did leave lineal descendants, so his children will take his share.

7. **Option (d) is the best answer** since the UTATA (Uniform Testamentary Additions to Trusts Act) does not require that the unfunded trust be in existence or be funded either prior to execution of the will or that it be funded before death. In fact, so long as the trust was in existence before Jackson's death, it is considered an inter vivos trust and can dispose of the property pouring over from the will. Although the law used to be that the trust had to be in existence, funded, and unchanged prior to execution of the will in order to dispose of probate property, the UTATA has changed that in all states, thus making **option (a) incorrect. Option (b) is also incorrect** because in all but 2 states (Florida and New York), revocable trusts do not have to be executed with the will formalities. **Option (c) is incorrect** because if the trust failed, a court would not impose a constructive trust unless injustice would otherwise result. Since the pour over did not pass all of Jackson's property to Eric outright, which would be contrary to Jackson's intent, there is no need for a constructive trust. If the will and/or trust were to fail for some reason, the result would be intestacy and not a constructive trust.

8. **Option (b) is the best answer.** Mistakes in the expression are mistakes that are made in the will, something like a scrivener's error. Mistakes in the inducement are mistakes the testator has made about a fact that induces her to make a particular bequest. Helen had the appropriate intent to benefit her 16 cousins, but she used the wrong term in her will. She mistakenly believed that her heirs at law were her cousins and not her aunt. That is a mistake of law that is expressed in the will itself. Had she bequeathed her property to "my cousins" her intent would have been correctly reflected. **Option (a) is incorrect** because that would be a mistake of fact, as if she thought one of her devisees was a cousin when that person was actually not related to her. **Options (c) and (d) are incorrect** because mistakes in the inducement are mistakes about a fact or the law that causes someone to make a bequest they would not ordinarily make. If Helen had mistakenly believed that her siblings were deceased and made a bequest to her cousins instead, that would be a mistake of fact in the inducement (assuming she would have preferred to

leave her property to her siblings). If she mistakenly believed that the law would cause her to have a tremendous estate tax liability and therefore made a huge bequest to a charity, that would be a mistake of law in the inducement.

9. **Option (c) is the correct option.** Parties may enter into agreements to limit spousal rights, such as a share in the other's estate, spousal maintenance, or a particular distribution of property at divorce, but they may not limit child support provisions under the Uniform Premarital Agreement Act. This means that **options (a), (b), and (d) are incorrect** because these rights can all be waived or limited through a pre-marital agreement.

10. **Option (d) is the best option.** UTC § 503 provides the exceptions to a spendthrift provision. These are a) a beneficiary's child, spouse, or former spouse who has a judgment or court order for support or maintenance, b) a judgment creditor who has provided services for the protection of a beneficiary's interest in the trust, and c) a claim of the state or the US. This means that the spousal and child support judgments are superior and Penelope can pierce the spendthrift provision for payment of any arrears on these judgments. She cannot pierce the spendthrift for future payments, however. The IRS is also a privileged creditor and can seek payment from the trust. However, Mark's lawyer would only be entitled to trust assets if the legal services were expended to help protect Mark's interest in the trust. Since the lawyer's services were for Mark's divorce, the lawyer is not a privileged creditor and may not pierce the spendthrift provision. This means that **options (a), (b), and (c) are wrong** because these are valid exceptions to a spendthrift provision.

11. This is a very tricky question because some elements of each of these theories are present. However, **option (d) is the best answer** because it is the **least** likely to be successful. In order to have a bequest revoked under the slayer statute, the slayer must have intentionally and feloniously killed the decedent under UPC § 2–803. There is no evidence in the facts given that Elena intentionally or feloniously killed Rupert. Although she gave him fake news and that raised his blood pressure, he also was suffering from congestive heart failure that was the ultimate cause of his death. The other three options may not be successful, but they are more likely successful than option (d). As to **option (a),** Elena appears to have procured the will (she used her own lawyer rather than Rupert's) and she was in a close and confidential relationship with someone who suffered from some reduced capacity. Those facts support the claim of "undue influence," so this option cannot be the LEAST likely. **Option (b) is also possible** but also not a clearly successful argument since the test for mental capacity is whether the testator 1) knows the natural objects of his bounty, 2) knows the nature and extent of his property, and 3) understands the disposition he is making and its effect on the beneficiaries. In this case Rupert seems to understand the extent of his property, he knows about his trusts, and his surviving spouse is a natural object of his bounty. Although the congestive heart failure may have

caused him to hallucinate or lack capacity, the will itself is not an obvious indication of incapacity. Nevertheless, deviating from a long-standing estate plan to give everything to a new spouse of just a few months might be evidence of incapacity. Still, this seems a stronger claim than option (d). **Option (c) is also possible** but also not likely to be successful. Insane delusion requires that the testator believe something completely unbelievable and refuse to change his mind when provided with accurate information. If Rupert began to believe all of the conspiracy theories and fake news and would not change his mind when presented with facts, he could be suffering from an insane delusion. The question is how much that delusion **affected** his will. Technically it did not affect it at all unless the desire to leave all to his wife was affected by the delusion that everything he was reading about in the news was true. This option is probably the second best answer because it is a fairly weak claim on the facts. The weakest theory, however, is the slayer statute, **option (d).**

12. **Option (d)** is the best answer because a co-owner will take automatically any property held as joint tenants with rights of survivorship or tenancy by the entirety (a spouse only can hold as tenants by the entirety), and designated beneficiaries will automatically take any property held with a beneficiary designation. Thus, the family home and the bank account will pass automatically to Rebecca, and the securities account will pass to the children who are the designated beneficiaries. The tangible personal property and the cabin are the only items owned outright by Jason at his death that will pass by the laws of descent since he died intestate. Under the UPC, a surviving spouse takes the all of the intestate property if the children of the decedent are also the children of the surviving spouse (see UPC § 2–102(1)(ii)). There is no probate property left for the surviving children. In some states, **option (b)** will be correct if a spouse takes a "child's" share under intestacy. In all states, however, co-owned property and the securities account with a beneficiary designation will pass automatically and are not disposed of according to the default rules of intestacy. **Options (a) and (c) are also incorrect** because Rebecca is the parent of the surviving children. If Rebecca had not been the parent of the children, then under the UPC she would be entitled to the first $150,000 and then half the remaining intestate probate property, which would come out of the tangible personal property and the cabin. And the children would take all of the probate property only if there were no surviving spouse. But since she is the parent of the children, she receives 100% of the tangible personal property and the cabin. She will also receive the family home and the cash in the bank account by virtue of being a co-owner. The children will split the securities account by virtue of the beneficiary designation.

13. **Option (b) is the best answer** because under most state laws a nonmarital child is entitled to inherit from a father only if the parents 1) participated in a wedding ceremony before or after the birth of the child, 2) the paternity of the child is established by judicial adjudication before or after the death of the father, or 3) the father acknowledged the paternity in writing. The 2019 UPC provides that a parent-child

relationship can be established either through adoption or de facto parentage, but the latter requires either an adjudication or that the parent voluntarily act as a parent. Since Herbert did not acknowledge paternity in writing and paternity was not established by a judicial adjudication, the only grounds for Abigail being entitled to inherit is that Herbert and Julia eventually married. It is not necessary for Herbert to know that Abigail was his child either before or after the marriage. Although Abigail is Herbert's biological child, she is not entitled to inherit from him solely on that ground since she was born out of wedlock and Herbert had no knowledge of her existence which makes **option (a) wrong.** As noted above, if the father does not acknowledge the child, or in this case even know about her, one of the three statutory requirements must be met for Abigail to inherit. That means that **options (c) and (d) are not correct.** The fact that Abigail already inherited from Greg, her putative father, is also irrelevant to her right to inherit from Herbert. If Greg had adopted Abigail, or Abigail had sought a judicial adjudication that Greg was her adoptive father through an equitable adoption adjudication, then the adoption would have cut off her rights to inherit from her biological father, Herbert.

14. **Option (d) is the best answer.** Mental capacity requires understanding three things: 1) the natural objects of one's bounty, 2) the general nature of one's property, and 3) that one is making an orderly disposition of the property. Although the will appears to make an orderly disposition of Tony's property, it fails to even mention the natural objects of his bounty, which are his wife and children.

    Option (a) is incorrect because although the witness signatures are indecipherable, extrinsic evidence could be used to identify the witnesses and they could be summoned to provide testimony that the will was validly executed.

    Although leaving property to a computer may seem evidence of incapacity, many testators provide devises to corporations, charities, and in trust to perform benevolent deeds. If Tony otherwise had capacity, a gift to Jarvis could be interpreted by a court as a gift, perhaps in trust, to promote artificial intelligence research or to house, maintain, and protect Tony's actual computer system for the general benefit or society, i.e., as a charitable gift. Consider the fact that gifts to pets are often construed to be gifts in an "honorary trust" for the benefit of the pet. A similar solution might be available for a gift to a computer. Otherwise, a gift to a pet will fail, but will not invalidate the entire will. Similarly, standing alone, the gift to Jarvis, although it might fail, is likely insufficient to show that Tony lacked mental capacity. That makes **option (c) less than ideal but perhaps second best.**

    Option (b) is also not ideal. Testators may make gifts to strangers, as Charles Vance Millar did when he devised his estate to the woman in Toronto who could produce the most children in the decade following his death. Four women ultimately successfully claimed the bequest having each produced nine children during that time. And a mistaken description of a beneficiary is not sufficient to strike down the entire will on grounds of incompetence. (Remember, if he failed to devise property to his surviving spouse she would likely be entitled to an elective share, but that has no bearing on whether or not the will is valid.)

If it could be shown that Tony's will was the result of a super-hero complex, then the Jarvis and Bruce Banner devises could be evidence of an insane delusion, thereby invalidating the gifts on grounds of mental incompetence. However, that option is not specifically offered as an option in the question. And a will that suggests the testator does not know the natural objects of his bounty fails one of the most basic elements of capacity under law. That makes **(d) the best answer.**

15. **Option (c) is the best answer** because there is no indication that Albert would not want the gifts to Bonnie and Clyde to pass to their lineal descendants under the anti-lapse statute. Application of the anti-lapse statute results in a substitute gift being created for the lineal descendants of any devisee who is related to the testator through a grandparent. Since the anti-lapse statute would pass the house to all three of Bonnie's children, and the cash and securities to both of Clyde's children, Dania and Edward will share those bequests with their siblings. Then they will each take the bequests which were devised to them: Dania gets the artwork and Edward gets the car. Isabel takes the residue. However, **(d) is the second best answer** because if the anti-lapse statute is not applied, then the gifts to Bonnie and Clyde both lapse and will pass into the residue to go to Isabel. **Option (a) is incorrect** because a predeceased beneficiary cannot take a gift, so the devises would not pass to Bonnie and Clyde's estates. The UPC provides, instead, that the gift goes directly to the lineal descendants of the pre-deceased legatee or devisee. Finally, **option (b) is incorrect** because although Dania and Edward are descendants of Bonnie and Clyde, the anti-lapse statute would create substitute gifts in all of their descendants and not just those named in the will. It is an interesting question, therefore, whether Albert would prefer the gifts to lapse and pass to Isabel through the residue rather than to the nieces and nephews who were not named in the will at all. But without any additional indication, the presumption is to apply the anti-lapse statute so long as a beneficiary is of the required degree of relationship, which means that without more, Bonnie and Clyde's bequests would pass to their lineal descendants under anti-lapse.

16. **Option (a) is the best answer.** Under UPC § 2–707, all future interests in trusts are deemed to be contingent upon surviving to distribution. The interests in Alexi, Barbie, and Connie are contingent by virtue of the fact that they are entitled only to life estates. That means that if any of them predeceases Linda, that child's interest is terminated because their interest in the property was not inheritable. Under normal common law rules, the five grandchildren would have vested remainders subject to open. But the UPC trust provision turns their interests into remainders that are contingent on surviving until distribution, i.e., the death of each of their mothers. Thus, Alexi's children have to survive her to take, and

Barbie's have to survive her to take, etc. **Option (c) is the next best answer** because under traditional common law rules the children would have vested remainders in life estates and the grandchildren would have vested remainders subject to open. But because UPC § 2–707 makes the grandchildren's interests contingent on survival, their remainders are both contingent on surviving and contingent on ascertaining the full class of grandchildren at the death of all the children. **Option (b) is incorrect** because Linda clearly has a life estate and not a defeasible fee interest and **Option (d) is incorrect** because a pour over into an unfunded trust is valid in all states under the Uniform Testamentary Additions to Trust Act or its equivalent.

17. **Option (b) is the best answer** assuming we are in a UPC state that allows for revival of a prior revoked will if that is the intent of the testator. Will 2 is validly executed under the UPC 2–502 even though the witnesses were not present at the time each of them signed. UPC 2–502 requires only that each witness sign within a reasonable time of witnessing the testator sign. The facts support that. And, besides, if there is any question whether or not these facts are sufficient to comply with 2–502, the UPC will validate the will under 2–503 under the "harmless error" doctrine. So if the testator intended this will as his will at the time he signed it, and there is clear and convincing evidence of that fact (which there appears to be) then 2–503 will validate the will. If the state were a strict compliance state, then will 2 was never properly executed because the witnesses were not present at the same time. **Option (a) is incorrect** because the first will was revoked by the second will by writing, and that second will was valid under the UPC and Juan had the intent to revoke Will 1 when he executed Will 2. **Option (c) is incorrect** because he revoked will 3 by physical act when he tore it up with intent to revoke it. **Option (d) is incorrect** because the UPC does not permit a revoked will to be revived if the testator did not have the intent to revive that will. In this case Juan revoked will 3 with the intent of reviving will 2, not will 1. So answer (d) would not reflect Juan's intent.

18. **Option (c) is the best answer** because the other three options clearly do not apply. Under the UPC, a testamentary writing whose material provisions are in the testator's handwriting is valid as a will. Technically, the writing may be seen as a codicil or amendment to the earlier attested will, but it is also a will in and of itself as to the gift of the poodle. Its validity doesn't depend on there being a prior valid will. **Option (a), which refers to a codicil, is incorrect,** however, because republication by codicil does not validate the codicil. Instead it validates a prior, otherwise valid will, by making it speak as of the date of the codicil. That doctrine is unnecessary in our current fact situation Because Raleigh had forgotten about his poodle at the time he wrote his will and did not mention either a separate writing or any other dispositive document, neither Incorporation by Reference nor Separate Writing Doctrine can be used. That means that **options (b) and (d) are incorrect.**

19. **Option (c) is the best answer** because Kurt deliberately lied in order to influence the bequest that Valerie was making. **Option (a) is incorrect** because duress requires a threat to do an illegal act, usually an act of violence. Kurt lied but he did not threaten to do anything illegal. **Option (b) is incorrect** although it is likely the second best option. The only questionable action by Kurt is his lie. It was her decision to make a will, her decision to go to the lawyer, and she asked Kurt to drive her there. He did not pressure her at any stage in her decision to redo her estate plan. He did not give instructions to the lawyer or otherwise participate in drafting the will or securing witnesses to the will. In a state like California, there is a presumption of undue influence in cases involving the elderly if an unrelated person becomes a caregiver (unless they were a pre-existing close friend of the elderly person). But that presumption is rebuttable and so even if a state recognizes such a presumption, **option (c) is a better option** because these facts raise a clear case of fraud in the inducement. **Option (d) is incorrect** because fraud in the execution requires proof that the wrongdoer intentionally misrepresented the character or contents of the will and that it did not represent the testator's intent. Kurt's lie was instead fraud in the inducement.

20. **Option (c) is the best answer** because a surviving spouse is always entitled to a forced, minimum share (elective share) under common law (except in Georgia and the community property states). However, if Esperanza and Pablo live in a community property state, or in Georgia that does not provide for an elective share, then **option (b) is likely the next best answer.** Pablo is certainly a pretermitted spouse because the marriage occurred after the will was executed and he was not provided for. However, most pretermitted spousal statutes do not apply if the testator clearly intended to exclude the spouse. In this case, Esperanza knew that she and Pablo were going to marry, so he was not accidentally omitted. Since Pablo is guaranteed an elective share, but might not be guaranteed a pretermitted spousal share because of the timing of the will, the elective share is a better challenge. Pablo might be able to argue that the mental upset of the cancer diagnosis was sufficient to render her incapacitated, and then **option (a) would be plausible.** However, that same argument might backfire because the cancer diagnosis arguably caused her to ask Pablo to marry her. And although the mental capacity required to marry is usually lower than that to make a will, any argument that the cancer diagnosis affected her mental capacity could put the validity of the marriage into question. The fact that Pablo was not appointed personal representative is irrelevant; a testator can name anyone as personal representative who will take priority over the statutory defaults, so **option (d) is incorrect.**

21. **Option (a) is the best answer** because UPC § 2–605 and most state ademption rules do provide that beneficiaries of stock will receive different amounts or even stock in different companies under certain circumstances. These are a) securities acquired by reason of action initiated by the organization (that would mean the stock split is covered and any additional shares acquired because of the split would pass to

Jason), b) securities acquired by a plan of reinvestment (that would mean the shares purchased with the reinvested dividends would pass to Jason). Additional securities purchased by the testator or acquired by inheritance would not pass as part of the bequest. This means that if we go through the question carefully, **option (b)** is permissible under the facts stated if Janice purchased the extra 40 shares, **option (c)** is permissible if 20 extra shares were acquired by stock split but the other 20 were inherited by Janice. **Option (d)** is permissible if all the extra shares were acquired by reinvestment or stock split. Since options (b), (c), and (d) would all be correct under the facts given, option (a) must be incorrect.

22. **Option (a) is the best answer.** Although open-ended, indefinite, and vague descriptions of trust beneficiaries are generally too vague to be considered ascertainable, a settlor may designate an indefinite class so long as the settlor grants the trustee sole discretion to choose from within that class, and membership in the class can be confirmed. To be valid, Molly must identify who attended Penelope's funeral and choose from among those. Molly must exercise her power within a reasonable time, but no person not chosen can complain unless Molly were to choose someone who did not attend Penelope's funeral. **Option (d) is the next best answer** because if the trust fails for lack of ascertainable beneficiaries, the property would lapse and pass by intestacy in this case since it was a residuary bequest. **Option (c) is incorrect** since Penelope made it clear that Molly was not to take the property for herself, but was to give it to others, thus showing intent to create a trust. **Option (b) is also incorrect** because failed gifts do not escheat to the state unless the decedent had no legal heirs. But since Jackson was alive and is her brother, he would take before the state if the trust failed.

23. **Option (c) is the best answer** because at the time Alex removed the funds and put them into his sole name, they became part of his probate estate and would pass according to his will. Although **option (a)** seems like the right answer, it is not because whether Alex intended to make an irrevocable gift to Elizabeth when he added her name to the account as a joint tenant depends on his intent, and since he intended for her to receive the funds only at his death, and he never gave up possession or control over the funds, he did not intend to create a true joint tenancy. In most states, a joint bank account is never viewed as a true joint tenancy since the depositing joint tenant has to right to withdraw all the funds thereby totally destroying the other joint tenant's interest. That makes it unlike a joint tenancy in land where the donee joint tenant actually owns the equivalent of a 50% undivided interest in the land. **Option (b) is also incorrect** because even though the will expresses a mistake, it is not clear that the mistake tainted the will. And even if it did taint the will, there is no indication of how Alex would want the funds to pass. Since he clearly intended to remove Elizabeth from the account after he had executed the will, whatever mistake may have existed at the time he wrote the will is of no moment. A testator can always dispose of property during life if he so chooses, and such gifts will be considered adeemed by extinction. In this case, his change of the funds in the account was

intended to remove Elizabeth as a taker at his death, and any language in the will to the contrary is not relevant since the will was executed prior to his change of mind. **Option (d) is also incorrect** because Alex has a valid will with a valid residuary clause leaving all to Sebastian, so the funds do not lapse and pass by intestacy.

24. **Option (d) is the best answer** because once Hazel gave the ring to Ethan, it was adeemed by extinction. Only if Ethan were to give back the ring to Hazel, so that it was hers at her death, would Isabel be entitled to it. Furthermore, a recipient of a specific devise is usually not entitled to the monetary value of the bequest unless the item is missing from the estate due to an action by a third party, such as sale by a guardian or condemnation. However, UPC § 2–606(a)(6) would give a devisee of specifically devised property a pecuniary devise equal to the value of the item "to the extent it is established that ademption would be inconsistent with the testator's manifested plan of distribution, . . . [or that at] the date of distribution or otherwise, the testator did not intend ademption of the devise." Without any other facts, it seems that Hazel clearly knew she was giving the ring to Ethan and it was reasonable to believe that Ethan and Carol's marriage would last, so the ring was permanently gone. As between Carol and Ethan's entitlement to the ring, that is a different matter. The traditional rule when engagements are broken is that the ring is returned if the wearer was responsible for the broken engagement or the donor can prove it was a conditional gift. However, Ethan and Carol were married and subsequently divorced, which means that the ring would have been accounted for as part of the property settlement at divorce. Assuming Carol was entitled to the ring, Ethan could not recover it and the court could not order Carol to give it to Isabel, so **option (a) is incorrect.** As between **options (b) and (c), (b) is better** because if a court were to order a pecuniary devise to Isabel, it would come from Hazel's general estate and not from Ethan's share specifically. But that would only happen if Isabel could show that Hazel did not intend for the ring to be adeemed when she gave it to Ethan, a showing that would be very difficult to make.

25. **The best answer is option (c).** This is a private trust for the benefit of Kamala's family and so it does not qualify as a charitable trust. Therefore **option (a) is incorrect.** The trust does violate the Rule against Perpetuities because we don't know about future vesting. As a result, **option (b) is correct at common law.** Under the analysis of the Rule, this trust could last for 500 years, well beyond lives in being plus 21 years. BUT, most states have adopted the Uniform Statutory Rule Against Perpetuities, which would at the very least allow this trust to exist for 90 years (the statutory period). If you think about this rationally, the trust may well be exhausted in 90 years. Given the high cost of college and university tuition, one million dollars could be spent easily within that period. And if it is, then there is no violation. And so option (c) would in effect validate the trust. The statutory rule would at least require waiting 90 years to see if the trust had vested. We should also point out that some states have repealed the rule altogether. And others have adopted judicial

doctrines, such as "wait and see" to determine whether or not the rule is violated. Nonetheless **option (c) is the best answer. Option (d) is wrong** because the gift does violate the Rule Against Perpetuities.

EXAM VIII
ANSWER KEY AND EXPLANATIONS

California Exam

1. **Option (c) is the best answer.** Under California law, the surviving spouse takes 100% of the deceased spouse's share of the community property. Some students confuse the wording in California Probate Code § 6401, which says "(a) As to community property, the intestate share of the surviving spouse is the one-half of the community property that belongs to the decedent under Section 100." They think that means that the surviving spouse only takes one-half of the decedent spouse's community property. But the statute says she takes "the" one-half that he owns. All he owns is one-half so she takes all of his community property. So she takes it all. Thus, **option (d) is wrong.** However, separate property is split between the surviving spouse and any children of Harry. Section 6401 says that if he has more than one child (and he does) then the surviving spouse only takes one-third. Under Section 6402 any of the estate that does not pass to the surviving spouse will go to the issue of the decedent, taking equally if they are all related in the same degree (which they are here because they are all children). This means that Wanda will take one-third of the separate property and the two minor children will each take one-third. That makes **option (c) the best answer.**

2. **Option (d) is the best answer.** A gift in trust that is revocable by the trustor is an "at-death transfer" under California Probate Code § 21104. And under CPC § 21109, beneficiaries of an "at-death transfer" must survive the death of the Trustor in order to take. That makes **option (a) incorrect.** Option (a) would be correct under the common law because there is no express requirement of survival attached to Steve's gift. At common law, Steve has a vested remainder and so at his father's death the remainder would pass to Steve's estate. But the CPC changes this result for an "at-death transfer." The transferee, Steve, must survive. So where does the property go? Absent the application of a statute, the failed gift to Steve would revert to Trustor's estate. That would make option (b) the correct response. But **option (b) is incorrect.** That is because, under California law, the anti-lapse statute applies. See CPC § 21110 which provides that if the transferee fails to survive the transferor, the lapsed gift shall pass to the transferee's issue. Here, the issue is Diane and so she takes because Steve, her father, was the beneficiary of an "at-death transfer." **Option (c) is incorrect** because there is no California statute that requires future interests in trust to survive until the time of distribution. There is such a statue in the UPC, but California has not adopted that statute.

3. **Option (d) is the best option.** Under the UPC both options (a) and (b) are possible. Under the UPC, the intent at the time of creation of the account is what matters. If Jane wants to provide that the funds go elsewhere because of a change in her intent then she would have to do so in accord with the bank's rules about how to change beneficiaries on a joint account. That would mean the funds go to Jules. But if Jean could prove that Jane's intent at the time she created the account was not to create a true joint account, but rather something akin to an agency account, under which Jules would have the power to withdraw funds, but only for the convenience of Jane, then Jules would not take. Parents sometimes create these accounts to give a child the power to access the parent's funds in the event the parent is ill or otherwise unable to pay his or her bills. But the point is that the intent at the time of the creation of the account is determinative. California, however, has a statute that provides that "Sums remaining on deposit at the death of a party to a joint account belong to the surviving party or parties as against the estate of the decedent **unless there is clear and convincing evidence of a different intent."** See CPC § 5302. Note that the statute does not say when that evidence or when that different intent must occur. A California appellate court has ruled that the intent expressed after the account was opened in a revocable trust is sufficient to satisfy the statute's requirement of a "different intent." See *Araiza v. Younkin,* 188 Cal.App.4th 1120 (2010). This case holds that the change of the beneficiary in a living trust is valid because it provides evidence of a "different intent" as of the trustor's death. Commentary from the California Law Commission also supports this conclusion. It says "the intention to negate survivorship may be shown to have existed after the time of creation of the account." Therefore **option (d) is the best answer. Option (c) might apply** if the change had been made in a will rather than a revocable trust. There is a California case, *Placencia v. Strazicich*, 42 Cal.App.5th 730 (2019), which holds that the "different intent" as to distribution of the funds in a joint or other form of survivorship account may be expressed in a will. But unlike the trust case, *Placencia* holds that the funds must go to the estate and be distributed under the will rather than distributed directly to the newly named beneficiary. But, under the facts in this question, the change was made in the revocable trust and not the will and so *Placencia* is not applicable.

4. **Option (d) is the best answer.** Here is why.

   The question asks you to identify statements that are NOT true, i.e., false. To answer any question like this, the best approach is to consider each statement and mark it as T or F. You are looking for statements that are false. **Option (a) is false.** In the absence of issue, parents, issue of parents, grandparents or their issue, the child of a predeceased spouse can inherit as a stepchild. So, although it is rare, it is certainly possible that a stepchild may inherit. Option (a) may appear to be the best answer, but you must read all options before you decide.

Option (b) is also false, The California intestacy statutes provide that distribution by right of representation is determined by a modern per stirpes rule (sometimes called per capita with representation) and not the strict or classic per stirpes rule. Strict per stirpes requires a division into shares at the first generation below the intestate, whether or not any of the members of that generation survived the intestate. Modern per stirpes tells us to make the division at that generation only if there is someone in that generation who is alive. Otherwise, the division will be made at a lower generation. The best example of this difference is a decedent who had two children who predeceased him, where those children had surviving issue. Strict per stirpes tells us to divide the estate into two parts and the children of the first child share that one half, whereas the children of the second child share that one half. Consider the difference in shares when child one is survived by only one child and child two is survived by five. Classis or strict per stirpes required the five children of child number two to share the parent's one half, giving them one-tenth each. But modern per stirpes would divide at the grandchild level and each of the 6 grandchildren would receive one-sixth of the estate.

Option (c) is true and so cannot be the best answer. An heir must survive by 120 hours. California has not adopted the 120 hour survival rule generally as under the UPC. But it has adopted this requirement of survival for intestate heirs.

Since both options (a) and (b) are false, the best answer is (d).

5. **The best answer is (b).** Under the UPC, the antilapse statute would apply and then (a) would be correct. But **(a) is not correct under California law** because the California anti-lapse statute does not apply whenever a testator specifically requires the beneficiary (here, Samuel) to survive. The justification is that T must have thought about the consequences of non-survival and is presumed to have known what the California rules are. The California rule is that failure to survive by a specific legatee means that the gift lapses and falls into the residuary. That is why Deb takes. **Option (c) is wrong** because it is irrelevant that T failed to provide otherwise, at least specifically. (The application of the lapse rule does provide otherwise and the presumption that T was aware of that rule really means that T did provide otherwise, implicitly.) T did provide a condition of survival and if that condition is not met then the gift lapses. The rules take over from there. A lapsed specific gift (which Blackacre is) falls into the residuary. **Option (d) is wrong** because Deb takes and there is no theory upon which to give Sam anything.

6. **The best answer is (a).** The applicable California statute says that a trust may be revoked either by the method provided in the will or by a writing, not a will, delivered to the trustee. Despite the fact that the statute says a will cannot revoke a trust, a will is nonetheless a writing which is signed by the testator, Alice, and necessarily delivered to the trustee, Alice, at the moment that she signs the writing. Therefore, the method provided in the trust, a "writing delivered to the trustee during the trustor's life" was satisfied and the gift in the trust was revoked. See

Gardenhire v. Superior Court (2005) 127 Cal.App.4th 882. The will leaves everything to Carl so **answer (a) is correct. Answer (b) is incorrect** because the will did revoke the trust, not because it was a will, but because it was a writing. **Answers (c) and (d) are incorrect** because the will effectively leaves everything to Carl.

7. **The best answer is (d).** CPC § 6122 revokes the will provision in favor of Mary. Therefore, **option (a) is wrong.** CPC § 5040 applies to any nonprobate transfer of property at death if the transfer is revocable. Therefore it applies to revocable trusts and it revokes any gift to an ex-spouse if divorce occurred after the execution of the document. As a result, the property in the revocable trust does not go to Mary. Therefore, **option (b) is wrong.** But § 5040 explicitly exempts life insurance from its coverage even though life insurance is revocable. As a result, Mary will get the life insurance proceeds. Therefore, **option (c) is wrong** and only **option (d) is correct.**

8. **The best answer is (c).** The gift to Wilma lapses but the gift cannot be saved under California's anti-lapse statute. That statute only applies to gifts made to Herman's "kindred" or to his wife's "kindred." And "kindred" has been construed by the courts to mean related by blood. Wilma was related by marriage and so is not "kindred" to Herman for purposes of the anti-lapse statute. See *In re Est. of Dye*, 112 Cal. Rptr. 2d 362 (Ct. App. 2001). Therefore, **option (a) is wrong.** Herman did die intestate and his adopted son Sam is clearly an heir. But so are the issue of Herman's other son Quince. Children, such as Quince, who are "adopted out," may still qualify as intestate heirs under CPC § 6451. Normally an adoption of a child will cut of the right of inheritance between the natural parent and the child who is "adopted out." But § 6451 provides that the relationship will be recognized for inheritance purposes if two requirements are satisfied: (1) The natural parent and the adopted person lived together at any time as parent and child, and (2) The adoption was by the spouse of either of the natural parents. Both of those conditions are met here. Therefore Quince and his issue will be recognized as Herman's heirs. Since Quince failed to survive he cannot take. Therefore **option (d) is incorrect.** Quince's issue can take in his place by right of representation. Therefore **option (b) is incorrect.** Under California's modern per stirpes approach the inheritance is divided at the child level because Sam is alive. Sam takes half and the other half passes by right of representation to Quince's three children, making **(c) the best answer.**

9. **Option (d) is the best option.** CPC § 6111 requires only the material provisions be in the Testator's handwriting. These include the names of the beneficiaries and the description of the gifts and some indication of testamentary intent. That test is satisfied here by the words "Everything to Betty." The word "to," written by T is likely sufficient indication of testamentary intent. Alternatively, we might rely on such words printed in the will form. The statute provides that testamentary intent may be shown by words in a commercially printed will form if that is what is used. A will downloaded from a legal documents web site likely meets the

required of a "commercially printed form," even though the actual "printing" was done by T. Regardless, the word "to" likely satisfies the testamentary intent requirement. If the requirement of showing testamentary intent, either in Tom's handwriting or in the words of the printed document, is not met, then (b) might be correct, but **(b) is not the best option** because the argument that "to" shows testamentary intent or that the form used was a commercially printed form are stronger arguments. **Option (a) is clearly not correct** because California no longer applies the "wholly in the handwriting" test for holographic wills. **Option (c) is not correct** because even if Betty can prove testamentary intent, there still needs to be sufficient satisfaction of the formalities. And further, proving by clear and convincing evidence is not the ONLY way she can win, since this will is most likely a valid holographic will.

10. **The best answer is (b).** California law does have dollar limits on gifts that can qualify under the statute for distribution of personal property by memorandum. The memorandum will control so long as it is sufficiently identified in the will and, unlike common law incorporation by reference, the memorandum does not need to be in existence at the time the will is executed. Therefore **option (d) is wrong.** The dollar limitations are that such memos cannot dispose of property which altogether is worth more than $25,000 and it cannot dispose of an item of property that is worth more than $5,000. The painting of Spot is worth only $4,000 and so it qualifies. The gift to Ned is valid. But the statute does not authorize disposition of cash gifts and so the $4,000 gift to Jane is not valid. That means that both **options (a) and (c) are wrong.**

11. **The best answer is (c).** California retains the common law rule against perpetuities. Therefore, **option (a) is wrong.** Under the traditional rule there is no life in being that can validate this gift. That is because the gift is to the first child of Amir to graduate from college. We don't know who that will be at Ursula's death. And Amir is still alive and so it is possible that he will have another child. Let's call him Seth. Then Amir and Sam, who were lives in being at Ursula's death might die and there is no certainty that this afterborn child, Seth, will graduate from college within 21 years of their deaths. Seth is a potential beneficiary who was not a life in being at Ursula's death. But California has adopted USRAP (the Uniform Statutory Rule Against Perpetuities). This statute acts as a savings clause when applied to any gift that does in fact violate the common law rule (which this gift does). But the rule allows us to "wait and see" what actually happens. So if contingent future interests do in fact vest within the period of the rule, that interest will be valid. That makes **option (b) wrong.** The gift to the first child is not absolutely void. We will have to "wait and see" what actually happens. **Option (c) is correct** under this "wait and see" approach because if it in fact turns out that Sam is the first to graduate from college then his interest will vest within lives in being (plus 21 years) under the rule. That is because he was alive at Ursula's death and can be used as the measuring life that validates his own gift. The USRAP does have a built in 90 year "wait and see" limitation. However, if Sam turns out to become the taker we do not

have to rely on the 90 year period. **Answer (d) is wrong** because it misapplies the 90 year limitation period. USRAP says, even it the future interest does not vest within the period of the rule (lives in being plus 21 years), if it does turn out to vest in anyone within 90 years of the creator's death (here that would be Ursula's death), then the interest is valid. So, in fact, even if there was an afterborn child, Seth, and even if Amir and Sam died more than 21 years before Seth graduates from college, nonetheless Seth would take so long as that event occurs within 90 years of Ursula's death. But, as stated, option (d) asks you to apply the 90 year rule at the time of creation of the interest. That is wrong. The 90 year rule allows you to wait and see whether the gift vests within 90 years.

See Lawrence W. Waggoner, "The Uniform Statutory Rule Against Perpetuities," 21 Real Prop. Prob. & Tr. J. 569–602 (1986).

12. **The best option is (d).** The question here is what is the effect of the "amendment" to the will. If it has no effect then the terms of the 2015 will control and that will leaves everything to all six children. The best conclusion is that the "amendment" has no testamentary effect.

    Option (a) is wrong. The amendment is wholly in the handwriting of the testator, but it is not signed. To be a valid holographic will, it must be signed. Indeed, to be a valid will of any kind it must be signed. Option (a) suggests that the "amendment" might be validated under the harmless error rule, which does apply in California so long as there is clear and convincing evidence. But the harmless error rule cannot be applied because under the California statute the will must be signed by the testator. Signing is not an error that can be corrected under harmless error. See CPC § 6110(c)(2).

    Option (b) is wrong. The doctrine of integration requires that all pages of the will be present when it was executed. Here, all pages are together but the only document executed was the 2015 will and the amendment was not present at that time.

    Option (c) is also wrong. There is no signed testamentary document that incorporates the amendment by reference. The amendment was not in existence when the 2015 will was executed.

13. **The best option is (a).** He has no claim against the estate because Helen can leave her own property to anyone she chooses.

    Option (b) is wrong because California does not recognize a spousal elective share. Each spouse is entitled to dispose of his or her half of the community property however he/she desires. So Helen can disinherit William to the extent of her half of the community.

    Option (c) is wrong because William is not a pretermitted spouse. They were married at the time Helen executed her will.

    Option (d) is wrong because he has no rights in her half of the community. She can dispose of her interest in the community property however she likes.

14. **The best option is (b).** The California rule on taking by right of representation is a modern per stirpes rule. That means you determine how to divide the property at the first level where there is a taker who survives. Here, none of Buck's siblings survive. But nieces and nephews did. Making the division at the niece/nephew level results in a division into fourths. Three survived and a fourth failed to survive but left issue. The share of the 4th niece, Deb, then passes by right of representation to her two children, so that they each take 1/8.

    Option (a) is wrong because there is no justification for dividing into thirds or sixths.

    Option (c) is wrong because after the niece/nephew level, the grandchildren take by right of representation and not per capita.

    Option (d) is wrong because issue of siblings take by right of representation and not based on who is the closest kin.

15. **The best option is (c).** California still has the Uniform Simultaneous Death Act, which provides that if there is no clear and convincing evidence that either Jack or Jill survived the other then the property will be distributed as though each survived. But here there is evidence that Jack survived, even though only for a day. Under California law, survival by one second is enough if it can be proved with clear and convincing evidence. Therefore, Jack survived Jill. As the surviving joint tenant he becomes the sole owner of Blackacre. At his death, Blackacre will pass under his will to the Red Cross.

    Option (a) is wrong because Jill died before Jack. As a result she had no interest in Blackacre to pass to her son, Saul.

    Option (b) is wrong because Jack did not die intestate. Sam may be his heir, but Jack disinherited him when he executed a will leaving all his property to the Red Cross.

    Option (d) is wrong because Jill had no interest in Blackacre to pass to her son, Saul.

16. **The best option is (c).** California has a 120 hour survival rule, but it only applies to intestacy, and not to wills (unless the will is a statutory will). Chet survived by more that 120 hours and so he inherits from Ted, but then he died intestate so the property will ultimately go to his son, Graham.

    Option (a) is wrong. Two of the sons failed to meet the 120 hour survival requirement. As a result they cannot inherit.

    Option (b) is wrong. Cam survived Ted but since Ted died intestate, the 120 hour survival rule applies. Cam does not meet this requirement. It is true that the facts don't tell us who inherits from Cam. For example, if his mother survived, she might well be his intestate heir. But this is irrelevant as to Ted's estate because Cam takes nothing from Ted.

    Option (d) is wrong because Ted's son Chet is Ted's only intestate heir. If Ted had left a will leaving anything to someone other than Graham,

Graham would not end up with all of Ted's property. Graham does not inherit directly from Ted, but only through his father, Chet.

17. **The best option is (b).** California no longer requires privity for an intended beneficiary to bring a negligence claim against a drafting attorney. See *Lucas v. Hamm,* 56 Cal.2d 583 (1961). But the exception to the privity requirement is only available in cases when the plaintiff is identified in the badly drafted estate planning documents as the intended beneficiary. Therefore, a named plaintiff who is unable to inherit because the will violates the rule against perpetuities (*Lucas v. Hamm*) or because the will was not executed properly does have standing despite lack of privity. But the facts in this question do not involve a badly drafted or executed document. Here, the documents were not drafted at all. As a result Wanda cannot show that Tom clearly intended her to be a beneficiary of the lawyer's services. We don't know why the documents were not executed. Perhaps Tom had not really made up his mind. The facts in this question are similar to the facts in *Chang v. Lederman*, 90 Cal. Rptr. 3d 758 (Cal. Ct. App. 2009), where the court held: "an attorney who drafts a will or trust owes no duty of care to a nonclient potential beneficiary in absence of an executed will or trust instrument expressly reflecting testator's intent to benefit nonclient."

    Option (a) is not the best option. In most cases it is likely that failing to complete estate planning documents in a timely manner is not negligence, but it probably depends on the facts. One can imagine a fact situation in which it might be negligence. E.g., testator is terminally ill and calls lawyer every day to bring documents for him to sign, but lawyer never gets around to it. Given the importance of facts to determine negligence, a court should not dismiss the case at the demurrer stage. It would be more appropriate to do so at the summary judgment stage.

    Option (c) is not the best option. If she can show she was the intended beneficiary she should have done so in her complaint, but there are no stated facts that can show that intention with the clarity required to get around the privity requirement.

    Option (d) is not the best option. It is possible a trial judge might do this, assuming that negligence is likely not to be proved. But it is a waste of judicial time when it is clear that Wanda cannot meet the "intended beneficiary" requirements of California standing law.

18. **The best option is (c).** Remember that the question asks for "not true" statements so it is best to go through all statements and mark them as True (T) or False (F). The IRS and other federal agencies do not recognize RDPs as spouses even though the states do. But the IRS does recognize the fact that RDPs are subject to the state community property system. Applying the old Supreme Court ruling of *Poe v. Seaborn*, 282 U.S. 101 (1930), the IRS has privately ruled that the community property rights of RDPs will be recognized even though they are not recognized as spouses. As a result, a partner earning $1M will not be viewed as making a taxable gift just because the state's community property system causes half of that

million to vest in the other partner. See PLR 201021048. That makes this statement False.

Option (a) is wrong because it is True. The state recognizes that RDPs are the same as married couples and therefore applies married filing rules to them. The federal government, by contrast, has determined that RDPs are not spouses and therefore cannot file as married.

Option (b) is wrong because it is True. Federal tax law recognizes the community property rights of registered partners and therefore only half of the community property is included in the estate of the first to die, whether or not that person was the earner of the income that produced the community property.

Option (d) is wrong because it is True. Generally, the federal government does not recognize registered partners as spouses. As a result, one might assume that the Social Security Administration will not award survivor benefits to a partner. But there is a provision in the Social Security Act that provides that if a "person" is entitled to an intestate share of the deceased worker's estate, that "person" can claim a survivor's benefit. The section was included to provide for "putative spousal" claims, but given the language it applies to any registered partner so long as the state provides that partner with spousal intestacy rights, which the California statute does.

19. **The best option is (d).** Foster children have no right to inherit. The only way for Frank to inherit would be through a claim to adoption. There are two possibilities, equitable adoption (under California case law) and California Probate Code § 6454. But, unfortunately, none of the conditions were met to warrant applying either theory.

    Answer (a) is wrong because California has never adopted a "functional parenthood" doctrine. California's Unified Parentage Act is quite liberal and recognizes parenthood whenever a parent holds out a child as his or her own. But functioning as a parent or a child is not enough.

    Answer (b) is wrong because under California's equitable adoption case law, there must have been a promise by Howard to adopt Frank and under these facts there is no such promise.

    Answer (c) is wrong because the Probate Code requires that there be some impediment to Howard's potential adoption of Frank. Once Frank's mother's rights were terminated there was no legal impediment to such an adoption.

    These facts are based on the California case, *Estate of Ford,* 32 Cal.4th 160 (Cal. 2004), which held that the foster child, although considered a child by everyone who testified in the case, could not meet the California standards for either statutory adoption of a foster child (§ 6454) or equitable adoption.

20. **The best option is (c).** The gift to grandchildren per capita is vested in the grandchildren who were alive at T's death (which includes Ginny) plus any afterborns (who for RAP purposes would become vested upon birth,

i.e., within 21 years of lives in being at T's death). There is no survival requirement linked to the gift to grandchildren. Under the UPC, by contrast, a future interest taker in trust must survive until the time of distribution. But this is not required under California law and so Ginny is vested at the time of T's death.

Option (a) is incorrect. The life estate given to children was clearly to children who survived T. Sam did not survive so neither he nor his issue have any interest in the life estate.

Option (b) is incorrect. Ginny is not claiming through her parent, but rather based on her status as a grandchild, which she is.

Option (d) is incorrect.

21. **The best answer is (a) Mary.** Under California's intestacy statute, Hal's heir is Mary who is a descendant of Hal's great grandparents.

    Answer (b) is wrong. Deb is a stepchild—or was a stepchild when Hal and Wang were married. A stepchild can inherit under California law if there are no living descendants of grandparents (which is true in this case), but only if the stepchild is a child of a predeceased spouse. Here, regardless of Hal's close connection with Deb, she is a child of a divorced spouse and so does not qualify as an intestate heir.

    Answer (c) is wrong. The state only takes if there is no intestate heir and under California intestacy law, issue of grandparents, or great grandparents, or beyond are heirs. It is difficult to die without an heir in California.

    Answer (d) is wrong. A divorced spouse can never take from her deceased husband as an intestate heir.

22. **The best answer is (b).** As in every state, a testator must have sufficient mental capacity to execute a will.

    Option (a) is wrong. Under California law, as in other states, there is no requirement for the will to be notarized.

    Option (c) is wrong because under California law, the testator need not sign in front of the witnesses so long as the testator acknowledged his or her signature on the will to both witnesses.

    Option (d) is wrong because under California law, as in other states, so long as the will was validly executed in the state of residence at the time of execution, the will is considered valid in California.

23. **The best option is (a).** The cost and the time required to go through probate are what lead California attorneys to use a living trust rather than a will. Of course, a pourover will is normally required to make sure that everything the decedent owns passes in accord with the dispositive plan in the trust. The trust only avoids probate to the extent it is funded with the decedent's property.

    Option (b) may be true, but it is not totally correct. Once a living trust has been established, it can control the distribution of property before testator's death. For example, the living trust normally would distribute property to the testator, the creator of the trust, if necessary.

Option (c) is absolutely false. A living trust is revocable by the creator and as a result everything in the trust is included in the trustor's taxable estate.

Option (d) is not best. Yes it is true that gifts to minors can be made through a living trust. But that is not the primary reason for using such a trust.

24. **The best option is (c).** The *Marvin* case held that promises of support or to share an estate, even oral promises, if proved, can be enforced. Willie promised both, so if Susie can prove the promises, they can be enforced. See *Byrne v. Laura*, 60 Cal. Rptr. 2d 908 (1997).

    Option (a) is wrong. Cohabitants are not listed as intestate heirs in California. There have been proposals to add cohabitants as intestate heirs under the UPC, but no state has yet adopted such a proposal.

    Option (b) is wrong. The Statute of Frauds does apply to any promise that cannot be carried out within a year, such as a promise for lifetime support. The Statute probably applies to all of Willie's promises. But given Susie's reliance and change in position (she quit her job and moved in with Willie), Willie's estate would likely be estopped from pleading the Statute. That is what the California Court of Appeal explained in *Byrne v. Laura*, 60 Cal. Rptr. 2d 908 (1997), which involved facts very similar to this hypothetical. Citing the fact that *Marvin* had approved of oral promises, the *Byrne* court explained that the *Marvin* Court had to have realized that estoppel would prevent application of the Statute of Frauds under the right facts.

    Option (d) is wrong because, even if Susie has a claim to *quantum meruit*, it is not her best claim. Damages for a *quantum meruit* claim would be limited to the fair market value of Susie's services during the relationship. In addition, she might have trouble proving such a claim, since it is based on an understanding between the parties that Willie would pay her for her "wifely" services. The facts in this hypothetical do not suggest any such understanding. Rather the understanding is that she would be supported for life or receive everything Willie owned at his death.

25. **The best option is (c).** Under the will, only surviving sons can take Blackacre and since none did survive, that gift lapses, and falls into the residuary. The California anti-lapse statute will not save a gift for issue of a predeceased beneficiary, such as the sons, if the testator required survival, which Steve did. At Debby's death, everything in the residuary estate passes to Steve's heirs. California statutory law says that whenever a future interest is left to an heir of the testator, then the heirs will be determined as if the testator died at the moment the future interest becomes possessory. See California Probate Code § 21114. That means the takers have to be alive at that time and it is irrelevant whether or not

they survived Steve. If we determine Steve's heirs at the death of Debby, the only lineal issue surviving at that time are Garth and Cathy.

Option (a) is wrong. The anti-lapse statute cannot apply because Steve included a survival requirement for his sons to take.

Option (b) is wrong. If we determined Steve's heirs literally at his own death, those persons would be Debby, Gus, Garth. But, as explained above, California Probate Code § 21114 says we determine the "would be" heirs at Debby's death.

Option (d) is wrong for the same reason listed above. California Probate Code § 21114 says heirs are determined at Debby's death.